PENGUIN BUSINESS

# BRANDS AND THE BRAIN

Arvind Sahay is professor of marketing and international business; Prof. M.N. Vora Chair in marketing and entrepreneurship; chair, India Gold Policy Centre; chair, marketing area; and chair, NSE Centre for Behavioral Science at the Indian Institute of Management Ahmedabad. Prof. Sahay completed his PhD from the University of Texas, Austin. He obtained his MBA from the Indian Institute of Management Ahmedabad, and he also holds a degree in chemical engineering from the Indian Institute of Technology Kanpur.

# BRANDS & THE BRAIN

## HOW TO USE NEUROSCIENCE TO CREATE IMPACTFUL BRANDS

ARVIND SAHAY

BUSINESS

An imprint of Penguin Random House

PENGUIN BUSINESS

USA | Canada | UK | Ireland | Australia
New Zealand | India | South Africa | China

Penguin Business is part of the Penguin Random House group of companies whose addresses can be found at global.penguinrandomhouse.com

Published by Penguin Random House India Pvt. Ltd
4th Floor, Capital Tower 1, MG Road,
Gurugram 122 002, Haryana, India

First published in Penguin Business by Penguin Random House India 2022



10 9 8 7 6 5 4 3 2 1

The views and opinions expressed in this book are the author's own and the facts are as reported by him which have been verified to the extent possible, and the publishers are not in any way liable for the same.

ISBN 9780143452614

Typeset in Adobe Caslon Pro by MAP Systems, Bengaluru, India



www.penguin.co.in

*To Kaavya and Shabnam (Babu log, it took a while, but it got done!) and all the participants of my Neuroscience and Consumer Behaviour and Neuroscience in Marketing sessions, whose feedback and enthusiasm helped me to refine the ideas*

# Contents


1. Introduction 1
2. Brain Operating Principles: How and Why Neuroscience Can Help Improve Brand Management 19
3. Decision-Making in the Brain: How We Decide about Brands 50
4. Why Brands Matter and the Nature of a Brand in the Brain 96
5. Diagnosing the Nature of Your Brand and Steps to Building a Brand 129
6. Sustaining and Rejuvenating a Brand 165
7. Neuroscience and Building, Sustaining and Rejuvenating Brands on Social Media 191
8. How the Brand in the Customer's Brain Leads to Brand Value for the Firm 229

9. Organizational Structure and Design to Deliver the Brand in the Brain 256

10. Neuromarketing Tools and Measurement in Managing Brands 289

*Acknowledgements* 315

*Notes* 316

# Chapter 1

# Introduction

On 5 June 2015, Maggi, a popular brand of instant noodles consumed as a snack and as a meal in India, was, almost simultaneously, withdrawn from the market and banned by the government from being sold. The reason? Laboratory tests, conducted at a government laboratory, had shown that the lead content in the noodles had surpassed the permissible level of 2.5 ppm by a whopping 15.[1] Overnight, a 75 per cent market share brand disappeared from the market! Competitors like Yippee and Top Ramen rushed to fill the 38,000-ton void on the shelves of 3.8 million stores, from which the Bombay High Court had asked Maggi to recall its products.[2] However, they failed to fill the void in the market, which consisted of the millions of bachelors, college students, moms, kids and young professionals, most of whom continued to scan the shelves for their beloved Maggi. And in that desperation, some sought the black market, where the Rs 10 pack of Maggi was selling at a price of Rs 102.[3] Many took to Facebook and Twitter to post Maggi stories from their childhoods and lament not being able to enjoy their evening cup of tea without the hot slurpy snack.

This turmoil had been brewing for about fourteen months when the authorities in the state of Uttar Pradesh informed Nestlé India that there was more than the permitted level of lead in Maggi and that MSG had been detected in a sample of Maggi Noodles that carried a 'No added MSG' claim on the pack.

After the ban, customers started posting their reactions online. These included messages such as 'We miss you, Maggi' and 'Come back, man'.[4]

And then Maggi released the #WeMissYouToo ad campaign, the brainchild of its branding team. Maggi's 'I miss you, yaar' and 'Come back, man' dialogued 48-second commercials went viral.[5] The characters, mostly bachelors, related their longing for Maggi, a commodity that was their evening snack and their midnight respite and how without it, they were being forced to change their lifestyle. According to MindShift Metrics, a digital agency that maps reach and trends on social media, the #WeMissYouToo hashtag received 5 million impressions.[6] The advertisements had more than a million views on YouTube.

Despite having been off the shelves for five months, Maggi was able to build back its market share. Within six months it had a 35 per cent market share and in two years it had a 60 per cent share of what was now a slightly larger market.[8] Hardly a small feat for a product blamed for harming the body. While much of its resurgence could be owed to its brilliantly planned contingency advertising campaigns, could just any company have made this possible armed with an emotion-triggering ad plan for the duration of its product's ban? And without a brand that was already deeply embedded in the minds of its customers?

Probably not! But brand Maggi came back. Stronger. Tens of millions of Indians are back with Maggi. By early 2020, four years after the ban and relaunch, it's almost as if Maggi never left. A powerful brand to begin with and a carefully crafted branding and communication strategy during the ban and after the relaunch turned things around. It gave emotional branding a new meaning. A new direction. Seven years down the line, in March 2022, Maggi may not have the monopoly of yesteryears, but it still commands over 60 per cent of the instant noodle market in India.[9] And COVID-19 just gave it a boost.

This brings me to the subject of the book, branding—the act of promoting a product or a company in the minds of customers. The book is also about how our brains evaluate a brand, choose one and relate to it—sometimes so strongly that in the presence of the brand, the emotional centres of the brain become more active and the reasoning and logical areas become less so[10] in a way that the brand becomes a loved brand, anthropomorphic in nature and an integral part of the lives of its customers.

*Our goal in this book is to connect brands to the key aspects of the brain's functioning and to use that understanding to develop better brand-related interventions. To do this, we will also endeavour to understand the functioning of the brain: how it works and how it takes decisions. It is intended for all those who are interested in understanding branding at the level of brain operations and in using the understanding to design and implement appropriate brand-related actions.*

It's fair to state that from the moment we wake up to the moment we fall asleep, we interact with hundreds of brands, whether we realize it or not. We make decisions about brands almost every other hour during the course of a normal day. From the second we turn on our phones in the morning, check Instagram, WhatsApp and Facebook notifications and pick an app to hail a taxi to get to work, to the very place we choose to work at, everything is all about brands. We are constantly making choices between the brands we associate ourselves with, consciously or unconsciously. Right from very early on—why we pick one school over another for our kids, the locality we choose to buy an apartment in, the kind of car we drive, the clothes we wear, the movies or television shows we watch, the celebrities we adore, the political parties we support, the places we eat at, the kind of spouse we seek—all of these decisions boil down to us preferring one brand over another.

But what is branding? Branding goes beyond just a logo or a graphic element. When we think about a brand, it encapsulates the sum total of the entire customer experience: everything from the logo, the website, the product or service use experience to the social media experiences, the way the firm answers the phone, the after-sales service, the word-of-mouth impressions and the way customers experience its employees—all of this as it exists in the mind of the customer. In short, the brand is the way a customer perceives the product and/or the firm. It is the lived experience of the customer. It is critical to be aware of the customers' brand experience and have a plan to create the brand experience that the firm wants to present. After all, a good brand doesn't just happen. It is a carefully considered strategic plan, well implemented over time. Brands have to be built in the brain, countless hours must be put in and sleepless nights spent figuring out how one wants to portray one's brand to the target customers. This brain-racking led to Nestlé's intelligent branding and Maggi's integration into the Indian human story, earning customers' trust and, finally, to putting the lead debacle behind it.

Building brands builds incredible value for companies and corporations. Thanks to the International Financial Reporting Standard's IFRS 3's official direction to include the brand value of acquired assets under intangible assets in the acquiree's balance sheets, it has only become easier to translate this 'incredible value' into monetary terms[11]. In the $27 billion acquisition of LinkedIn by Microsoft, LinkedIn's 'marketing-related' (trade names) evaluation came to just under $2.15 billion.[12] But we don't even have to look that far! When India's Tata Motors bought Jaguar and Range Rover from Ford, it was buying the brand. Goldman Sachs and Morgan Stanley helped Ford sell the brands to Tata for $2.56 billion, and the brands were worth more than all other ingredients combined.[13] Likewise, when Kraft bought Cadbury for $19.5 billion, what did they buy? The chocolate? The industrial units? The recipes? The candy makers? No, they bought the brand.[14] So what is in a brand?

Short answer: everything! Long answer: a brand is something that empowers a company enough to establish a presence in the minds of consumers. It enables recognition, which in turn familiarizes the consumer with the brand, thereby making it an easier, safer and almost automatic choice. This familiarity translates into a biased preference towards the brand. Neurally, this happens because the ventromedial prefrontal cortex, a part in our brain engaged in decision-making, responds to this preference by associating the preferred brand with a higher reward value, which in turn directs our decision towards the said brand. Thinking about the brand, choosing the brand, talking about the brand or using the brand leads to higher levels of certain neurotransmitters in the brain; which neurotransmitter depends on the positioning of the brand. *In fact, a study found that individuals processed brand information even before they started the decision-making process*![15] Consistent branding is capable of putting the consumer's mind at ease during a brand interaction by alleviating the perceived risk. A powerful branding strategy impels people to talk about the brand and generate referrals, banking mostly upon the human desire to imitate others. The bottom line is that it eases our consumer experience by making an emotional connection and making the experience emotionally rewarding.

Our brains want the certainty of a strong brand; our brains feel rewarded neurophysiologically with increases in the levels of neurotransmitters like dopamine, serotonin and oxytocin that gets triggered with a liked brand. Our brains conserve energy with brands; our brains (and therefore, we) feel secure with a preferred brand. In some ways, if brands did not exist, our brains would create brands, whether offline or online, as brands satisfy the need within our brains to create and/or see patterns. Arguably, as more commerce moves online and people's brains being wired to want to connect (if not to people, then to objects), the need for brands in the brain will rise even more.

Consider the Chinese mobile brand OnePlus. Its smartphones managed to take up 36 per cent of the Q4 2018 Indian market share in a very short time,[16] an impressive feat accomplished largely due to a clever initial branding strategy: you could buy a OnePlus phone only through an invitation. This became the driving force in creating momentum behind these phones, for the brand successfully appealed to the human desire for exclusive products. The 'by-invitation-only' system allowed the manufacturer to gradually fulfil the demand while customers were kept in a constant state of anticipation. This anticipation only added to the phone's appeal as a 'VIP product' for only a 'select' group of people. The nucleus accumbens in the brains of consumers were anticipating the 'gain' of buying the brand:[17] the anticipation of the gain was from the exclusivity promised.

With the launch of its third model, OnePlus 3, in December 2014, less than nine months after entering the market, the company brought the 'invite only' scheme to a strategic end[18] and announced an exclusive partnership with Amazon India,[19] having achieved a substantial customer base. In 2019, Amazon India announced that OnePlus's latest OnePlus 7 had become the fastest-selling premium smartphone in the first seven days of its launch![20] And so the right approach to branding conveys an idea to the consumer base and can provide the company with a differentiating strategy in the brains of its target consumers in a competitive market.

Before diving further into the book, let's briefly recapitulate what a brand does for the seller of the brand.

**The first thing that a brand does is that it enables recognition.** People tend to do business with companies they recognize and can identify with. If your branding is consistent and easy to recognize, it can help people feel at ease purchasing your products or services. Recognition brings about a sense of familiarity that reduces the customer's perception of the risk involved in engaging in your brand (making a person feel more secure and increasing the serotonin in the brain) and thus enhances their purchasing experience.[21] A strong brand helps customers know what to expect. A brand that is consistent and clear puts the customer at ease, because they know exactly what to expect each and every time they experience the brand. Surprises are not always welcome in scenarios like banking, housing, transportation, etc. On top of that, with age, our tendency to engage in risky propositions declines significantly.[22] Branding helps develop a relationship of trust with consumers, which, in turn, helps alleviate any risk perception.[23] All of these reduce marketing support requirements over time.

**The second thing that a brand does is that it differentiates its owner from the competition.** A strong brand helps set a company or product apart from the competition. With advances in the technology of production, differentiating between the intrinsic nature of rival products is becoming increasingly difficult due to a reduction in attention spans and the plethora of brands clamouring for our attention. Brands are no longer competing on a local stage; they now compete in the global economy. And how does a firm stand out from the thousands or millions of similar organizations around the world? Through branding.[24] The brain likes the dopamine spike that a 'different' brand provides.

**Thirdly, a brand provides the 'vehicle' to capture the customer's preference.** Whenever there is a conflict between item preference and brand preference, we are more likely to lean towards buying the item from the brand we like, the one that gives us more dopamine (or serotonin, oxytocin, vasopressin or acetylcholine or a combination). The mere presence of a brand logo can result in a greatly biased decision. In a behavioural science study, it was found that individuals processed brand information even before they started the decision-making

A brand's management and efforts at engagement should be coordinated to reflect the variance on the connection dimension that exists on social media.

Chapter 8 is about the economic value of brands. Brands are special intangibles that in many businesses are the most important asset. Brand value is not just a financial number. Brand value influences the choices of customers, employees, investors and government authorities. Brand valuation would comprise technical valuation, which can be utilized for balance sheet reporting, tax planning, litigation, securitization, licensing, mergers and acquisitions, investor relations purposes and commercial valuation, which is operational for the purpose of brand architecture, portfolio management, market strategy, budget allocation and brand scorecards. Brand valuation approaches for this purpose are discussed, throwing light on which approach would be best suited to which business. We discuss the neuroscience-based drivers of the valuation, which is at the market level, and connect these to the financial numbers. The stronger the neural imprint of, and the greater the emotional attachment to a brand, the greater the likelihood of purchase and customer loyalty, leading to the success of a brand as reflected in the firm's balance sheet.

In Chapter 9, we discuss how to deliver the brand promise through organizational structure and design. Given the importance of brands as intangible assets, a well-implemented brand architecture strategy can provide a product road map to the future for a brand, clarifying where it can go and how it can get there. We discuss how various organizations have created internal structures that are intended to shepherd brands in the markets, and internal organizational structures that provide incentives to managers to work at creating, sustaining and rejuvenating brands in the channel and among customers.

A clear organizational structure that is consistent with what a brand is trying to deliver to its customers is necessary to manage and maximize the value and equity of a brand. This chapter deals with the alignment of corporate strategy and values with brand values and mindset and how managerial mindsets and the brains of managers can influence the brand performance in the marketplace.

We conclude with Chapter 10, which takes the reader through examples of some existing and potential neuromarketing tools that can be used to generate customer insights in general and also specifically about decision-making in relation to brands. How can we use neuromarketing tools to improve the brand management process in the firm? It also connects neuromarketing tool usage to existing organizational structures: how does one fit neuroscience and neuromarketing into the organizational processes seamlessly? To aid the reader, we also provide an illustrative list of firms that provide neuroscience-based services.

Let us start our journey by first looking at the brain and brain operating principles.

# Chapter 2

# Brain Operating Principles: How and Why Neuroscience Can Help Improve Brand Management

To understand how neuroscience can help improve brand management, it is important to understand how the human brain functions, to understand key brain operating principles. Brands are, after all, perceptions and images in the brain, a presence in the 1500 cc mass of tissue inside our heads. It's all, therefore, grounded in the tenets of biology, and psychology that arises from biology. If one looks at a cross-section of the human brain, from the top down, it appears as if it is broken into three major components. Our newest brain, our *Homo sapiens* brain, the neocortex, the forebrain, corresponds with the conscious and reasoning level, where decisions (apparently) are made, where we see and hear. The neocortex is responsible for all of our rational and analytical thought and language.[33] The middle two sections make up our limbic brains (*the midbrain*—the hippocampus, the amygdala, thalamus, etc.). Our limbic brains are responsible for all of our feelings, like trust, love, affection, fear, anger and loyalty;[34] it is also where conscious memories are formed. It's responsible for a significant proportion of human decision-making, and it has no capacity for language;[35] it is also where a lot of our unconscious emotion is centred. The third section is the hindbrain or the reptilian brain, the oldest part of the human brain, located at the back of our heads (the brain stem, the ventral tegmental area, basal ganglia, the cerebellum, etc.), which is responsible for the automatic functions of the brain, but more importantly, for unconscious memories and emotions; it is where many of our habits are embedded.

Figure 1 below shows the basic brain structure.

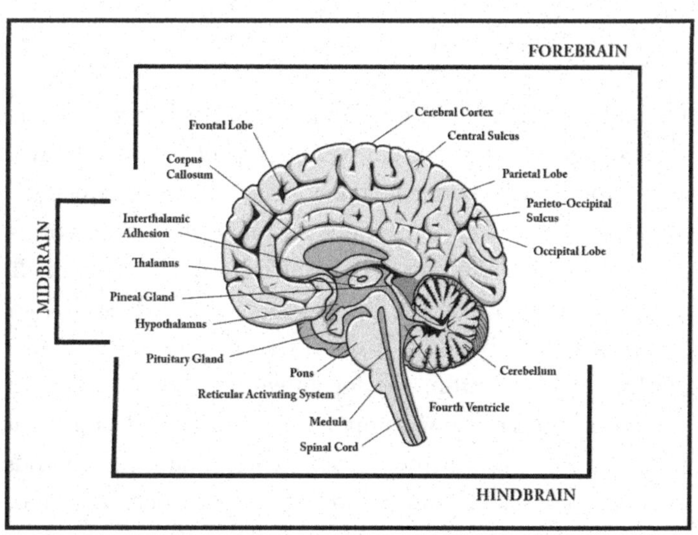


*Anatomy of the Human Brain*

From a branding and decision-making perspective, the six key brain operating principles that influence and drive behaviour are as follows:

First, the brain has objectives that it wants to achieve in pursuit of the survival and health of the organism that it inhabits: the human being (this sounds almost as if the brain were a separate creature!). It wants to feel good, to avoid pain, to feel secure, to get rewards and so on. These objectives arise from the midbrain and in some measure from the hindbrain. Each of these 'brain states' (feel good, feel secure, etc.) corresponds to levels of neurotransmitters like dopamine, serotonin, acetylcholine, oxytocin, vasopressin, testosterone, oestrogen, BDNF, etc., in the brain. Most of these are produced in the brain; some are produced elsewhere in the body. 'Optimal' levels of these neurotransmitters lead to 'feel good', 'feel secure', etc., sentiments and are linked to stimuli in the environment. The brain likes to go for brands that give it the neurotransmitters that it is looking for.

Secondly, relative to other organs in the body, the brain is an energy guzzler. However, the total energy available is limited, and what can be used in a confined space is also limited given the need to maintain homeostasis. The brain is designed, therefore, to conserve energy. The brain conserves energy by having a distinct tendency to push processing into the unconscious—into automatic processing that is more efficient. Conscious thinking and focus are the most energy-intensive activities that the brain does. Brands are a way of conserving energy.

Third, the brain is designed to look for patterns, to see groups, to categorize, to create patterns, sometimes when there aren't any, and to be comfortable with patterns, to look for meaning before detail. Brands are a way of fitting into a pattern to create meaning. Patterns make the brain feel comfortable. Patterns are both consciously and unconsciously present in the brain. The unconscious patterns reside in the midbrain and the hindbrain. Patterns make us feel secure and comfortable. They adjust serotonin in the brain to the desired levels. Familiar patterns make us feel secure and comfortable and increase the serotonin and vasopressin in the brain. Familiar brands are the pattern that the brain wants and seeks. The more familiar the brand, the stronger the pattern.

Fourth, and in direct contrast to the third brain operating principle, the brain remembers and engages with contrasts that break a pattern; contrasts excite attention. Contrasts provide variety and increase dopamine in the brain. Variety and attention keep brands alive and interesting. Brands need to both fit into a pattern and be different at the same time; a brand, therefore, needs to be different from the competition and ***also*** different in some ways from its earlier avatars. The brand, simultaneously, should fit into an expected pattern of what a brand in its category is supposed to be like. Differences may be perceived consciously or unconsciously. The brain wants dopamine. Dopamine leads to feeling good. Ceteris paribus, brands that give more dopamine will be selected over the competition.

Fifth, human brains are designed to mirror, to imitate, to conform socially to others. We tend to do what others around us are doing. We imitate. Neurophysiologically, when we observe others doing an action, the same neurons fire in our heads, literally. When a fan watches Roger Federer execute his tweener shot, that person is literally using the same neurons in their head—without the physical action. When we see COVID-induced fear in the person in front of us, we feel the same fear, literally. This is how human brains connect. Human brains are wired to connect. Powerful brands create their own self-reinforcing cycle through imitation. Mirroring actions make us feel good through higher levels of relevant neurotransmitters in our brains.

In the rest of this chapter, we develop these points further to illustrate the idea of why using insights from neuroscience helps to improve brand management. And then we derive some action implications.

## Brain Operating Principle #1 (BOP#1)

*The brain wants to feel good, to avoid pain, to feel secure, to get rewards and so on. Each of these 'brain states' corresponds to levels of (and combinations of) neurotransmitters like dopamine, serotonin, acetylcholine, oxytocin, vasopressin, testosterone, oestrogen, BDNF, etc., in the brain. Optimal levels of these neurotransmitters lead to 'feel good', 'feel secure', etc., sentiments and are linked to stimuli in the environment. So the brain looks for these stimuli to get the required 'rewards'. (the figure below is an illustration).*

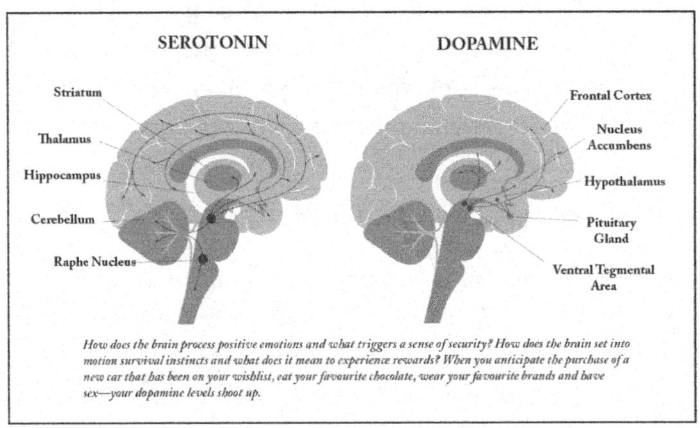


*How does the brain process positive emotions and what triggers a sense of security? How does the brain set into motion survival instincts and what does it mean to experience rewards? When you anticipate the purchase of a new car that has been on your wishlist, eat your favourite chocolate, wear your favourite brands and have sex—your dopamine levels shoot up.*

*Neurotransmitters*

Each of these 'objectives' in the brain leads to improvement in the well-being of the organism. When the customer drives the BMW that he had been eyeing for the past year on a road holiday, he feels rewarded, his dopamine levels go up, he feels good. When she buys 'comfort' food, like Maggi, for instance, she feels secure and her serotonin levels go up. When the salaried employee invests his bonus through a relationship manager that he feels comfortable with in a mutual fund, his serotonin and dopamine levels go up. In older times, the reward would have been finding food or surviving an attack from a predator, both conducive to survival and a better life, but the modern equivalents are product and service stimuli in the environment, obtaining which improves the situation of the organism. And the brain is configured to want these dollops of neurotransmitters. Brands are a means of delivering these dollops of neurotransmitters to the brain. In the aftermath of the COVID-19 pandemic in 2020–22, safety-related brands and even other brands that can increase serotonin in the brain will get greater traction as more people's brains want to feel 'safe' up to a point. The key, of course, is how does my brand make the consumer feel more safe? At the time of publication of this book, the waning of the pandemic should drive behaviours through other neurotransmitters as well.

## Brain Operating Principle #2 (BOP#2)

*The brain is the most energy-intensive organ in the body. It is 2 per cent of the body weight but has 20–25 per cent of the body's energy consumption. So it tries to conserve energy by pushing things into the unconscious, by making things automatic. Automatic processing in the brain is more energy-efficient. Brands are shortcuts to making choice decisions and are energy savers; without brands, customer brains would face a perpetual overload.*

Consider the following table relating to the brain—the brain that accounts for a mere 2 per cent of the total body weight.[36]

| | |
|---|---|
| Percentage of the body's oxygen consumed by the brain | 25 per cent |
| Percentage of the body's glucose used by the brain | 70 per cent |
| Percentage of the body's nutrients consumed by the brain | 25 per cent |
| Number of neurons in the brain | 100 billion |
| Number of connections in the adult brain | 1 quadrillion (100 billion × 10,000) |
| Number of new neurons formed daily throughout the life of a person (neurogenesis) | 7000 |
| Energy consumption by the brain | Approximately 30–60 watts |

The brain is a vast network of connections that requires an enormous amount of energy to keep it running. Of all the activities that the brain does, deliberate conscious thinking and reasoning are the most energy-intensive.[37] The brain, therefore, has an automatic tendency to reduce the amount of effort spent on conscious, deliberate reasoning and conscious thinking.

Yale researchers have demonstrated how the brain saves energy while processing a deluge of sensory information in the primary visual cortex. 'There are over one hundred billion cells in our brain and each of them makes over ten thousand connections with other brain cells. While the large number of possible combinations of cell connections allows for higher-ordered thinking, this is a big problem evolutionarily in terms of energy cost,' said researcher McCormick. 'Therefore, the brain has to encode things efficiently to save energy.'[38] To conserve energy and to become more efficient, our brain does one of two things. It either forgets or remembers, and when it remembers, the brain has a tendency to push things into the unconscious to conserve energy. Pushing things into the unconscious and making things automatic conserves energy.[39] And the brain tends to remember those things, events, brands and people (even unconsciously) that are relevant, that have an emotional meaning.

The brain also forgets in order to conserve energy. Our brains contain not only learning mechanisms but also forgetting mechanisms that erase 'unnecessary' learning.[40] Brains do this to reduce work and to reduce the energy expenditure on the conscious brain.

But what determines what enters our unconscious store and what gets erased? This answer constitutes the fundamental difference between success and failure for a brand. A powerful brand, therefore, is one that has been 'learnt' well, and not only that, the brand has also entered the unconscious of the target customer and is entrenched there. By being entrenched in the unconscious, it becomes an automatic choice for the consumer and reduces the brain's energy consumption. The extra effort required to process a new brand is, therefore, not needed. Paradoxically, even if the brand resides in the unconscious, it needs to be used or consumed or remembered in some way periodically; otherwise, without a strong emotional imprint, the brand will be erased from the memory. The brain is like a muscle. Without use, it atrophies. Or, to be precise, without the exercise of remembering, thinking, buying, talking about and using a brand, it gets erased from the brain—especially if it does not carry a strong emotional imprint.

Current tools in neuroscience allow us to peek into the brain at a granular level. Neuroscience uses tools like functional Magnetic Resonance Imaging (fMRI), electroencephalography (EEG), eye tracking, face tracking, etc., to find out and understand how consumers feel and react when exposed to products and/or related stimuli.[41] Neuroscience investigates the unconscious processing of information in consumers' brains.[42] Human decision-making is both a conscious and an unconscious process in the brain. In fact, unconscious decision-making happens more often than conscious decision-making. Human brains process a majority of information unconsciously, below controlled awareness; this unconscious information has a large influence on the decision-making process.[43,44]

Conventional market research, such as focus groups or surveys, are usually employed to understand behaviour. However, these research methods may not reach the unconscious thinking of consumers in a granular and accurate fashion and are more subject to the skills and interpretation of the facilitator. This leads to incompatibility between the findings of market research and the actual behaviour displayed by the target market at the point of purchase. Neuroscience focuses on enhancing our understanding of the brain through tools such as the fMRI and EEG scans. These peek into the brain directly as it is trying to conserve energy while making a decision. Market researchers can use this information to determine if products or advertisements stimulate responses in the brain linked with the emotions[45] that are more likely to increase liking and/or purchase.

When making buying decisions, customers use heuristics (also known as cognitive biases). These are short and simplified methods of making decisions and finding solutions; they reduce the energy consumption of the brain. For example, the distinct smell of a certain food product, or an idea or slogan such as Subway's 'Eat Fresh', are different ways that can be used to benefit a product.

That brands are present in the unconscious is demonstrated by studies that find that even as customers claim that their reason for buying a brand is completely rational, the unconscious emotion centres of the brain are activated when they talk about and choose the brand. Thus, a clear understanding of how a brand can get into the unconscious and reside there will help a firm improve its brand management capabilities and outcomes.

The brain also conserves energy by using habit formation.[46] Habits form through incremental experience over time and do not shift readily with changes in people's goals and plans. Habit knowledge is protected from short-term whims and occasional happenings. When confronted with options, habits are likely to be favoured due to the ease with which they can be performed when compared with the alternatives. Thus, the brain prefers exercising familiar choices over new ones because of the difficulty of learning new usage behaviours. Habits also are likely to be favoured positively due to the fluency or speed and ease of processing that comes with frequently performed behaviours. High fluency is experienced as positive, partly because it evokes familiarity over uncertainty and makes people better at processing and understanding. Habits thus exploit a physiological aspect that favours what feels easy because it is well-practised, over what feels more difficult because it is new. Change increases risk perceptions in the anterior insula and changes serotonin levels from where they should be. The brand that has become a habit has, therefore, attained brand nirvana.

Additionally, repeated behaviours, such as a customer's buying of the same brand, heighten feelings of comfort, confidence and control, although these choices might initially be random. Furthermore, actions performed out of habit promote coherence or comprehensibility of experiences and thus enhance meaning in life. The switching costs one incurs can discourage deviating from habits, and the subsequently experienced fluency can further contribute to an increase in the liking for products and brands that are habitual. Indeed, one could argue that the goal of branding should be to make one's brand habitual!

## Brain Operating Principle #3 (BOP#3)

*The brain is designed to look for patterns, groups and categories; to create patterns, put products, people and events into categories, sometimes even when there aren't any, and to be comfortable with patterns; to look for meaning before detail. Patterns reduce perceived risk. Brands are a way of fitting into a pattern to create meaning. These patterns can exist both in the conscious and the unconscious parts of our brain. Patterns allow things, people and events to become familiar and less of a threat. When we become more comfortable with them, their perception uses less energy. A higher feeling of security and comfort enhances serotonin. More serotonin enhances a feeling of security and comfort.*

Throughout our lives, we build association networks in our brains; we learn how to decode symbols and visuals and unlock mental concepts or meaning from them. For example, when we see two people holding hands and we immediately understand that there is some level of caring between them, it is because we learnt in childhood that our parents held our hands because they cared for our safety. If we are an investor in the stock markets, and the stock that we bought has gone up two days in succession, then our brain automatically and uncontrollably expects it to go up on the third day as well. The brain has created a pattern, even if there is no pattern, because it looks for a pattern all the time. Scientists even have a name for this phenomenon: 'the hot hand fallacy'![47] Gamblers who are on a winning streak in a casino, for example, will be reluctant to get up because they see the pattern of wins and associate that with continuing to sit at the gambling table to continue the 'pattern'; they do not want to break the pattern.

The brain's desire for patterning is rooted in the 'safety' that it feels when an object belongs to a particular category or pattern that can then be recognized as familiar or safe. Neurally, recognizing a pattern quietens the amygdala, a fear centre in the brain;[48] it reduces perceived risk and the activation of the anterior insula that heralds risk perception.[49] For a brand, this reduction can improve brand perception, adoption and use. Any feature that falls within a pattern reduces risk. Colgate is an oral hygiene product line of toothpastes, toothbrushes, mouthwashes and dental floss. In its brand communication, it displays all the certifications it has received from the Indian Dental Association, a trusted body in that domain. It also portrays itself as the number one brand recommended by dentists. The intention is to alleviate doubts consumers would have about its authenticity and safety, to establish the pattern of the trusted toothpaste.[50]

Some colours, for example, reduce risk in the brain. Consider the following.

Take the colour red. It is one of the most passionate colours. Red is associated with action, adventure, fire, lust, anger, courage and rebellion, for example.[51] Red would lead to a higher perception of risk for some people and a decreased perception of pattern; it would fit into the pattern for other kinds of people who are looking for excitement and greater risk.[52] Red tends to be a colour best used for action-oriented products and brands. Red, for example, is the predominant colour in the Virgin logo—which is perfect for that brand, as founder Richard Branson is widely perceived to be adventurous and rebellious. People will gamble and make riskier, more impulsive decisions if surrounded by the colour red. Guess what the dominant colour of Las Vegas is? Clearance sales are also famously marked with red.

Blue stands for security, trust, productivity and calmness of mind.[53] As a result, blue is the colour of choice for the UN flag. It is also the most popular colour in the corporate world, where it is a symbol of trust and security. JP Morgan, IBM and others are well-known firms that use blue as a symbol of trustworthiness. They use the pattern associated with the colour blue. Evidence has shown that a green colour scheme in a workplace results in less absenteeism due to illness.[54] Workers at a certain factory complained that the black boxes they had to lift were too heavy. So the boxes were re-painted mint green. The load didn't change, but the workers were happier.[55]

At another company, people working in a blue room complained that the office was too cold. When the walls were painted a warm peach, sweaters came off, even though the temperature had not changed.[56]

A strong brand forms a part of a pattern in the mind of the customer. It may be a part of a ritual. It may be associated with certain events. It may be a habit. It may be the pattern itself. The brain associates the brand with the pattern and feels comfortable. The brain gets the rush of neurochemicals that make the person feel good or safe and motivates the person to repeat the pattern; the emotional centres of the brain get activated.[57] A loved brand can trigger oxytocin in the brain.

A brand can better fit into the pattern of the customer's brain by asking itself questions such as: how are customers experiencing the sale? Is there a pattern in the experience? Does my brand fit into that experience pattern? How welcoming or comforting is the brand? Is that the pattern the customer is looking for? What do the customers see, hear and feel immediately upon encountering the brand? Does this fit their pattern? Or fall outside it? Should the brand be a part of the pattern? Or should it be outside it?

Consider the above in the context of cultural codes that constitute a significant pattern for many consumers. For brand owners and designers, this means a need to understand which cultural codes, symbols and visuals will unlock the right meaning. Take the design of the coffee brand Nescafé Azera, designed to create out-of-home coffee cues with an identity reminiscent of enamel-badged Italian coffee machines. When Netflix, an American online entertainment streaming company, made its entry into the Indian market, it brought with it a concept that was relatively new to the Indian crowd. It rolled out 'Nothing like some steaming filter kaapi over your favourite show', connecting to existing behaviours of many Indians (especially in the south of India) who are known for their love of a hot cup of coffee—and fitting into a pattern.

*Thus, a brand that recognizes and fits into a pattern that the customer has in their mind is likely to increase its adoption and acceptance.*

Interestingly, while the brain looks for and creates patterns, it is also looking for contrasts from the pattern at the same time!

## Brain Operating Principle #4 (BOP#4)

*The brain remembers and engages with contrasts/differences/peak shifts from existing patterns; contrasts excite attention. Attention keeps brands alive and interesting. Contrasts provide dopamine. Brands need to both fit into a pattern and be different at the same time; to be able to differentiate themselves from the competition; and to keep the interest of the customer alive if it is already an established brand. Contrasts from existing patterns that exist in the brain are detected very quickly in the unconscious mind through the automatic, faster, reflexive path in the midbrain and hindbrain. The conscious mind also looks at the contrast in the forebrain. Contrasts lead to more dopamine, something that the brain wants. Contrasts will get the customer to consider and buy at first and, later, will keep the brand interesting, new, novel, and prevent the customer from getting bored.*

A contrast is something that is different from an expected pattern. It is a surprise, it is unexpected, it is a peak that is a shift from a base level of perception. A surprise breaks the expected pattern. The brain pays attention to a contrast because at a very basic level, that attention has survival value—is this thing that is different good for me? The difference from the base level, from the expected pattern, triggers a dopamine spike in the brain. The figure below shows a contrast in imagery for Timotei—the other image is what one expects to see in a shampoo advertisement.

*Contrast Shift*

The hippocampus has been found to be the part of our brain that tries to predict what happens next.[58] When something happens that has not been predicted or expected, the brain tends to engage and pay attention. When we interrupt the actions of the pattern-predicting hippocampus, our brain stands to attention. Surprise makes us jump into a decision-making process as opposed to consuming information passively and encourages us to reassess our beliefs. So you will pay more attention to Timotei automatically!

This gives marketers a great opportunity to pitch their product and ensure their efforts are not ignored.

One study showed another benefit of surprise: it releases pleasure chemicals such as dopamine, which implicitly create a neural association between your product and the good feeling.[59] Ferrero, an Italian confectionery company, produces Kinder Joy, which is a candy and one of Ferrero's Kinder brand products. Its egg-shaped packaging splits into two; one half has layers of cocoa and milk cream while the other has a toy. Although there are many other chocolates with the same taste, kids prefer this brand for the surprise element it offers each time they open the egg. A similar concept is used by cereal companies.

Pokemon tazos included in bags of Cheetos and Uncle Chipps are other such examples. What was then a surprise has now shaped the childhood memories of millions of kids in India. Making certain tazos rare encouraged further consumption of Cheetos by the curious kids who wanted to complete their collection.

Associations can change over time. And that is why brands also need to evolve with time. The brain looks for surprises, for contrasts, for new things. It is essential to keep up with evolving trends. The brand Amul keeps itself contemporary by using spoofs on recent events with a familiar protagonist in their advertisements. The cartoons have a twist that is unexpected, which provides the dopamine (BOP#4) , and the protagonist is familiar, increasing the comfort and security and the serotonin (BOP#3).

Fevicol, Indian adhesive manufacturing company Pidilite's most famous product, has now become synonymous with adhesives. When you walk into a store, you are more likely to ask for Fevicol without even realizing that what you actually want is any adhesive! This is because the consumer is not thinking about the product's functionality separately and is associating it with the brand name itself, which has been possible because the usage of the product has been made much easier by this particular brand association.

Fevicol has employed a very famous ad film—which showed an overloaded truck with people literally stuck to it with Fevicol—to generate surprise and contrast in the mind of the customer. Thus, a visual feature of the product that evokes fond emotions, memories or surprise in an effective way helps to create memories and therefore brands. Marketing emphasizes constructing positive, unforgettable experiences in the minds of consumers; these impacts are measured by neuroscience.[60]

Why does a contrast or a peak shift help to increase brand attractiveness? A contrast gives the brain a dopamine spike. A contrast is paid immediate attention to, because from an evolutionary perspective, anything that is different from a pattern can be dangerous (exciting), can be of possible benefit and needs attention; the brain gives a dopamine spike that leads to and comes from that attention.

The brain looks for dopamine spikes. It likes these spikes. Dopamine makes the brain feel good. Dopamine is a reward in and of itself. A brand is a stimulus that can lead to a dopamine increase. *So, a brand that helps to create dopamine spikes that are higher than those provided by the competition will be liked by the brain and will be more likely to move into the memory systems of the brain. The formation of memories also depends on dopamine.*

## Brain Operating Principle #5 (BOP#5)

*Human brains are designed to mirror, to conform socially with others, to interact with people, animals, objects around us. We tend to do what others around us are doing. We imitate. We copy. We are wired to connect—to humans, to objects, to machines and also to brands. The mirror neuron system in the brain is thought to drive this behaviour from a very early age, as shown below.*

*Powerful brands create their own self-reinforcing cycle through imitation. Imitation makes us feel secure. It is one of the bases of influencer marketing. Imitating a key influencer whom we like by using the same brand or the brand that they endorse increases serotonin and oxytocin. We feel part of a collective.*

A chance incident during an experiment led scientists to the discovery of mirror neurons in the brains of monkeys. A monkey that was observing another monkey eat a banana started to show increased activity in the F5 area of its brain, the same area that the other monkey was using to actually eat! The neurons in the F5 area of the brain of the monkey watching the other monkey eat were called mirror neurons. Humans are thought to have a mirror neuron system (MNS) rather than localized mirror neurons. These neurons, speculated to be present in the human inferior frontal cortex and superior parietal lobe, fire up both when we see an individual carrying out an action and when we carry out the same action.[61] Although the MNS is not fully understood, it is theorized that it is this system that enables us to understand others' intentions, learn actions, empathize,[62] imitate (even unconsciously) and mimic actions. Some even suggest that it is engaged in self-awareness and consciousness.[63]

Consider a typical social scenario. The popularity of Facebook and Instagram had everyone flocking to these platforms, sharing similar kinds of photos and posts, and holding mundane and trivial conversations, often with semi-strangers. The now-normal standards of social media have been achieved through acts of mimicry[64] and a very human instinct to try and fit in.[65] The MNS pushed us to conform with the established social standards and to 'imitate' the actions of friends by opening a social media account and posting content that was very similar to that of the people connected to us through the account. Facebook doesn't come with instructions about the content we need to post, and yet, most of us don't take chances lest we stand out in the crowd and appear 'non-conformist'.

Brands have, in many ways, exploited the human urge to conform and imitate without knowing its neural basis. Airbnb's 'That's why we Airbnb' campaign is a great example of this. It shows people arriving at their Airbnb, and their clear elation that their cultural experience has already started even before they have stepped out to explore beautiful places such as Berlin and Goa. It makes them feel like a local in a foreign location. It doesn't take a lot of time for the viewer to imagine themselves on their next vacation, checking into an Airbnb with their loved ones and 'mirroring' the experience of the protagonist in the ad. Through the protagonist of the ad, the MNS of the viewer plunges them into the immersive world of Airbnb and this imagined experience could actually motivate the viewer to consider renting an Airbnb for their next vacation. It would even have triggered a subtle motor simulation of the viewer actually going through the imagined visit themselves!

In a study that looked at the role of mirror neurons, researchers examined the effect on memory as subjects watched an advertisement. Half of the participants watched a mineral water bottle commercial in which the protagonist grasps the bottle and brings it to his mouth, and the other half watched the one in which the protagonist doesn't make any contact with the bottle. It was found that the first half recalled and recognized the product after watching the ad much better than the latter half. The researchers surmised that MNS pushed the first half of the participants to imagine and simulate the act of grasping and drinking and therefore, formed a stronger brand memory.[66]

A brand striving for a powerful impact on consumers could therefore focus on making consumer interaction easily imitable, stimulating mirror neurons and affecting brand memory in the process. Every subsequent brand interaction would re-invoke both the memory and the motivation to imitate, thereby strengthening brand memory. Such a cyclical process could help a brand have a strong influence on the consumer brain, gradually embedding itself in the consumers' unconsciousness; the more people that are then using the brand, the better off the brand will be, because of our instinct to imitate others!

In addition to the five brain operating principles (BOP), particularly in the specific context of brands, there is a sixth BOP that has to do with our conscious and unconscious memories. Humans are the sum total of our conscious and unconscious memories. Brands depend on being a part of our memory; the more deeply embedded a brand is in the memory, the better off is the brand.

*Our memories are mostly unconscious ones; these memories come into play when choosing a brand and when engaging with a brand. Powerful memory creation in the brain requires following some rules such as repetition (varied and chunking), meaning before detail, emotional engagement and getting enough sleep. The most powerful brands are those that are the most deeply embedded in our unconscious memories. Their retrieval from memory and choice requires no conscious thought!*

A study[67] was carried out to investigate the difference in branding between Pepsi and Coca-Cola . This study reported that, in blind taste tests, there was no difference in consumer preference between Coke and Pepsi; both produced equal activation in the ventromedial prefrontal cortex, an area of the brain known to process sensory inputs. When informed that they were tasting Coke/Pepsi, however, this changed.

The study, therefore, implies that drinking the Coke brand is rewarding beyond simply the taste itself because more subjects preferred Coke when they knew it was Coke than when the taste test was blind. Interestingly, there was also significant activation in brain areas like the hippocampus and dorsolateral prefrontal cortex (DLPFC) when subjects knew they were drinking Coke. The hippocampus and DLPFC are known to play a role in *memory* and *recollection*, which suggests that subjects connect their present drinking experience to previous brand associations. What are the decision-making implications? It would appear that separate processes contribute to consumer decision-making: the ventromedial prefrontal cortex responds to sensory inputs; the hippocampus and DLPFC recall previous associations to cultural information. The results of this study, therefore, suggest that the Coke brand is more deeply embedded in certain brain areas for the respondent set at the time that the study was done.

This reaffirms not only the importance of branding, but also shows that the contents of memory influence perceptions about and reactions to a brand. Why was Coke better received? Why did it evoke the response and feelings that it did? Through a combination of brand communication and consumer experiences, Coke created a stronger bond with people, placing itself more firmly in the arena of positive emotions in the affect centres of the brain as compared to Pepsi. Coke was, thus, more deeply embedded in the emotional memory of the customer than Pepsi, at least for the set of respondents in this study.

A lot of consumer research has been carried out to study the influence of brand associations on consumer preferences and how this association is reflected through brand memories. Brand memories can be defined as 'everything that exists in the minds of customers with respect to a brand (e.g., thoughts, feelings, experiences, images, perceptions, beliefs and attitudes)'. 'Studies have shown that different areas of the brain are activated when exposed to a brand as opposed to a person, and decisions regarding the evaluation of brands in various product categories activate the area of the brain responsible for semantic object processing rather than areas involved with the judgement of people.'[68] These two findings suggest that brands are not processed by the brain in the same manner as human personalities, indicating that only personality theory cannot be used to explain brand preferences.

fMRI scans of customers show that for loyal customers, during the choice task, the presence of a particular brand serves as a reward—which is not the case for less loyal customers. Loyal customers also showed more activation of brain areas concerned with memory and emotion, suggesting the presence of an affective bond with the brand.[69]

Changes in neural activity in the striatum (a part of the human reward system) get reflected in brand loyalty levels.[70] When the brain chooses Brand A over Brand B, the brain makes predictions of expected rewards (dopamine, serotonin, oxytocin, etc.) and moves towards loyalty with repeated doses. Over time, the brain learns that the expected outcome from a brand is more rewarding. A helpful salesperson makes one feel good and encourages loyalty. As may a discount in price for a certain customer type. Researchers think that networks in the striatum and amygdala are used by the brain to learn and make better predictions.

Consumer behaviour can now be investigated at the level of both, an individual's conscious choices and the underlying, unconscious brain activity level.[71] The most powerful brands are those that get into the unconscious memory and have an emotional meaning so that the brand almost becomes a habit—a part of a person's life. Neuroscience provides insight into neural differences seen in individuals even when no behavioural differences are observed.[72] For instance, some consumers may recall quite a few memories while exercising a choice whereas some may not at all. The greater the number of positive memories retrieved, the more likely that the behaviour will continue. If, therefore, as a marketer, most of my customers are in the category with positive memories, then one would have a higher success rating. On the other hand, one would be concerned that if the behaviour were not backed by memory, the customer's potential to switch becomes higher.

This insight needs marketers to develop an understanding of the cognitive processes and activities in the consumer's brain at an unconscious level. They can then advertise the product so that it communicates and meets the needs of potential consumers with different predictions of choice.[73] The pandemic of 2020–22 has caused several experiences for potential customers that are now a part of their conscious and unconscious memories (involuntary incarceration, eating at home, preparing food at home, working from home, exercising at home, consuming content from home, etc.) with a high degree of emotional imprinting. The emotional imprints, of course, may be negative as well, which provide opportunities for brands to provide contrasts in powerful ways. Arguably, there is only a small window of opportunity for 'real world' brands to come back to their former levels or more, post pandemic.

Brands that, therefore, seek to establish a connection between consumers and the products they are buying either by forging an emotional connection or by establishing a particular image in a relatable fashion (for example, related to COVID) will get greater traction (at least till signs of COVID remain in our conscious and unconscious memories). It is known that consumers prefer a choice task where there is at least one familiar brand. In addition, the evocation of desired emotions helps. For instance, the brain's reward centres (e.g., the ventral striatum) show significantly higher activation when consumers looked at a sports car as compared to a sedan—presumably because the sports car may be associated with a status symbol or excitement in some way.[74] Many corporations, including Delta Air Lines, General Motors, Home Depot, Hallmark and Motorola, have conducted similar MRI studies to investigate the effect of their brand on consumers, but the results have not been made public.

Neuroscience, thus can help to diagnose steps to be taken that will make the brand emotionally more meaningful and push the brand deeper into the unconscious memory. Essentially, the most powerful brands are those that lead customers to use System 1 processing only—fast, automatic, unconscious and reflexive—as a rule, and System 2 processing (slow, deliberate, considered) only as an exception. Neuroscience has shown that a significant proportion of our decision-making is automatic, intuitive and instinctive—and it's done in System 1, the 'rapid response' part of our brains.[75] After that initial 'autopilot' response, we then rationalize those decisions in the System 2 part of our brains—the reflective and logical section.

*A powerful brand, therefore, provides increases in relevant neurotransmitters more than the competition, reduces energy consumption of the brain, fits into a pattern and provides a contrast at the same time, commands high mirroring among people and is deeply embedded in the unconscious memory of the customer.*

In the following section, we propose some actions that help to improve memorability and to plant memories more firmly in the mind of the consumer.

## Push the Customers to Use Their Imagination

When the brain is forced to use its imagination, it will automatically view a campaign as personal. Leave something open for the imagination when selling a brand.[76]

Take, for example, Nike's 'Just Do It' slogan. This is generally interpreted by customers as whatever 'it' is in their life at the time. Nike has reportedly received mail from people who have left unhappy marriages or taken new jobs that they were afraid to—all despite the company's core demographic being people engaging in sports—having been encouraged by the slogan. Personalization increases serotonin, makes the person more comfortable and reduces perceived risk.

The act of visualizing the use of a brand in the brain leads to it becoming more firmly embedded in the brain. Golfers use the tactic of visualizing the swing of the club to improve the distance and the accuracy of their ball striking. The combination of, and alignment between, visualization and physical action improves distance and accuracy.

## Use the Olfactory Senses

Smell is actually a very important sense for sales and branding. It appeals viscerally because the olfactory bulb, the seat of sensing smell in the brain, is directly linked to the limbic system[77] and the memory system in the brain.[78] For example, Singapore Airlines, one of the most successful airlines in the world, has not only made sure all of their staff uniforms match the aircraft aesthetic, but also has all of their staff wear the same perfume.

Another study of Nike shoes found that 84 per cent of participants rated shoes as superior when in a scented room as opposed to when in a neutral room.[79] Because the smell is such a primitive sense, it can often override higher functioning processes like reasoning and logic. As Gerald Zaltman notes, 'Olfactory and other sensory cues are hardwired into the brain's limbic system, the seat of emotion, and stimulate vivid recollections.'[80] Car companies that changed the interiors of their car from wood to plastic spend time to put in the right smell—that was a part of the customer's memories of what a new car interior should smell like.

## Make the Brand Easily Usable (or in Digital Parlance, Make the UX Intuitive)

The usability features of a product, which help with touch and improve ease of use so that one can use a product without having to think, makes a brand stronger, more deeply embedded in the memory. 'Google it!' has become a popular catchphrase that almost everyone uses nowadays and people have actually forgotten about the actual activity they are doing. Google as a search engine, and more so as a brand, has made the entire process of searching for or looking up anything on the Internet so easy that users actually prefer calling it 'googling' instead of referring to the activity of searching. This trend is so pronounced that even the other search engines struggle to not use the phrase mentioned above.

## Use Shapes

In many cases, shapes can be used to evoke memories in customers. Heart-shaped chocolates remind people of love. Diya-shaped lights commonly used at Diwali in India remind people of the joyousness of the festival of lights. Christmas tree-shaped cookies and themes prompt people to dig into their memory store and evoke the holiday spirit.

Neuroscience helps to assess where the brand is at a given point in time in terms of how the customer's brain thinks and feels about it, whether they trust the brand. While marketers have taken a largely social science approach to understanding the role of trust and applying those insights, neuroscientists have been studying trust from the standpoint of brain function and how that influences behaviour. While the findings of neuroscientists are not inconsistent with what marketers believe to be true about trust, they offer an additional and deeper level of explanation and validation. Moreover, they point to additional levers that marketers can use to build brand trust and engagement.[81] It helps in determining the position of the brand in the minds of the customers and assists in designing a plan for future growth.

We desire the sleek minimalism of an Apple product or the elegant lines of a BMW first, then convince ourselves it's because of the interface or engineering.[82] As brand owners, brand strategists or brand designers, this knowledge can be used to create brands that connect with System 1 (that seduce the unconscious), while also talking to System 2 (convincing the conscious) and thus go deeper into the memory of the customer—of different types and segments.

## The Role of Market Segmentation

An example of where neural research can serve as a tool for marketers is when targeting the youth segment to get into their memories. Young people form a high percentage of buyers in many industries, including the fashion and electronics industries. Due to the development of brain maturation, adolescents are subject to strong emotional reactions, although they can have difficulty identifying the emotional expression of others. The ability to recognize emotions seems to abandon its pre-puberty linear relationship with age and enter a stagnant phase until the ability is picked up again after a few years.[83] This neural information can be used by marketers to target adolescents with shorter, attention-catching messages, and the ones that can clearly impact their emotional expressions. Teenagers rely more on 'gut feeling' and don't fully think through consequences as the executive command centres of their brains are not fully developed. Their decreased ability to judge trustworthiness results in misjudgement in social situations, which implies that they are more prone to risky behaviour.[84] It is for this reason that teenagers are the main consumers of products based on excitement and impulse and those are the products that are more likely to get into their memories easily. Their BOP#1 and BOP#4 drive decisions which are largely influenced by dopamine, adrenaline and norepinephrine. The larger notion, however, is that segments based on emotions are now more possible than ever as emotional profiles of people get captured through their online presence. In a sense, neuroscience can be used to obtain more precise market segments by targeting specific brain functions and accurately entering the memories of target customers. These segments can be on the basis of psychological and neurophysiological profiles by using online data; at least two firms that one knows of are already doing this. In the November 2016 elections in the US, Cambridge Analytica famously used Facebook data to segment and target voter segments.

The question that naturally arises at this point is that if the brain is subject to brain operating principles that brands can tap into and if brands are a part of our memories, if the best brands are deeply embedded in our memories, then how does a customer decide between brands? In our next chapter, we turn, therefore, to decision-making in the brain—especially with respect to brands.

# Chapter 3

# Decision-Making in the Brain: How We Decide about Brands

While the six key operating principles discussed in the previous chapter provide us with an explanation of why the brain does what it does, how the brain arrives at a decision requires equal attention from the branding point of view. How do we decide which political party we should support? Which locality would be best for spending our old age in? Which mutual fund should we invest in? Even a decision as small as which brand to go for, for a bath towel requires decisions.

In this chapter, we first consider the role of reason, emotion, the conscious and the unconscious in decision-making. We then build in inputs from the brain operating principles, including memory, to construct a picture of how the brain takes decisions; this includes a mapping of the neural correlates of decision-making—which part of the brain is doing what in the decision-making process. We conclude by looking at factors such as homeostasis, mood, personality and culture and how they influence the process of brand-related decision-making in the brain.

Decision-making is triggered when we are exposed to stimuli combined with a felt need. Stimuli can take various forms. They can be external advertisements, word-of-mouth information, or a stimulus that drives the need for a product in a category. We could be driving through the city when a billboard catches our attention. It may be a commercial aired during our favourite TV programme, or even what catches our eye as we browse through aisles in a store. We may see products cleverly integrated in movies: an actor riding the latest Honda bike or the actress putting on a certain brand of lipstick on screen. Or a friend may suggest a product to us.

Consider the stimulus of watching the Surf Excel ad. Surf Excel is a Hindustan Unilever product famous for its '*Daag Achhe Hain*'—'Dirt is good'—brand proposition. It urges everyone to celebrate stains. When two kids, a brother and a sister, walk back home from school in their white uniforms, the little girl falls into a puddle, dirtying herself. As she starts crying, the brother decides to seek revenge for his little sister. He dives into the puddle and starts beating it with a barrage of blows. As he fights the puddle for hurting his sister, the girl cheers her brother on. The boy emerges out of it totally dirtied, in soiled white clothes, but with a triumphant smile on his face as he proclaims, 'Sorry *bola*'. The sister is happy that she has been avenged. As they walk back elated with their victory, the brother warns the puddle not to do it again, with a smiling sister in tow. A female voiceover then concludes,

'*Daag lagne se kuch achha hota hai, toh daag achhe hain na.* Surf Excel: Daag Achhe Hain (If getting soiled results in something good, then isn't dirt good? Surf Excel: Dirt is good).' The brain of the viewer has just received a dollop of reinforcement of some patterns and a contrast at the end when the mother smiles to see the dirty kids that makes it more likely that she will buy Surf Excel.

Or picture yourself on a day out at the mall with your friend. As you casually stroll through the lanes of stores, admiring the displays in the windows, your friend mentions that he got a great deal on running shoes at the Adidas store. You are now intrigued by the idea he planted in your head and you respond with, 'Let's go check it out.' If this is a trusted friend or a close associate, and you are also a runner, you may find yourself in the Adidas store in a few minutes browsing through the racks of shoes, contemplating which pair you'd like to buy. Although your original intention was probably just window-shopping, you were prompted to make a purchase.

How does the brain make decisions relating to Surf on viewing the advertisement? Or what drives the reaction to your friend's observation? The advertisement appeals to emotions and the unconscious and reduces energy consumption of the brain (Brain Operating Principle [BOP] #2), fits a pattern in our minds (BOP#3; that of a child fighting for their sibling, that of school kids returning from home), provides a contrast (BOP#4; the fight is with a puddle that has made one child's clothes dirty—this is unexpected; the smiling mother at the end of it saying, '*Daag achhe hain*' is also unexpected), and because of all of these, is memorable and engaging. The same is true for the friend's recommendation. It is low on energy consumption: you do not think too much because it is your friend doing the recommending. It fits into your pattern of looking for deals (Indians are known to be value-conscious). For some, it might be the sheer unexpectedness of the recommendation. And it could be emotionally relevant depending on how much you trust or depend on this friend's recommendation.

## Decision-Making in the Brain: the Role of Reason, Emotion, the Conscious and the Unconscious

A second-level detailing of the processes in the brain that lead to decisions explains the combination of reason and emotion along with conscious and unconscious parts of the brain in the decision-making taking place.

The decisions we make are determined by brain activity ahead of time. It has been found that the outcome of a decision can be encoded in the activity of the prefrontal and the parietal cortex up to 10 seconds before it enters awareness.[85] That is, we are not conscious of the decision as it takes place and become aware of it on many occasions after the decision has already been taken in the brain.

Figure 1 shows the current understanding of the combination of reason, emotion, conscious mind and unconscious mind in decision-making and provides a sense of the relative proportions in influencing decision-making, depending on the nature of the decision-making.

## Figure 1

### Reason, Emotion, Conscious and Unconscious in Decision-Making[86]

| | **Conscious** | **Unconscious** |
|---|---|---|
| Primarily cognition and reason-based | 20–50 per cent (deliberate and conscious reasoning) | 20–40 per cent (heuristics) |
| Primarily affect and emotion-based | 10–30 per cent (recognition of emotions as they are happening) | 30–60 per cent (below the radar completely) |

So if a large proportion of the decisions are made unconsciously or a significant proportion of any decision has an unconscious influence, what about free will?

In early 2016, Proceedings of the National Academy of Sciences (PNAS) published a paper[87] by researchers in Germany in which the authors tried to find out if human subjects possessed the ability to disapprove an action in their own brains (in this study, a movement of the foot) after the detection of its Bereitschaftspotential (BP, which indicates that an action is about to happen). Discovered in 1965, the BP shows unconscious electrical activity in the motor cortex and occurs before the motion is actually undertaken by the person. The 2016 study suggests that the unconscious BP can be overridden by conscious effort even though the brain has prepared for action unconsciously.[88]

So there is evidence for the existence of at least some degree of free will in humans—that conscious reason can override unconscious emotion. However, it also appears that a person could prevent the motion from happening only if they attempted to cancel it 200 milliseconds or more before the onset of the movement.

The study showed that subjects were able to 'override' these signals and stop short of performing the movement that was being anticipated by the BP. Furthermore, researchers identified what was termed a 'point of no return': once the BP is detected for a movement, the person could refrain from performing the movement only if they attempted to cancel it 200 milliseconds or longer before the onset of the movement. After this point, the person was unable to avoid performing the movement. The 1965 paper underlined that the absence of conscious will during the early BP (termed BP1) is not proof of the non-existence of free will, as also unconscious agendas may be free and non-deterministic. The paper, therefore, suggested that human beings have relative freedom, i.e., freedom in degrees, that can be increased or decreased through deliberate choices that involve both conscious and unconscious processes.

In a sense, emotion causes rationality. Not the Aristotelian concept of rationality, nor the rationality that is assumed by economists. Rather, rationality in the context of the organism. Damasio describes this rationality as 'the quality of thought and behaviour that comes from adapting reason to a personal and social context.'[89] So we cannot be rational if we are not also emotional. This may seem quite contradictory. After all, what has emotion got to do with rationality, right? In fact, you may argue that emotion gets in the way of being rational. It is what we are often told by friends, work colleagues and others—to 'separate your emotions from your logical reasoning and be rational'. Research in neuroscience flowing from the works of Antonio, Bechara and colleagues is now increasingly pointing towards the conclusion that human beings cannot reason without a modicum of emotion; that emotion is a part of all reasoning.[90] So decision-making in the brain is a combination of reason and emotion and of the conscious and the unconscious. And strikingly, a lot of this decision-making takes place through unconscious emotion. We can roughly categorize our decisions as Conscious–Cognition, Unconscious–Cognition, Conscious–Emotion and Unconscious–Emotion interactions, or the RECU Framework (Reason, Emotion, Conscious and Unconscious).

**Conscious–Cognition:** On average, about 20–50 per cent of our decision-making is influenced by this condition. This relates to deliberate and conscious reasoning, i.e., controlled processing. For example, when you are asked to multiply two numbers, say 5 and 6, you arrive at the product 30 through deliberate reasoning. When you evaluate an Ashok Leyland 22-ton truck that provides 5 kmpl, requires servicing every 10,000 km and has a life of 3,00,000 km when carrying full load, you compute the lifetime value of the truck as a factor in the decision-making. This is conscious reasoning.

**Unconscious–Cognition:** This accounts for approximately 20–40 per cent of the decision-making process, on average. Under these conditions, we employ what are called 'heuristics'. 'Heuristics are general decision-making strategies people use that are based on little information, yet very often correct; heuristics are mental shortcuts that reduce the cognitive burden associated with decision-making.'[91] These are essentially the brain's go-to rules, energy-conserving shortcuts, when faced with a choice. Heuristics range from general to very specific and serve various functions. For instance, the price heuristic, in which people judge higher priced items to have higher quality than lower priced things, is an example of unconscious cognition and is specific to consumer patterns; the outrage heuristic, in which people consider how contemptible a crime is when deciding on the punishment, is unconscious emotion. The representativeness heuristic leads people to categorize objects according to what they look like rather than statistical probability—and an example of the application of Brain Operating Principle #3, that of looking for patterns that make one feel comfortable.

**Conscious–Emotion:** Around 10–30 per cent of a decision, on average, can be attributed to this. What it means is that we are able to identify emotions as they play their part. For example, if you have vertigo, a fear of heights, you're likely to avoid outdoor activities like bungee jumping and skydiving due to this fear. As you view a BMW car that your friend has just arrived in, you feel a twinge of admiration and envy and are able to identify the emotion as you feel it as it influences you to make decisions.

**Unconscious–Emotion:** A relatively large 30–60 per cent of decision processing for many choices that we make happens below the radar, in the unconscious, and is emotion-based. This is done without our realization. Across all decisions, emotions arising unconsciously are responsible for a major chunk of our decision-making processes. It happens without our knowledge. It is present in most of the things we do—where we go on vacation, the spouse we seek, the products we buy, the school and residence we choose and whether we choose to buy Surf Excel or not.

Let us now examine the decision-making process in the brain in more detail and how it leads to a decision in favour of a brand. Stimuli are processed in the brain along with input from memory, which lead to decision and action outcomes. Figure 2 provides the overall framework for decision-making that builds on the brain operating principles outlined in Chapter 2.

**Figure 2**

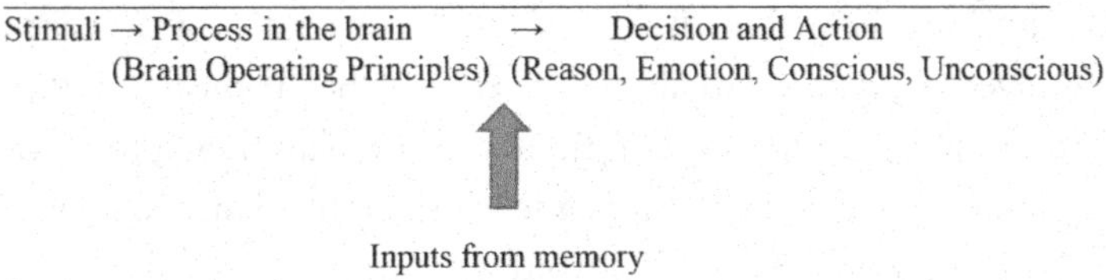

Stimuli → Process in the brain → Decision and Action
(Brain Operating Principles) (Reason, Emotion, Conscious, Unconscious)

Inputs from memory

Most existing approaches to decision-making are based on what was observed in response to a stimulus. One constructed frameworks and models that attempted to explain the reasons for the stimulus response data that was observed. With our current knowledge of neuroscience and biology, we can now also observe what happens in the brain in response to stimuli and how these translate into decisions and actions.

Stimuli come in many guises. When you are casually strolling through a clothes store checking out the various options, your brain utilizes what you see as stimuli. The sensory neurons then relay the visual image to the primary visual cortex (V1), which is located at the back of the brain (posterior end) in the occipital lobe. When you hear a friend recommending a product, what you hear serves as a stimulus. The primary auditory cortex part of the temporal lobe in the brain then processes this auditory information.

Our brain is constantly picking up things whether we notice it or not, consciously or unconsciously. Visual, auditory and sensory inputs get the decision-making process started; they launch a complex process that leads to an end result, be it purchase, perception reinforcement or perception change. So the advertisement, as a stimulus, leads to some processes in the brain, which are partly explained by the brain operating principles, the meta principles behind the decision-making. Apart from the creation of new memories and immediate drivers of action, depending on the context, because of the advertisement, the viewer is also recalling, either consciously or unconsciously, memories that already exist relating to the brand and the category.

These stimuli, in the form of verbal and visual signals, odour and taste, reach our brain's sensory cortex for processing. The neurons in the related cortex respond to the stimulus by firing up and sending neurotransmitters to the different parts of the brains that lie in the path of the decision-making process. For example, a typical visual signal (the 'Daag Achhe Hain' advertisement, or the sight of Surf on the supermarket aisle) enters the eye, reaches the retina, goes through the optic nerve to the Lateral Geniculate Nucleus (LGN) in the thalamus, and then to the visual cortex.[92] Simultaneously, a part of the stimulus also reaches the amygdala, a part of brain which has the primary role in the processing of memory, decision-making and emotional responses. The Surf stimulus fires up neurons in the amygdala and invokes the appropriate emotions towards the stimulus, say, in this example, the emotion of joy.[93] The hippocampus then invokes all the joyful memories of a more innocent time in life, in the context of the stimulus, and thus a memory (or the emotion associated with it) is invoked.[94] Combining responses from both the visual cortex and the hippocampus, the orbitofrontal cortex and the ventromedial prefrontal cortex then evaluate the various options in terms of expected utility of every option and go with the one that appears the most advantageous, the one that provides a better, relevant mix of neurotransmitters! And hopefully, Surf gets bought!

Before we come to the influence of memory on a decision related to brand choice, let us dive into the neural correlates of the decision itself.

## Neural Correlates in Combining Conscious, Unconscious, Reason and Emotion in Decision-Making

Let's look at the decision-making process at a third level of detail (level one was brain operating processes, level two was reason versus emotion and conscious versus unconscious). In level 3, we examine how the brain codes the value of incommensurate alternatives on a common scale to combine conscious and unconscious and reason and emotion in the decision-making process.

Consider a situation where a choice has to be made between consuming an attractive food and seeking a source of warm, pleasant touch. To decide between these fundamentally different rewards, the brain needs to compute the values and costs associated with two multisensory stimuli, integrate this information with motivational, cognitive and contextual variables and then use these signals as inputs for a stimulus-based choice process. The brain uses a common scale for these different 'products'. And, therefore, for brands as well.

New understanding of how value-based decision-making processes are implemented in the brain allows us to integrate neuroeconomic and computational approaches with evidence on the neural correlates of value and experienced pleasure to describe how systems for valuation and decision-making are organized in the prefrontal cortex of humans and other primates.[95] The orbitofrontal and ventromedial prefrontal cortices (OFC and VMPFC) compute expected value, reward outcome and experienced pleasure for different stimuli on a common value scale. Attractor networks in VMPFC area 10 then implement categorical decision processes that transform value signals into a choice between the values, thereby guiding action (I prefer the warm food over the pleasant touch!). This synthesis of findings across fields provides a unifying perspective for the study of decision-making processes in the brain.

Humans are often faced with deciding between two courses of action with entirely different characteristics. For instance, we often need to decide between spending money on a luxury such as a painting or a holiday, and paying for piano lessons or better car insurance. That such incommensurable choice options are comparable with any consistency at all is remarkable, and suggests an efficient neural system that channels options into a core comparative valuation system.

We know now that activation in the medial orbitofrontal and perhaps posterior cingulate cortices is correlated with the difference in value between presented options.[96] This implicates these regions in encoding value comparisons, not simply of the form that one option is better than another, but assigning a quantity that reflects by how much. This finding echoes other evidence of the existence of a cardinal, or cardinal-like, valuation scale in the orbitofrontal cortex (OFC) of the macaque. Previous findings also suggest that the OFC area indexes simple (ordinal) preference.

For example, in a study, respondents were asked to compare goods and choose which item or bundle they preferred. Choices involved both gains and losses; however, subjects did not make decisions that involved a trade-off between a gain and a loss; the trade-offs were between different levels of gains or between different levels of losses. The findings indicated the involvement of the OFC in comparative valuation for choices that involved gains and losses and then a combination of the scores into an overall evaluation score. This suggests that options are compared in a similar manner, whether the aim is to choose the smaller of two losses or the larger of two gains.

The data from this study provides neurobiological evidence that attributes a central role to the OFC in value comparison, where the critical weighting is based on the differences in value between presented options. These differences appear to be assessed using an abstract valuation scale that functions similarly in both gain and loss domains, and is used to influence choice probabilities. The findings speak to a growing understanding of the neural processes related to object valuation executed in this cortical region of the forebrain, processes that are essential in underpinning choice.

The VMPFC and striatum encode the subjective value of different goods or actions during decision-making in a way that can guide choice. But how do these subjective value signals arise? One of the most critical sources of value information is undoubtedly past experience. Evidence with primates indicates that dopaminergic neurons in the midbrain encode a teaching signal that can be used to learn the subjective value of actions.[97] In 2008, we obtained direct evidence regarding the activity of dopaminergic neurons in humans that showed BOLD (Blood Oxygen Level Dependent—the measure of the activity of a part of the brain) prediction error signals in the ventral tegmental area (VTA) using fMRI.[98] BOLD activity in the VTA was significantly correlated with positive, but not negative, reward prediction errors. In 2006, researchers[99] demonstrated a causal role for dopaminergic signalling in both learning and striatal BOLD prediction error signals. What are the implications of this research for decision-making in general, and decision-making in the context of the brand?

The VTA sits at the intersection of the hindbrain and midbrain areas and is largely in the unconscious domain. The OFC sits in the forebrain just behind the forehead and is largely in the conscious domain. Thus, the coding of the relative valuation of decision alternatives is a combination of conscious and unconscious. The figure below provides a sense of the areas of the brain involved in the decision-making process generally and also in relation to brands.

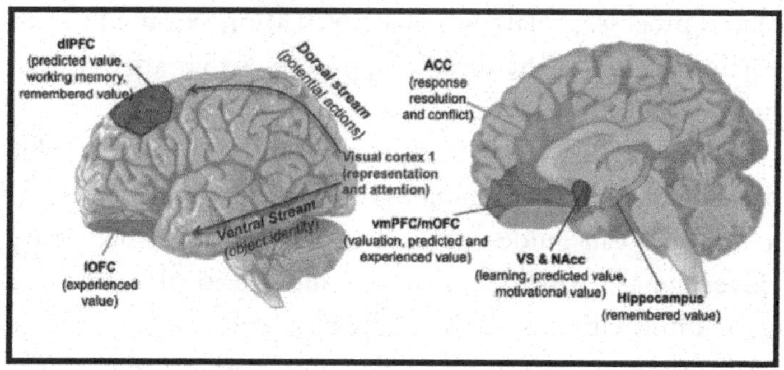


*Brain Areas Involved in Brand Decisions*

## What about Reason and Emotion?

Emotions are the mental states we experience in association with thoughts, behaviours and external stimuli. Neurobiologically, emotions are brought about by the changing levels of neurotransmitters like dopamine and serotonin, oxytocin and acetylcholine, emitted by neurons in specific parts of the brain. Emotions are neurotransmitter levels in the brain and vice versa! For example, a person feeling very scared is going to have a hyperactive amygdala, a spike in dopamine, acetylcholine, cortisone and adrenaline. A person feeling secure, comfortable and very interested will have high levels of dopamine and serotonin. A person getting the feeling that a gain is on the way will have a very active nucleus accumbens[100] and high levels of dopamine. A person feeling a heightened sense of risk will have increased activation levels in the anterior insula[101] and reduced levels of serotonin. A person feeling on a 'high', feeling 'rewarded', is having a surge of dopamine from the ventral tegmental area into the prefrontal cortex area of the brain. And in the context of brands, all of these are in play at different levels in different places for different people.

Emotions are generated by many antecedents. Consider the emotional perception of high risk in the face of an external stimulus that may be pleasant or unpleasant—an advertisement for example. We know that high levels of arousal led to people paying less for insurance against potential losses and greater willingness to pay for lotteries. Arousal leads to risk-seeking behaviour, unpleasantness leads to a greater propensity to protect oneself from harm and pleasantness to gain-seeking behaviour.[102]

Note also that emotion and attention are different and are independent. Strong brain imaging support for the idea that emotion processing is independent of attention comes from an influential fMRI study done in 2001.[103] In this study, attention was manipulated by asking subjects to attend either to pairs of houses or faces, which were presented in a four-picture display. The pictures in the house pairs were either identical or different, whereas the faces were either fearful or neutral, and the subjects were asked to attend either to houses or to faces and to make the same or different judgements. Supporting the view that emotion processing occurs automatically and independently of the attentional focus, fMRI results revealed increased amygdala activity in reaction to the fearful faces, regardless of whether they were attended to or not. What was also consistent with the traditional view was how response times to houses were slower when fearful faces were displayed as distractors. A brand needs to keep drawing attention on an ongoing basis to be able to sustain the emotions associated with it.

## The Role of Memory in Decision-Making

The interesting thing is that most of our decisions are influenced by our emotions and the memories they invoke or the memories that invoke associated emotions; sometimes the memory itself is an emotion. This is what brands do! Invoke memories and emotions. The hippocampus helps in invoking these memories in the context of the emotions received from the amygdala. Since inputs from memory influence play an important role in decision-making, let's have a look at what kinds of memories there are and how they are formed.

We draw from our memory any previous experience: events, facts, WOM, post-purchase experience and evaluations. This can be consciously recalled and are called declarative memories. Past experiences impact future decision-making.[104] It is evident that positive results have a positive impact on people's decision-making. Therefore, if one decision under a given situation yields positive results, a person is likely to make the same decision in a similar situation in the future. However, in case of negative outcomes, people generally do not make the same decisions that led to those negative outcomes. They, in fact, avoid repeating their past mistakes. It, however, does not essentially mean that the decisions made based on our past experiences are always the best decisions. For 'Daag Achhe Hain', this would mean prior experience with Surf or detergents. When my friend suggests I look at a particular shop, that may trigger prior memories of excellent advice from that same friend.

There is also a part of our memory that is accessed without us being consciously aware of it happening. It is a type of long-term memory which is acquired and used unconsciously. It affects our behaviour and thought. This is the non-declarative memory. It is the reason we immediately associate the colour green with peace and why we recall the lyrics of a song when we hear the first few words.[105]

Procedural memory is one of the most common forms of non-declarative memory, which flows effortlessly through our actions. It is invoked each time we are required to carry out a commonly learnt task without much conscious awareness of our previous experiences.[106] It's our 'how to' knowledge. Riding a bike, tying a shoelace and washing dishes are all tasks that require procedural memory. Turning automatically to Colgate toothpaste in the morning. Buying Cadbury as a 'sweet' to be given for celebration in the Indian cultural context. What we think of as 'natural' tasks, such as walking, require procedural memory. Though we can do such tasks fairly easily, it's often hard to verbalize exactly how we do them. Habits and cultural norms also constitute procedural memory. Powerful brands such as Marlboro and Maggi are associated strongly with procedural memory; there are certain actions and contexts that are very closely associated with those brands. The sub-cortical system (inside the cerebral cortex) that is essential to procedural memory function is the basal ganglia system, particularly the striatum (or neostriatum), which is important in the formation and retrieval of procedural memory.[107] A successful brand that is deeply embedded in the unconscious memory should preferably be a part of the procedural memory. As a brand marketer, I would want to associate unconscious automatic actions with the brand for the consumer. Colgate is a great example here.

Studies of memory retrieval also showed that emotional memory is particularly resilient to time; emotional stimuli that are associated with a memory will enable the memory to stay in place up to one year after exposure to the stimuli.[108] So how does memory formation take place?

The cerebral cortex plays a key role in memory, attention, perceptual awareness, thought, language and consciousness. It is divided into four main regions or lobes, which cover both hemispheres: the frontal lobe (involved in conscious thought and higher mental functions such as decision-making, particularly in that part of the frontal lobe known as the prefrontal cortex; it plays an important part in processing short-term memories and retaining longer-term memories which are not task-based);[109] the parietal lobe (involved in integrating sensory information from the various senses, and in the manipulation of objects in determining spatial sense and navigation);[110] the temporal lobe (involved with the senses of smell and sound, the processing of semantics in both speech and vision, including the processing of complex stimuli like faces and scenes; it plays a key role in the formation of long-term memory);[111] and the occipital lobe (mainly involved with the sense of sight).[112]

The medial temporal lobe (MTL, the inner part of the temporal lobe, near the divide between the left and right hemispheres), in particular, is thought to be involved in declarative and episodic memory.[113] Deep inside the medial temporal lobe is the region of the brain known as the limbic system, which includes the hippocampus, the amygdala, the cingulate gyrus, the thalamus, the hypothalamus, the epithalamus, the mammillary body and other organs, many of which are of particular relevance to the processing of memory.[114]

The hippocampus, for example, is essential for declarative memory function, particularly the transference from short- to long-term memory, and the control of spatial memory and behaviour. Active London black cab drivers have up to a 40 per cent larger hippocampus. The hippocampus is one of the few areas of the brain that is capable of actually growing new neurons.[115] The amygdala also performs a primary role in the processing and memory of emotional reactions and social and sexual behaviour, as well as in olfactory memory.[116]

What we usually think of as 'memory' in day-to-day usage is actually long-term memory, but there are also important short-term and sensory memory processes, which must be worked through before a long-term memory can be established. The different types of memory each have their own particular mode of operation, but they all cooperate in the process of memorization, and can be seen as three necessary agents in forming a lasting memory.[117] Powerful brands should exist both as an unconscious procedural memory and as a conscious episodic and semantic memory.

Episodic memory represents our memory of experiences and specific events in time in a serial form, from which we can reconstruct the actual events that took place at any given point in our lives. It is the memory of autobiographical events (times, places, associated emotions and other contextual knowledge) that can be explicitly stated.[118] Individuals tend to see themselves as actors in these events, and the emotional charge and the entire context surrounding an event is usually part of the memory, not just the bare facts of the event itself. When we watch the Surf Excel commercial, the visual stimuli are encoded as sensory input and trigger a recall in the medial temporal lobe of our brain. This accesses our episodic memory, evoking some of our strongest memories. This retrieved memory is even updated during retrieval by gently weaving in the message that Surf Excel conveys.

Working memory is the memory that temporarily holds information for processing and is vital for reasoning and decision-making. Recent functional imaging studies detected working memory signals in both the MTL, a brain area strongly associated with long-term memory and the prefrontal cortex, indicating a powerful relation between long-term memory and working memory.[119] However, the considerably higher working memory signals found in the prefrontal lobe indicate that this part in the brain plays a far more significant role in working memory than the MTL.[120] Encoding of working memory involves the spiking of individual neurons induced by sensory input, which persists even after the sensory input disappears.[121]

**Consolidation and reconsolidation:** Short-term memory (STM) is temporary and subject to disruption. Long-term memory (LTM), once consolidated, is persistent and stable. Consolidation of memory involves synaptic consolidation and system consolidation. The former involves a protein synthesis process in the MTL, whereas the latter transforms the MTL-dependent memory into an MTL-independent memory over months or years.[122] 'Recent findings on reconsolidation fit with the behavioural evidence that retrieved memory is not a carbon copy of the initial experiences, and memories are updated during retrieval.[123,124]

How big a role does memory really play in decision-making, though? Engaging in logical introspection and a methodical review of all the options does seem like the better way to proceed through decision-making. But an Aristotelean rationale can lead to cognitive overload if implemented on all occasions of decision-making and sometimes leads to bad decisions. That would lead to lower levels of dopamine, which goes against the 'feel good' motivation of our brain. Our brain likes to feel good and it looks for rewards to feel good. It feels good and rewarded when it has a dopamine spike (Brain Operating Principle [BOP] #1); it feels good when it expends less energy (BOP#2). It feels good when it sees familiar patterns (BOP#3). The brain (and you as an individual) feels good when it has a surge of oxytocin and vasopressin, the 'bonding' neurotransmitters.[125] Decisions, therefore, that lead to the appropriate changes in the neurotransmitter levels in the brain are taken more often.

Memory provides us with an answer to the brain's wanting to feel good. It reminds us of previous times we faced the same decision and how at those times, we successfully made it so. It leads us towards choosing one option over the other quicker than the hefty analytical part of our brain does. A brand, therefore, needs to ensure that good memories get associated with it. For example, a recent Super Bowl ad for Volkswagen Passat had a child enacting the role of a popular *Star Wars* character, Darth Vader, as his parents neglected him. When it came to making a buy decision between the many options, many *Star Wars* fans were reminded of this ad and memories of their *Star Wars*-struck childhood. The feel-good neurotransmitters would likely be released, leading to an increased inclination towards Passat in the brains of these fans.[126]

Companies could, therefore, follow the lead and try to improve their memorability by triggering a dopamine spike with appropriate levels of serotonin in consumers' brains. For long-term bonding with the brand, they need to generate oxytocin[127] and vasopressin, or their equivalent, in the brain.[128]

When a customer chooses a Cadbury chocolate over an Amul, or an Amul over a Mars, a combination of neurotransmitters, as above, is coursing through the brain, which makes the brain feel better with that choice as compared to the competitor. When a teenager uses their favourite Nike shoes in front of their peers, a similar thing happens. The figure below captures the conscious and unconscious pathways to decisions and the role of memory.

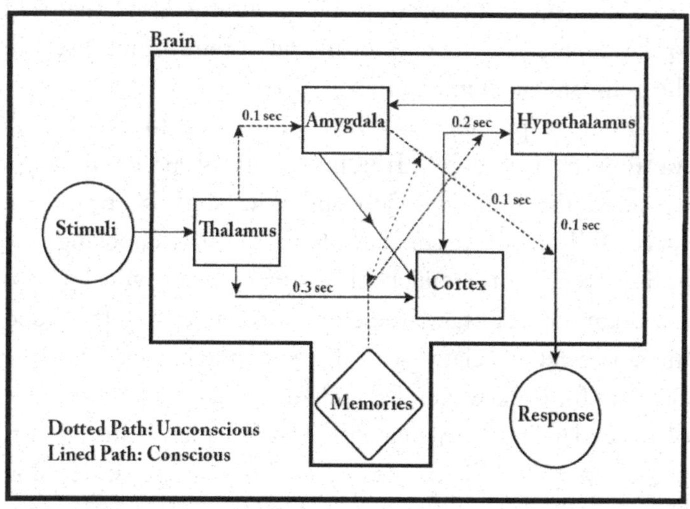


*The Conscious and Unconscious Paths to Decision-Making and the Role of Memory*

Let's look at two studies that further examine the role of memory on decision-making. An experiment was conducted to examine how people arrived at decisions when they were required to choose between options. They were asked to choose from various desserts. The researchers were building upon a previous similar experiment,[129] in which people were asked to memorize either a two-digit or a seven-digit number and were offered a choice between two snacks: chocolate cake (tasty–favourable feelings but unhealthy–unfavourable cognitions) and fruit salad (less tasty but healthy). The idea was to test whether a person would opt for the more emotional-laden (sinful) dessert or the healthy alternative (fruit salad). The hypothesis was that if the mind was cognitively overloaded (trying to remember a seven-digit number), then it would opt for the 'easy' emotion-laden alternative (dessert).

This experiment presented choices between four desserts: chocolate cake, cheesecake, crème and fruit salad. The four-option set was chosen with the rationale that recall and maintenance of just two options may not strain mental resources enough to engender meaningful stimulus–memory differences. Fruit salad was viewed as healthier but less tasty than the other desserts. Fruit salad would thus be more popular in stimulus-based choice than memory-based choice.

It was seen that the observed results were consistent with the notion that memory-based choices are guided more by feeling-based considerations (say, an urge for tasty food), whereas stimulus-based choices are guided more by cognitive or deliberation-based considerations (say, the need to obey a sensible diet). This difference arises because, as compared to stimulus-based choices, memory-based choices are made in circumstances in which cognitive resources are relatively depleted.[130] *As a brand marketer, therefore, an implication is that engaging the reasoning process of a customer in an unrelated task during the decision-making process will lead to a decision that is driven more by emotion.*

This conclusion is further substantiated by a second experiment[131] that also examined a decision pitting a hedonic option against a more sensible option. Students at the University of California, Los Angeles, were asked to indicate which of four colleges they would prefer to attend, assuming that they did not attend their current school. Some participants encountered a choice set composed of Duke University, University of Michigan, University of California, Berkeley and Princeton University. Others encountered a choice set in which Northwestern University replaced Princeton. It was seen that when schools were undifferentiated in fun and academics, no memory–stimulus difference arose, but when schools were differentiated, a memory-based choice would favour fun and a stimulus-based choice would favour academics.

These two studies examined decisions that pit immediately compelling, higher-affect, hedonic, fun options (e.g., chocolate cake) against lower-affect but more sensible or appropriate options (e.g., fruit salad). As predicted, it was seen that memory-based choices favoured the higher-affect, hedonic options, whereas stimulus-based choices favoured the more sensible or appropriate options.

It seems profitable, therefore, for a company to find a way into the into the memory of the customer. There could be many ways of doing so. Cadbury found an interesting way of using advertising within the cultural contexts and Indian traditions that form a part of the procedural memory of many Indians. Consider its Dairy Milk '*Shubh Aarambh*' campaign. This was a shift from its notion of celebrating happy occasions with chocolate to the concept of anticipating the occurrence of something good after consuming the chocolate. The campaign is based on the concept of the Indian tradition (procedural memory) of having something sweet before or during every auspicious occasion ('*Kuch Meetha Ho Jaaye*'—let's have something sweet), with the belief that it leads to a favourable outcome—'*Kaam Achha Ho Jaaye* (the work will go well)'.

One of these commercials[132] opens with a young girl standing at a bus stop relishing a bar of Dairy Milk, as a young boy comes up to her and requests her for a cube of the chocolate. Astonished, the girl asks if she knows him, to which he shakes his head and says no. The girl then asks him for a reason for her to share her Dairy Milk. The boy explains to the girl that his mother told him that before starting anything auspicious, it is a must to have something sweet, so as to be successful in the task. The girl ponders over this and reluctantly gives him a cube of her chocolate. She then asks him what auspicious work he was planning to do. To this, the boy tells her that he was thinking of dropping her back home. The girl looks at him, amazed; the boy smiles at her, and she starts to blush. The voice-over then states, 'Shubh Aarambh. Kuch Meetha Ho Jaaye.'

What is the memory that is sought to be planted? It appeals to the culture embedded deep within us. It tries to change the procedural memory (a synonym for culture) of having a traditional sweet at an auspicious new beginning to having a Cadbury chocolate. Indians grow up with the procedural memory of having sweets to celebrate, for an auspicious beginning or a new venture. The campaign focuses on making the Cadbury brand the centre of this memory. People should automatically think of and buy Cadbury when they think 'Kuch Meetha Ho Jaaye' and 'Shubh Aarambh'. The 'emotional relatability' of the context for the target group increases the probability of the message sticking in the memory.

Talking about the creative concept, Abhijit Avasthi, national creative director, Ogilvy & Mather India, said, 'Shubh Aarambh is yet another cut on our long-running and immensely successful "Kuch Meetha Ho Jaaye" thought for Cadbury Dairy Milk. Though it is rooted in the cultural truth of auspicious beginnings starting with something sweet, we've tried to give it a youthful, contemporary flavour.'[133]

Now that we have a sense of how prior memory works as an input in the decision-making process, and about its importance in decision-making, let us ask the next question: how do we integrate the three levels of decision processes in the brain along with memory to understand how decisions related to brand choice work?

When we watch the Surf Excel advertisement of a boy's love for his little sister, we relate it to our experiences from when we were younger, which are derived from our memory. For most people, there is an evocation of an unconscious summary of emotions from their childhood that is stored in their amygdala, perhaps also the basal ganglia and the ventral tegmental area (VTA), which makes them react positively. Many good memories we have date back to our childhood days. For others, there may be a recall of an actual sibling event that is related to the one being shown in the commercial. This emotion, coupled with the associated past experiences, makes it more likely that the customer will react favourably to the commercial.

Research suggests that when time allowed for a decision is low, basic or relatively automatic emotions are more likely to drive choice behaviour when cognitive load, i.e., the amount of working memory used, is high rather than low, and the emotionally desirable outcome will be selected (e.g., chocolate cake).[134] When the time allowed is high and exposure to choices is high, higher level emotions are more likely to drive choices under conditions of low versus high cognitive load and the affectively desirable outcome will again be selected. In contrast, when time allowed is high and exposure to choices is low, and when cognitive load is low, higher level emotions are less likely to be influential and higher level cognitive processes are more likely to operate, leading to selection of the cognitively desirable outcome (e.g., fruit salad). Hence, the role that task-related emotions play in decision-making is highly context-dependent.

We may also think of emotion-based and reason-based decisions as System 1 and System 2, respectively. Systems 1 and 2 are conceptualized as distinct modes of thought; where System 1 is automatic and emotions-driven, System 2 is controlled and deliberate.[135] Using System 1 and System 2 dichotomies, the choices we make can be classified as memory-based or stimulus-based. Memory-based choices tend to reflect relatively more System 1 processing, whereas stimulus-based choices reflect relatively more System 2 processing. Thus, memory-based choices tend to favour immediately compelling, emotion-rich options, whereas stimulus-based choices tend to favour emotion-poor options whose attractiveness emerges only after more deliberate thought.

Consider a consumer who is looking for frozen desserts at a local grocery store, intending to purchase one of these desserts for a dinner later in the week. Now, suppose that this same consumer is not at the grocery store but is instead at home, drawing up a shopping list of items, including frozen desserts that she will purchase on her next grocery store visit.

In the former circumstance, the consumer is selecting from items that are lined up in front of her at the store itself; in the latter circumstance, the consumer must attempt to recall the items available at the store and only then can select which item to include in her shopping list. The former circumstance illustrates a stimulus-based choice while the latter depicts a memory-based choice.

Recalling a consideration set of relevant options requires effort. In memory-based choice, a customer first has to identify a favourite from their consideration list while devoting resources to maintaining this set in their working memory. In contrast, under a stimulus-based procedure, there is no necessity for recalling the relevant options and thus no need to maintain them in working memory. Thus, the task of identifying a favourite occurs in a context of relatively plentiful mental resources. The memories that are recalled are from the unconscious, which is more efficient and conserves energy—a natural preference of the brain.

An important consideration is that the System 2 processing is easily hampered by cognitive load whereas System 1 remains unaffected by it. In other words, System 1 operates irrespective of whether cognitive resources are strained, while System 2 is expected to operate only when cognitive resources are in abundance. As a consequence of this, System 1 tends to guide memory-based choices, whereas System 2 tends to guide stimulus-based choices. This would mean that the more deeply a brand is embedded in the unconscious memory, in a manner that it is easily cued for recall, the more powerful it becomes in the market, the more likely that it will be the brand of choice.

Emotion has not only transient effects on cognitive processing, but also long-lasting effects, which will eventually lead to better memory for those events. Vivid memories for emotionally charged personal events support this notion, but there is also empirical evidence that emotional events are better remembered than neutral events. Emotional stimuli (including pictures, words and faces) are better remembered than neutral stimuli, an effect that tends to be similar for positive and negative stimuli. This finding suggests that the memory-enhancement effect of emotion is driven by emotional arousal (i.e., emotional intensity) rather than by emotional valence.[136] Also, emotional memories tend to be accompanied by a sense of re-experiencing, and these recollection benefits are also augmented relative to neutral memories over time.

Essentially, emotion enhances long-term episodic memory by modulating activity in two main memory-related brain regions, the medial temporal lobe (MTL) memory system and the prefrontal cortex (PFC). However, the effects of emotion on MTL and PFC regions may be related to different mechanisms: AMY (amygdala) and MTL are part of basic/direct neuro-hormonal mechanisms underlying the memory-enhancement effect of emotion (bottom-up mechanism), whereas PFC is part of a mechanism (also including the parietal cortex) that has an indirect/mediated involvement in the formation of emotional memories and works by enhancing strategic, semantic, working memory and attentional processes (top-down mechanism).[137]

We had earlier discussed how the hippocampus retrieves contextual memories in response to a nudge by the amygdala upon encountering a stimulus. The cue for decision-making acts as a peculiar stimulus to our brain and demands a similar engagement from the emotional and calculating centres of our brain. Once an emotion is invoked, the strong correlation of our memories with that emotion automatically invokes relevant memories. It reminds us, say, of all the joyful times we bought a particular chocolate bar and cherished it with our friends. Or of how disgusted we felt whenever we went to the shoe store next door because of the salesman's rude behaviour. This emotion, along with prior memories and experiences, gives us leverage over having an intense involvement of OFC and VMPFC to objectively choose among the many options. For instance, in the previous two scenarios, our emotions may lead us to choose the chocolate bar and to not go to that shoe store next door. And our brain happily accepts this shortcut in a bid to minimize cognitive effort (BOP#2). In fact, emotional decisions are automatic and far quicker. Moreover, the emotion and the context of the current decision-making leaves an imprint of the retrieved memory, thus re-engineering the memory to encode it within it our current decision. This feedback-like system essentially influences our future decisions, just as it does the current one. Therefore, a brand must seek to get into the procedural memory of its customers as much as possible.

A particular kind of unconscious memory, that we have discussed above (Kuch Meetha Ho Jaaye), procedural memory, is also related to habits. In the section below, we explore habits in more detail to understand how brands can become part of consumer habits—which can make the decision automatic in favour of the brand.

## How Habits Can Influence Decision-Making

During its formulation, a habit is an intentional activity and progresses with time to become automatic in nature. It is in essence an unconscious activity that eventually transforms into an automatic activity that gets done almost without effort. Brushing teeth with Colgate toothpaste is a habit for some. Smoking Marlboro cigarettes is a habit for others.

Habits reflect associative learning and the formation of context-response associations in procedural memory. Once habits form, perception of the context automatically brings the response to mind, and people often carry out that response. As habits strengthen, they gradually become independent of the incentive value of their consequences. In response, the neural activation shifts from associative processing (in the anterior cingulate cortex and VMPFC) towards sensorimotor cortico-striatal brain regions. When repeated in a sequence, habitual responses also may be chunked together and activated as a unit.[138] Brands that become a habit, of course, will have a stratospheric standing in the market: difficult to dislodge, depending on the strength of the habit. The stronger the neurotransmitter (dopamine, serotonin, oxytocin, vasopressin, acetylcholine, adrenaline etc.) response (Brain Operating Principle #1), the stronger the habit. Very strong brands and powerful political leaders become habits for many people—habits that are not easy to break.

Although habits are largely insensitive to changes in goal structure and value, they interact in three different ways with deliberate goal pursuit. First, habits are formed in daily life as people pursue goals by repeating actions in particular performance contexts.[139] Initially, goals and declarative task knowledge structure behaviour. With repetition, responses and associated context cues are captured in procedural learning systems. Goals also may contribute to habit formation by heightening attention to certain stimuli and identifying the value of action outcomes. Given the abundance of direct and indirect connections between neural circuits underlying goal-directed and habitual behaviours, goals can have a biasing influence on habit formation.[140] Goals, therefore, provide a means for cueing and strengthening habit formation.

Crosstalk between habit systems and more deliberative action control, especially during habit formation, is consistent with an evolutionary history in which neural systems supporting more sophisticated planning capacities evolved on top of neural mechanisms associated with habits.[141] Thus, marketing actions that can get a customer to repeat a behaviour would create desired habits.

A second interface between goals and habits emerges after habits form. Habits provide an efficient baseline response that likely integrates with more effortful goal pursuit only when necessary, as when habits prove unreliable in a given context or when people are especially motivated and able to tailor responses to particular circumstances. Various factors impede people's ability to deliberate and thus tip the balance towards relying on habits, including time pressure, distraction, stress and addiction. Addictive substances may, in addition, promote habit responses by accelerating habit learning.[142]

The third way in which goals integrate with habits is through the explanations that people generate for their habits. Because a person is not consciously aware of what triggers the habitual action (and this is why a brand that is a habit AND is associated with a strong neurotransmitter response is like reaching marketing nirvana), people must infer the reasons for their own responses. Under these circumstances, people are quite plausibly likely to infer that there are underlying motivations and goals that are driving the repeated behaviours;[143] the goals and the behaviour provide the pattern for the action (BOP#3). Of course, habits also reduce energy consumption by the brain (BOP#2).

## The Aftermath of a Decision

The culmination of the decision-making process is how we perceive the consequences of the option we finally choose. Sometimes we feel satisfied about our brand decisions, and sometimes, we feel unfulfilled by them.

Let's consider the sense of regret that often follows our decisions. A feeling of disappointment or dissatisfaction with a choice made is an important driver of decision-making. 'Anticipated regret is the belief that the decision will be a result of inaction.[144] Anticipated regret may prompt behaviour; if regret is experienced, it will impact future decisions and actions. People can often get consumed with the path not taken.'[145]

Regret is a function of how a decision was made.[146] The number and variety of options available during decision-making may determine regret. The remorse is a function of the nature of the choice forgone, perhaps, because not enough information was looked at. This regret may get magnified if an individual revisits the forgone options and thinks about the satisfaction from those other options. It is known, however, that people who are dissatisfied with their decisions tend to embrace the decision as a way of reducing anxiety about the quality of their decision.[147] A job applicant, for example, who does not get the job, may reason that he did not actually want to work for that company. A consumer that was unable to buy a brand because of cost considerations will reason that, that brand is not very good anyway.

However, individuals also experience satisfaction with their decisions. How pleased is the decision-maker with the outcome? Many things impact levels of satisfaction. Individuals prefer to make their own decisions and believe they will be more satisfied with their choices; however, when people are given only undesirable options, decision-makers are less satisfied than those who have had the choice made for them. The explanation is that the decision-maker assumes responsibility for the decision. Consequently, making bad choices may make them feel as if they are responsible.

Future decision-making is based on past decisions, as well as levels of satisfaction or regret.[148] While there is evidence to support this notion in many cases, particularly when the decision may be reversed, decisions may be based on the reversibility factor.[149] People are willing to pay a premium for the flexibility of being able to change their minds at a later date. When a shopper purchases using a catalogue or on an online marketplace, they have the option to decide whether or not they will keep the item after it arrives. Gilbert and Ecker concluded that people do have a preference to having an option to changing their minds. Interestingly, having the option to change one's mind inhibits satisfaction with one's choice.[150]

Regret combines reason and emotion and may also combine conscious and unconscious aspects depending on customer and context. On the other hand, feeling 'good' or 'happy' also drives decisions. Dopamine is the 'feel-good' neurotransmitter. When we feel good, dopamine is released. Conversely, when dopamine is released, we feel good. The more the dopamine, the better we feel. It has been proven that more dopamine is released in anticipation than in consummation. Thinking of something releases more dopamine than actually doing it. This is why the post-purchase dissonance occurs. It is why we do not feel as good as we expected we would after the purchase. A powerful brand counteracts this by providing the security of a familiar choice, thereby enhancing serotonin as well.

Therefore, emotions not only participate in at-hand decisions, they are capable of strongly influencing our upcoming decisions. Even when we are faced with a never-before-made decision, the feedback system would encode its aftermath and our emotion, say of regret over a poor decision or of pride over a brave one, and record it for the decisions to come!

Let us now circle back to the Surf Excel example. The advertisement along with prior experience with the product and the WOM feedback from other peers of the customer combine to create conscious and unconscious memories. At the point of consideration and purchase, depending on the strength of the arousal that these stimuli (advertisement, experience, WOM and point of sale stimuli) provide to the emotional unconscious and conscious, the consumer will make a choice. If Surf Excel has managed to provide a strong arousal to the VTA and OFC areas with positive valence and high arousal, through all the possible stimuli, then, at the point of purchase, the probability of choosing Surf Excel rises. When the arousal is very strong and positive from memory, and especially unconscious memory, then the choice becomes automatic! The customer starts using cues or stimuli in their environment to decide in favour of a brand (my detergent has run out; need to buy). Over time, the purchase becomes a habit. And one has achieved marketing nirvana.

And yet, there are other factors influencing the decision that the brain is making in favour of, or against, a brand. The brain is part of a living organism that is in a state of balance or equilibrium in the environment—in a state of homeostasis.

How do changes in homeostasis affect its decision? The brain has moods, or we as individuals have moods, which are a reflection of the nature of the neurotransmitter balance at a given point in time; moods also impact decisions. And then there is personality. The physiological structure of the brain is partly a function of the personality. Finally, culture influences decisions on brands; culture is part of the procedural memory in the brain and, of course, procedural memory can be altered through marketing actions.

In the final part of this chapter, we explore the impact of homeostasis, mood, personality and culture on decision-making. The figure below captures this in a nutshell.

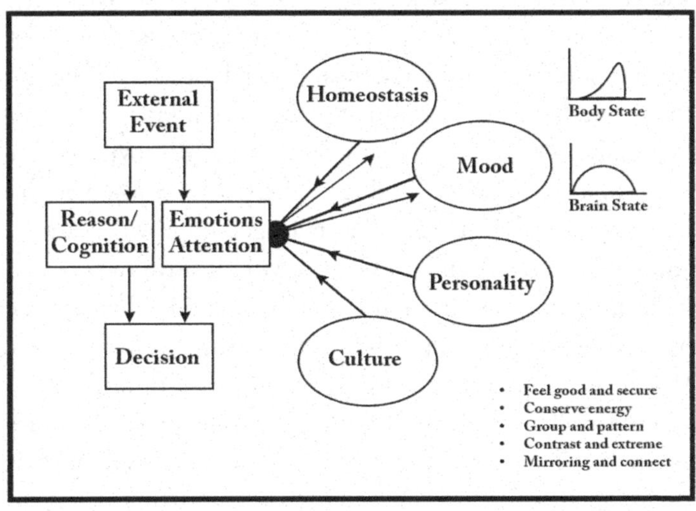


*Drivers of Emotions in Decision-Making*

## Homeostasis

Homeostasis refers to the bodily state of having a particular temperature, heartbeat in a particular range, a particular rate of sweating, etc. When these metrics are within a particular narrow range, we are in a homeostatic balance and are positively inclined from an emotional standpoint. The brand which is able to influence the homeostatic balance in the right direction can lead to positive emotions and greater likelihood of choice. Automotive manufacturers spend considerable amounts of time and money to provide the best homeostasis-promoting features in the car for their customers. Buyers who have bought a new car earlier are accustomed to a homeostasis that is partly driven by the smell of the interiors of a new car. The next car purchase will more likely lead to the same (expected) homeostasis with a similar or same smell. Car makers spend considerable time ensuring that the interiors of a new car smell in a particular way. Notice that this homeostasis is achieved unconsciously.

## Mood

Moods impact our emotions and decisions. For instance, two mood states such as sadness and anger, although both negative, can yield very different judgemental effects. Sadness not only coincides with appraisals of situational control in the immediate situation, but also triggers appraisal tendencies to perceive situational control even in novel situations.

Anger, on the other hand, coincides with appraisals of individual control and triggers appraisal tendencies to perceive individual control. Anger leads to greater risk-taking in men (as compared to women) while women took lower risks when disgusted.[151] People who experienced incidental anger were more likely to evaluate the ideas of others than those who were neutral or sad.[152] Angry people felt that evaluating the ideas of others would improve their mood especially when the expectation was that the evaluations would be low as compared to high.

Thus, sad people will attribute blame to situational factors whereas angry people will attribute blame to other individuals within the environment.[153]

A person can be happy or sad at any given point in time; they can be anxious or content. A study[154] reasoned that distinct affective states of the same valence might have different effects on decision-making. That is, distinct affective states provide people with nuanced information which may impact their implicit goals for an unrelated decision. For example, sadness implies loss or a sense of something missing, which should prompt people to seek rewards or replacements, while anxiety signals uncertainty and a lack of control, which should prompt people to reduce uncertainty and be risk-averse (seek serotonin). In three experiments involving gambling or job choice decisions, participants who were sad sought high risk/high reward alternatives while those who were anxious sought low risk/low reward options.

Antonio Damasio notes, 'We are more vulnerable when we are only vaguely aware that our emotions are being influenced, and most vulnerable when we have no idea at all that our emotions are being influenced.' In an environment of universal social media, where scraping/gathering data off the Net about individuals makes it possible to gauge moods, it is not just possible, but feasible to track moods and develop and deliver interventions for customers that increase the likelihood of a response given a mood. A leading housing company in India is already constructing and using profiles of customers by scraping data off different social media platforms.

Another framework that has caught the attention of researchers working on emotion is the Affect-based Evaluation and Regulation (AER) Framework. AER provides a simple but powerful approach to accommodating divergent streams of mood research under one overarching theoretical umbrella. AER broadly categorizes research on mood into those related to affective evaluation and those related to affect regulation. In the former category of research, emotions (affect) influenced the reasoning process (cognition) directly and indirectly by increasing the use of reason that is in tune with the emotion. Thus, positive moods generate favourable evaluations and proactive action tendencies. In contrast, negative affect has a propensity to generate less favourable evaluations, resulting in inhibitory action tendencies, e.g., buy less! A positive mood will increase the propensity to help if aided by a corresponding motivation. However, if events in the situation tend towards the negative, the motivation may become negative. COVID-19 as an external event has turned motivation negative for many people. Sadness as a mood can be thought of as being driven more by motivation rather than reason. When sadness is seen as being caused by ambiguous negative events that are thought of as circumstantial, people may use reason more than emotion.

In both cases, the mood will impact decisions through emotions.

It is important to keep in mind that mood-related appraisal tendencies are stable and reliable indicators of behaviour. It is known that the hippocampus plays an important role in the pre-attentive stages of encoding of the context of a stimuli.[155] Because appraisal tendencies appear earlier in the brain before the processing happens in the cortical structures, appraisals may be less influenced by cognitive load. That is the unconscious, which may drive more of the decision in the case of moods rather than the conscious and cognition.[156] Alternatively, it might be the case that appraisals occur at the PFC, which appears to maintain the representation of goals and the means to achieve them which would make appraisals less reliable—the unconscious would then be less reliable. If the hippocampus is involved for the activation of appraisal themes and dimensions and the PFC for the subsequent links to judgement and behaviour, then memory and cognition would play a larger role.[157,158]

## Personality

There are many dimensions of personality: introversion and extroversion, risk aversion and risk seeking, accepting and judgementalism, agreeableness, neuroticism, conscientiousness, etc. In this section, we will address a few and look at the implications for decision-making and brand choice.

Studies have suggested that the brains of extroverts pay more attention to human faces than the brains of introverts. In fact, the brains of introverts respond to faces in the same way they respond to images of flowers, whereas extroverts' brains show a stronger response to faces. This suggests that human faces, or people in general, hold more significance for extroverts (which, perhaps, partially explains why they seek other people's company).[159]

Extroverts exhibit more risk-taking behaviour. For example, researchers have found that risky sexual behaviour, such as having unprotected sex, is associated with 'sensation seeking', a trait related to high extroversion.[160] People with personalities that are low in conscientiousness but high in extroversion or neuroticism are also more likely to be the ones getting involved in high-risk sports, including paragliding and skydiving. Additionally, research has linked high extroversion (and high self-esteem, which may be influenced by extroversion) with adolescent smoking.

Unlike introverts, extroverts tend to go for immediate gratification and pass up future opportunities. Researchers have proposed that extroverts may feel greater happiness than introverts because they are more sensitive to rewarding social situations.[161] On the other hand, others have suggested that extroverts are happier because they engage in more social activities.[162] Some scientists think that extroverts' perpetual happiness stems from their greater mood regulation abilities.[163] Or maybe they're happy because they hold on tightly to all of those good memories.[164]

Our personality is part of what makes us who we are, so it's not so surprising that our levels of introversion and extroversion have wide-ranging effects on everything from our language to our risk-taking behaviours and our mental health and happiness.[165]

Extroversion positively related to higher activity in the lateral and the medial PFC and greater activity of the amygdala in viewing positive stimuli.[166] According to Eysenck's theory, the behaviours of introverts and extroverts are due to differences in cortical arousal (the speed and amount of the brain's activity). Compared to extroverts, introverts have naturally high cortical arousal and may process more information per second. This means, essentially, that if you put introverts into an environment with a lot of stimulation, such as a loud restaurant, they will quickly become overwhelmed or overloaded, causing them to sort of shut down to stop the influx of information. Because of this fact, introverts tend to avoid such active environments. Extroverts, on the other hand, are only minimally aroused, so they seek out highly stimulating environments to augment their arousal levels.

In 1999, scientists measured the cerebral blood flow of introverted and extroverted people with positron emission tomography (PET) scans while they thought freely.[167] They found that the introverts had more blood flow in their frontal lobes and anterior thalamus—brain regions engaged in recalling events, making plans and solving problems. Extroverts had more blood flow in brain areas involved in interpreting sensory data, including the anterior cingulate gyrus, the temporal lobes and the posterior thalamus. The data suggested that the extroverts' attention was focused outwards and the introverts' attention was focused inwards.

Research has also shown that introverts have more neuronal activity than extroverts in brain regions associated with learning, motor control and vigilance control, and that their premotor process external stimuli more quickly.

Studies show that the reticular activating system (RAS), which is responsible for regulating arousal, has higher basal activity for introverts than for extroverts.[168] Interestingly, the 'lemon juice experiment' also lends credence to the arousal theory. The RAS responds to all types of stimuli, including food—because introverts have increased RAS activity, they salivate more in response to lemon juice. In another published study,[169] researchers gave participants Ritalin, a drug that stimulates the release of the chemical dopamine, which is involved in reward and motivation. While on

Ritalin, the participants watched videos showing various scenes from nature. After three days, the scientists took away the drug, and then had the participants watch videos in the lab again—the extroverts were excited by the videos, while the introverts were not. The results suggest that Ritalin's effects on the dopamine system didn't translate into reward or motivation for the introverts. This suggests that introverts have a fundamental difference in how strongly they process rewards from their environment, with their brains weighing internal cues more strongly than external motivational and reward cues.

Gender also influences decision-making with respect to brands. Females at a younger age tend to have a greater affect-laden brand relationship as compared to males; this difference between males and females, however, narrows with age.[170] Both males and females at an older age tend to have a greater degree of cognition in their brand relationships as compared to earlier stages in life. During tasks related to emotional regulation, females recruited brain regions associated with emotion processing (amygdala and OFC), while males recruited regions associated with cognitive processing (PFC and superior parietal regions).[171] Unlike men, women develop brand relationships on affect rather than on cognition and the expressivity about their brand relationship also differs: women use greater emotional experiences whereas men use more factual experiences with the brand.

## Culture

Culture has been defined as the sum total of the experiences, the conditioning and the attitudes that determine a pattern of behaviour by a person—a pattern that tends to be relatively fixed. Many procedural memories that we have are a part of the culture that we have imbibed, such as having traditional sweets in India on an auspicious or festival day, or gifting red envelopes in China on New Year's Day, or having turkey on Thanksgiving in the USA. Cultural conditioning is an integral part of our unconscious procedural memories and culture has a large effect on how emotions are generated within a customer.

Let us look at some examples where firms have generated emotions based on homeostasis, mood, personality or culture, or a combination of these.

Diversified financial services company Edelweiss released new TVCs positioned on the thought 'Now you can'. According to Shabnam Panjwani, marketing head, Edelweiss, 'The key objective of this campaign was to establish mother brand Edelweiss's stature among a wider audience in readiness for Edelweiss's expansion in retail broking and mutual funds and entry in life insurance and housing finance. The second objective is to establish a positioning that resonates with the "New India" that is progressive, ambitious and confident of their own ability to make "change" happen.' This is designed for the personality that is ready to take some risks and wants to feel in control.

The idea behind this campaign? To provide the customer a sense of empowerment, a feeling of being 'in control', the emotion of being able to achieve personal financial goals. It focuses on the unstoppable new spirit of India, a country under construction, a nation being built, a country set to grow at a rapid pace. No goal seems unattainable, luxury is no longer a dirty word, and our legendary entrepreneurial spirit is burning brighter than ever. Today, the nation is no longer scared to dream. The campaign reflects this spirit and to help the customer achieve their financial goals—'now you can!' It seeks to elevate that emotion in the customer's mind and to have the customer associate that emotion with the Edelweiss brand. This advertisement pushes people to attain a positive 'can do' attitude to realize their potential and make their dreams come true. The emotions that are generated interact with reason, leading to decisions.

## Summing up Decision-Making in the Brain

Many attributes, like emotions, mood, affect, reason and certain conscious and unconscious factors, join hands to determine decision-making. When a decision is formed, it enters the implicit memory.

As the brain makes and executes decisions, it wants to feel good—essentially, the brain is looking for a reward in the form of a dopamine surge or calming levels of serotonin, or other neurotransmitters. The greater the perceived level of 'reward' by the brain, the higher the likelihood of the action that leads to the reward in terms of the relevant neurotransmitters in the brain; this reward is influenced by the contents of the memory, and the cognition and the affect. The argument is almost circular. More dopamine, serotonin, norepinephrine, oxytocin, etc., mean the brain feels more rewarded. And more external rewards (finding a mate, being able to buy an Audi or Mahindra Thar, wearing one's favourite shoes, going to a preferred theme park) lead to more dopamine, serotonin, oxytocin, etc., in the brain!

So how do we use our understanding of brain operating principles and the way decisions are taken in the brain to improve the design and implementation of brand building and sustaining activities? This forms the subject of the next few chapters.

# Chapter 4

# Why Brands Matter and the Nature of a Brand in the Brain

*'Your brand is the single most important investment you can make in your business.'*[172]

Steve Forbes, chairman and editor-in-chief, Forbes Media

Successful brand management comprises various value components that include identity, functionality, usage experience, emotion and brand relationship-related value that is formed with frequent interaction with and use of the brand.[173] So far, we have touched on how branding has many positive consequences, like recognition, referral generation and differentiation, and how brain operating principles and reason, emotion, conscious and unconscious in the brain drive decisions that can relate to brands. In this chapter, we will explore how brands matter in the brains of customers and, therefore, for firms. We consider the reasons why brands matter, how brands exist in the brains of customers and why and how managers can diagnose, build and sustain brand relationships using ideas like brand love and brand promise, transcending the product in an era of increasing individualism.

Brands matter for three reasons. First, being a 'presence' in the mind of the customer, they can exist independent of the product—and can sometimes transcend the product and even survive there for long periods with no product. This provides enormous leverage to firms that are able to develop powerful brands. In the 1990s, Thums Up—a cola in the Indian market—was absent for six years after Coca-Cola withdrew it from the market under the HQ imperative that the beverage Coca-Cola should be the most prominent brand in the Coca-Cola stable, not some other soft drink brand. It did not work. Coca-Cola Ltd ultimately ended up bringing back Thums Up, which then very quickly became the number one soft drink brand in the country, the position it had occupied earlier.

Second, as a greater proportion of the perceived value in the customer's mind becomes intangible, firms and organizations need to understand the nature of this intangible value so that their efforts to develop that value can be more focused and they can better leverage the presence in the consumer's mind. There is evidence that intangible value constitutes from 50 to 80 per cent of the total market value of a firm.[174]

Finally, as consumers are bombarded with an increasing number of choices and messages, given that humans have limitations on their cognitive abilities (our rationality is restricted), brands are the tools that consumers use to decide and choose; brands become energy-saving devices

(Brain Operating Principle [BOP] #2); brands provide patterns (BOP#3); powerful brands also simultaneously provide contrasts and excitement (BOP#4) and the most powerful combine these with mirroring of lots of people (BOP#5) and strong memory presence (BOP#6). Because brands become the shortcut for choosing many products, services, politicians and other objects, their importance rises further.

## It's All in the Mind

Brands can be said to operate in the mind of the customer at one or more of the following four levels.

Brands are, first and foremost, identifiers. My brand is different from yours. Yours is different from mine. When the American Midwest was settled, ranchers needed to be able to identify their cattle from those of other ranchers in cases of theft and overlap. So they 'branded' their cattle with the mark of their ranch, and so everyone could identify a particular animal as belonging to the Circle K ranch. The logos that we see today can be thought of as direct descendants of these brands. The identifier makes a brand familiar and easily identifiable, fitting (or not) into the pattern in the buyers' mind. But brands are more than a different name, logo, colour, design or shape.

At the second level, brands are a promise of, and deliver, a certain quality, performance and functional benefits. Buying Surf detergent from Unilever is a guarantee of the 'whiteness' of the wash that the consumer obtains. A Grundig tape recorder of the 1960s from Germany was a guarantee of longevity and good sound quality. The Maruti Suzuki car brand in India is considered to be excellent for fuel efficiency and reliability. The consumer uses primarily cognitive pathways in the brain on this second level. A certain level of functional benefit leads to a certain level of valuation in the orbitofrontal cortex (OFC) when a person is comparing one brand with another. The promise of performance and benefit sets expectations; delivering or exceeding expectations leads to positive contrasts and dopamine. Of course, the valuation also includes other components.

It is at the third level that brands become more interesting. In addition to functional benefits, brands are about *transaction-specific emotional benefits*. Buying a BMW 320i makes the customer feel good about themselves, it gives them higher status among peers and it offers high performance. The nucleus accumbens in the brain fires up in anticipation of the reward (i.e., the good feeling of the high status along with the attendant dopamine). The consumer uses affect pathways in the brain by providing transaction- and usage-specific affect benefits. By the 1980s, most top brands had reached this level.

Transaction and usage-specific benefits lead to a desired order and structure rather than chaos; customers often achieve structure by believing that they are in control of the outcomes in their lives.[175] However, life-altering events will often shake this belief. Events such as random violence, severe economic downturns and natural disasters. The COVID-19 pandemic of 2020–22 is one such life-altering event. Sometimes even minor events like a favourite product not being available at the local store can cause the feeling of loss of control and influence the level of perceived transaction-specific affect. It is at these times that people look for other signs of structure and affect. One manifestation of this desire takes place in the arena of brand choice. People will impose narrower boundaries on the brand—what it can do and not do, where it belongs, what is okay and what brand actions are not in order to derive the emotional satisfaction (affect) from the product/service.

At the fourth level, consumers begin to form relationships with brands. The brand has a personality and becomes anthropomorphic in nature.[176] Take, for example, the way people talk about Apple iPhones, or how attached people are to consumable products like Maggi noodles. It becomes personal to the consumer and is a part of the consumer's life. If the brand is missing, the consumer feels as if they are missing something. Consumers can develop relationships with brands on the basis of brand attributes or brand personality. For instance, consider luxury brands like Versace, Armani or Rolex. Their sophistication is exemplified through their advertising campaigns, and attracts consumers who can associate with this personality. The consumer feels connected to the brand, feels love and passion for the brand and feels incomplete without the brand; relevant brain pathways and neurons display long-term potentiation that persists over time. When faced with a preferred brand, the VMPFC, an emotion centre of the brain, becomes more active; simultaneously, the dorsolateral prefrontal cortex (DLPFC), a part of the brain closely associated with reasoning and logic, becomes less active. Indeed, some evidence suggests that at a deep level, a brand relationship is akin to love—brand love. Customers love their brands and, therefore, it would not be amiss to claim that some levels of oxytocin and vasopressin are involved at this level of a brand relationship.

Our present understanding, derived from research in marketing and neuroscience, strongly indicates that at the brand relationship level of something called a 'brand ladder', customers bond with the brand. Brand relationships are created along dimensions such as brand partner quality, love and passion, self-connection and interdependence, commitment and intimacy.[177] The customer's preferred brands activate the regions of the brain (paracingulate gyrus and temporo-parietal junction) used for emotional meta-representations.[178] Figure 2 summarizes the brand ladder. Brand ladder is a term coined by Kevin Lane Keller that describes the nature of consumer engagement with the brand and determines where a brand exists in its journey towards having a meaningful long-term relationship with the consumers. New brands, typically, are competing only at levels one and two. The strongest brands compete at all four levels, with a large proportion of the value to the customer coming from level four; indeed, a large proportion of the customers may be at level four.

**Figure 2**

**The Brand Ladder***

Nature of Consumer Categories of Consumer Engagement with Brand

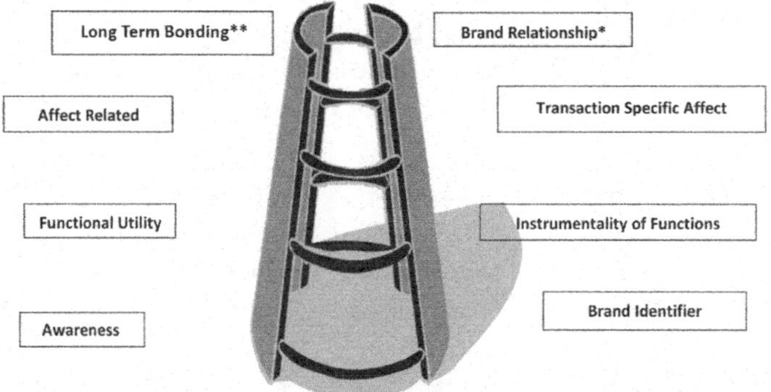


** Right side of the ladder: various categories of customer engagement with a brand.*

*** Left side of the ladder: nature of customer engagement at each level.*

Table 1 below captures the difference between brands in level three (that is primarily based on transaction-specific emotional value) and a brand that has developed a relationship with the customer (level four).

This table summarizes the differences between affect and brand relationships.

**Table 1: Difference between affect and brand relationship**[179]

| **Criteria Defining Level of Brand Engagement Categories 3 and 4** | **Affect-related (Category 3)** | **Long-term Brand Relationship (Category 4)** |
|---|---|---|
| **Level of affect** | Emotions generated can be because of the functional benefits/ social benefits; limited in nature. These emotions tend to be event- and time-specific. | There exists a very high level of affect/passion for the brand; this affect is at a qualitatively higher level compared to level three. Emotions are at the level of a bond and somewhat independent of functionality and time. Dopamine levels in the brain tend to be high. |
| **Longevity of use** | At this stage, a brand could be used once or more in the time to come. | It's a long-term commitment with the brand. |
| **Consumption pattern** | Varying levels of usage of the brand. | Consumer behaviour tends to approach ritualism. |

| Criteria Defining Level of Brand Engagement Categories 3 and 4 | Affect-related (Category 3) | Long-term Brand Relationship (Category 4) |
|---|---|---|
| **Post-consumption pattern** | Using the brand feels good to the customer. There is a dopamine surge specific to the event. | It becomes a part of one's life. Consumer feels connected and possessive about the brand. Absence of the brand leads to a sense of deprivation—serotonin levels fall. Long-term higher dopamine levels. |
| **Co-creation** | More focus on attracting and engaging customer. | Users participate in co-creation of brand value and the process has greater mutuality. |

Research, put together with anecdotal customer perspectives, conceptualizations and evidence in marketing and neuroscience research literature, substantiates the four levels of the brand ladder: customers bond with the brand; brand relationships are created along one or more of the following dimensions:[180]

- Brand partner quality: brand considered a reliable and trustworthy partner.
- Love and passion: these are the affect-based feelings related to the brand indicating warmth, affection and passion, possessiveness towards the brand, feeling of uniqueness and a biased positive feeling towards the brand.

- Self-connection: is the extent to which the brand becomes the focus of the consumer's life—the past, present and the future (expected) selves of the customer as connected to the brand.
- Interdependence: routine interaction with a brand, making consumption an important ceremony to be celebrated.
- Commitment: shows the longevity and stability of the brand relationship.
- Intimacy: represents strong beliefs about the superior performance, memory of personal associations and experiences; elements of person-brand congruity.[181]

Coca-Cola has been a global leader in branding under which a diversified portfolio of brands thrive. It has different brands on different steps of the brand ladder. Consider the Minute Maid Pulpy Orange launch in India: this was an example of a brand launch where Coca-Cola focused on the product attribute for the first two years ('Where's the Pulp' campaign). This is the first step of the brand ladder—it describes 'what it is' or product attribute-based differentiation.

Similarly, for Maaza Mango in India, Coca-Cola has celebrated the fact that Maaza is the best mango experience you can get in a bottle. The communication platform positioned Maaza as the best and the only way to quench the thirst for mangoes, a strong desire which hits most mango lovers in summer, through '*Aam Ki Pyaas*' (thirst for mangoes), and all the activities Coke did around it were to communicate superior quality and performance on mango taste. This is the second step of the ladder—it describes 'what it does' or functional differentiation. Both these products are on the functional step of the brand ladder, with Maaza having a foot on the affect rung because of the experience promise and the fact that since it is a summer fruit in India, there are many mango aficionados who have a particular fondness for mangoes.

Further up the ladder is Thums Up, a Coca-Cola beverage brand in India. It celebrates masculinity, the strong cola for the real man, with an apt tagline, 'Taste the thunder'. For many years, Coca-Cola has focused on establishing Thums Up as the ultimate male icon among beverages. A Thums Up drinker feels good drinking it in front of his peers (with a majority of consumers being male). This is the third step on the ladder—'how it makes you feel' or emotional differentiation.[182]

This would further turn into a brand relationship when a Thums Up drinker's sense of personal identity is tied to the brand, when he feels something is missing if the brand is not present, when Thums Up is present at significant milestones in the person's life and when it provides a sense of uniqueness.

Mountain Dew is another brand that strongly identifies with its target group. Its core target group is males, typically of the age group of twelve to twenty-nine years. The name Mountain Dew is very strongly linked to the mountains. Climbing a mountain means having enough physical as well as mental strength to be able to reach the top. It encourages an active lifestyle and supports taking on challenges and risks. Its tagline, '*Darr ke aage jeet hai*' (beyond fear lies victory) addresses the adventurous spirit of the youth and encourages them to be bold and daring. It is commonly associated with masculine prowess. Mr Pratik Pota, executive vice president, marketing–flavours, PepsiCo India, aptly said,

'Mountain Dew is a brand that exemplifies the adrenaline rush, exhilaration and a "can do attitude".'[183]

The next aspect to pay attention to is 'whether the brand increases the stature of the customer in the eyes of their social circle':[184] the social benefits. Those who own a Harley-Davidson are part of the elite HOG (the Harley Owners Group); buying a Ferrari allows you to enter the 'Ferraristi' clan with pride.[185]

Across different markets, brands are being imbued with personalities[186] and consumers are developing relationships with brands.[187] Some even love their brands and see them as part of their extended selves.[188] Many studies have shown that some of the reasons for unique and strong brand loyalty are habit, intergenerational influence, unique sensory stimuli, emotional security and right fit with personal identity. This has been the case even if respondents rationally claim that the brands were functional.[189] Such phenomena have implications for the development and management of brand relationships. Strong brand relationships are a way for managers to increase customer loyalty and, thereby, get marketplace advantage. Managers can diagnose, build and sustain brand relationships to obtain customer loyalty and competitive advantage.

The relationship between companies and the Indian consumer has visibly changed both parties. The MNCs among India's trusted brands, such as Samsung, OnePlus and others, have not succeeded with the same versions of their offerings elsewhere. The Indian consumer has demanded and received products and services with local relevance, innovative business models and appropriate pricing. What the consumers seek is a brand that strikes a chord with them. Indian companies, too, have had to innovate to sustain loyalty and many have acquired new capabilities and customers in the process.

Evidence on brand relationships provides some interesting insights. First, brand relationships exist across income strata—but there are product category effects and income effects.[190] Consumers are more likely to form brand relationships with products that they use more frequently and are dependent on for functional or emotional reasons.[191] Consumers who are above a certain consumption threshold (in terms of the variety and quantity of products and brands consumed) are more likely to develop brand relationships. Low price brands can also be candidates for brand relationships among lower income customers. Many owners of Hero CD100 Dawn (an entry-level motorcycle in India positioned as an alternative to public transport, which sells for around Rs 45,000 and serves as a commuting vehicle and family vehicle) display evidence of brand relationship along the dimensions of brand partner quality and interdependence.[192]

Second, age and gender have a significant influence on the nature of the brand relationship that is established. Across countries, young consumers, and teenagers in particular, form strong relationships with their brands. Younger consumers tend to establish stronger affect-based brand relationships as compared to older consumers. Research indicates that the age group of thirteen to nineteen years is higher on the affect dimension than young adults (twenty to twenty-five years); the older group also develops strong brand relationships, but they are relatively more rational about their brand relationships. In addition, females at a younger age had a more affect-laden brand relationship as compared to males; this difference between males and females, however, narrows with age. Both males and females at an older age tend to have a greater degree of cognition in their brand relationships as compared to earlier stages in life.[193] Unlike men, women develop brand relationships on affect rather than cognition and the expressivity about their brand relationship also differs—women use greater emotional experiences whereas men use more factual experiences with the brand.[194]

Third, brand relationship development is a function of opportunities in the 'market'. When Maggi was banned in India, it used the time that it was not present in the market to connect with its customers on a regular basis. It would update customers on the status of the legal cases. It would respond to customer comments on social media. Tweets from customers that '#We Miss You Maggi' were responded to in near real time with '#We Miss you Too'. TV campaigns were run to reassure mothers that they had done the right thing in feeding Maggi to their kids.

Fourth, in many instances, the desire for a brand leads to significant changes in the consumer's behaviour. For instance, when consumers develop relationships with luxury/high-end brands, they are ready to change themselves to suit the brand requirements to better fit the pattern that they have constructed in their brains (Brain Operating Principle [BOP] #3). Consumers who wear a Rolex watch change themselves to suit the brand requirement, their appearance, the way they carry themselves. Within this category, brands can be either aspirational—which make you change in order to develop a relationship—or inspirational, just as The Body Shop inspires consumers with its values and environment-friendly approach. This has also been called the Diderot Effect after the French philosopher, who had a rather cluttered office/study, and yet, after hanging on his coat stand in the office a robe of some distinction, found himself over time replacing other things in his office to match the robe, including his own clothing, displaying self-connection and intimacy. The effect was first described in Diderot's essay 'Regrets on Parting with My Old Dressing Gown'. Here, he narrates how the gift of a beautiful scarlet dressing gown leads to unexpected results, eventually plunging him into debt.

Diderot was initially happy with the gift. However, in comparison to the gift, the rest of his possessions seemed inadequate. And he slowly replaced his other possessions to match up with the elegance of his new possession. His old desk, for example, was replaced with an expensive new writing table. 'The poor man may take his ease without thinking of appearance, but the rich man is always under strain.'[195] In this instance, the purchase of the gown triggered a change in the pattern; the new gown became the keystone for an entirely new pattern, building on an unconscious desire in the philosopher's mind.

The gown provided the initial trigger, dopamine, to Diderot (BOP#4: the contrast effect). The underlying desire for a pattern (BOP#3) then took over, driven by the salience of the gown, somewhere in the recesses of Diderot's brain.

Fifth, in many brand relationships, there is a strong community of users (e.g., Harley Owner Groups, Mac User Groups, Java Community Centres); a significant part of the brand relationship benefits comes from brand community-based activities and the emotional benefits generated. Among American Harley-Davidson consumers, for example, there exists a hierarchy based on the status of the bikers. They reinforce the ethos and values with the community and show a ritualistic pattern in their usage (BOP#5 and BOP#3). The identity, the motives and the level of commitment of the individuals who are a part of the subculture evolve in patterns that are linked to the product and its usage.[196] Fellow riders develop relationships with others who have similar values and perspectives, indicating the co-construction of the Harley-Davidson brand experience. In this process of consumption, consumers also start entertaining each other and socialize, thus making consumption a socializing tool and the brand a symbol of that socialization.[197] Research supports the importance of purposively selecting, initiating and managing interactions among customers when facilitating brand communities.[198] Thus, the existence of brand relationships is influenced by product category effects, demographics, market opportunities, consumer-driven change in self-behaviour and the possibility of building brand communities; in each of these cases, neural pathways in the brain have undergone long-term changes.

## Brand Relationship

Given the social nature of humans, it is not surprising that we have the capability to form relationships with inanimate, and often intangible, objects like brands. Similar to the way we harbour relations of trust, protectiveness with other humans, we form relationships with brands. Brand relationships, just like interpersonal relationships, consist of four core concepts or expectations: that of reciprocity (participation of the partners involved), meaning provision (in psychological, socio-cultural and relational spheres), multiplicity (regarding different roles a relationship may play in the lives of the partners) and temporality (a space for evolution in response to changes in the environment).[199]

Brands as relationship partners may develop through anthropomorphization, association of a strong spokesperson with the brand or lending the partners human qualities of emotions, expectations or thought. Anthropomorphization is often a major consequence a brand expects would emerge out of its marketing tactics. It's not simply the portrayal of the brand as a human; rather, the brand must persuade consumers to associate human-like qualities with it. Consider the popular 'cleaning' brand Mr Muscle. Its commercials often feature an orange costume-donning muscular superhero called Mr Muscle who goes about fixing household cleaning crises. The brand's explicit efforts towards lending itself human-like features seems to have resulted in the creation of a mascot instead. On the other hand, when a customer explicitly relates something like 'But I can't possibly live without it!' a brand has successfully been anthropomorphized. Imagine that Netflix suddenly recalled its site. If you are an ardent binge watcher, you will be devastated and will scramble to watch and download all of its content before it shuts down. The drop in some neurotransmitters would be substantial (Brain Operating Principle [BOP] #1).

Once a brand has established itself as a partner, the consumer expects it to contribute to the initiation and maintenance of the relationship and the brand's everyday marketing tactics are seen as contributions. There are different kinds of relationships that enjoin the customers and the brand, all on the basis of seven categories: voluntary vs imposed, positive vs negative, intense vs superficial or casual, long-term vs short-term, public vs private, task-related vs personal and symmetric vs asymmetric. For example, a continued connection with a brand of detergent that one uses just because one's mother used the same can be classified as a 'kinship', an imposed connect with lineage ties—it forms a part of a familiar pattern of behaviour and is a part of procedural memory (BOP#3 and BOP#6). Or you swearing by a brand of perfume because it has always made you feel good could be classified as a 'committed partnership' wherein you have voluntarily committed to a brand for the long term because it has socially or psychologically helped your confidence on many occasions. Other categorizations include 'arranged marriages' (long-term imposed exclusive commitment), 'courtships' (interim state on the way to a committed partnership), and 'flings' (short-term, time-bounded engagements of high emotional reward, but devoid of commitment or reciprocity demands).

Finally, what good would a discussion on brand relationships be if we didn't have a way to measure the extent of the partnerships? On the basis of the brand's affective and socio-emotive attachments, behavioural ties and supportive cognitive beliefs, one could assess the quality, depth and strength of the brand relationship. The degree of interdependency, intimacy, commitment, self-connection and love and passion determine the brand relationship quality. For example, engaging a particular caterer every time there is a dinner party highlights the ritualistic nature of the bond between the hosts and the caterer, or an interdependency. Or a brand holding emotional significance in a person's life, or perceptions rooted in beliefs about the products, translates this intimacy into a strong bond.

Let's have a closer look at the result of a high quotient of the 'love' component for a brand.

## Brand Love

Neurologically, a distinctive feature of love is that just a subliminal verbal reference, of a loved person or brand, activates brain areas like the fusiform and angular gyri, which are involved in the abstract representations of others; this does not occur when referring to friends or a hobby.[200] In addition, similar brain reactions in the fusiform gyrus were recorded for people who felt passionate about a retail luxury store and where they spent much more in absolute and relative terms than others, suggesting that love and relationships can extend to a brand. Significantly, activity in the gyrus, the amygdala and the anterior cingulate cortex in the brain significantly correlated with the passion score.[201] Love is also associated with high levels of oxytocin (connecting to neurons in the nucleus accumbens) and vasopressin (acting in the ventral pallidum), which promote bonding (associated with brand relationships) that persist over time. Brand love is known to lead to higher purchase and positive WOM.[202] It is important also to note that symbolic, hedonic and experiential benefits of a brand[203] are subsumed under the affect-related activity in the brain, while functional benefits tend to be more cognitive in nature.

Brand relationships result from dopamine and oxytocin in the brain in the region of the nucleus accumbens and amygdala and, critically, have long-term neurological connections among neurons, which is physiologically different from the 'temporary' excitation of transaction-specific affect, hence the difference in the categories between affect and brand relationship. Consider the relationship that people have with Maggi. For years, Maggi has been synonymous with 'instant noodles'; the pattern in the mind that it evokes is instantaneous and strong, leading to a sense of familiarity, safety and security (BOP#3).

When Maggi went through adverse laboratory findings and the ban in 2015, warnings were plastered all over TV, print and online media notifying us of the excessive lead content in Maggi. Watching these, the anterior insula fired up, heightening the sense of risk. Levels of serotonin, vasopressin and oxytocin decreased, following the sadness, feeling of fear and uncertainty resulting from bad faith—a trusted brand like Maggi had betrayed us. The negative contrast from what was expected (Brain Operating Principle [BOP] #4) needed to be managed carefully through reassurance and other actions.

Evidence from neuroscience also suggests that brands always play a role for consumers, that consumer decisions have a brand and emotion-related dimension. For preferred brands, deemed a 'rational choice', there was still a significant response in the right ventral striatum, the reward centre of the brain that is connected to emotions, an important underpinning of brand value. Evidence also suggests a strong affective memory component through hippocampus and VLPFC activation for a preferred brand.[204]

In the research literature, the conceptualizations and operationalizations of brand relationship and brand love are closer to the neurological bases of love as emotion[205] rather than friendship.[206] Brands that customers have affect for but where customers have not reached a 'love' or 'relationship' stage are therefore, also represented differently—neurally.

This data suggests that brand love and, therefore, brand relationships exist at a different level of engagement as compared to simple 'affect', associated with transaction-specific affect (or 'friendship') that we postulate as being in the affect level of the brand ladder, i.e., brand relationships tend to be more System 1-driven.[207] This is very important because System 1 is the involuntary, quick response that is evoked; it is largely in the unconscious and determines which brand a person chooses over another.

## Brand Promise

At any given point, once a brand gets established in the minds of a large enough number of people, the brand is a promise of an expected amount of benefits at one or more levels (identifier, functionality, affect and relationship). The evolution of a brand towards relationships needs to happen at the customer end through customer actions, emotions, beliefs and attitudes. The expectation from the brand becomes an implicit promise or contract for the customer, who gets their brain objectives (BOP#1), whether it is security, reward or pain avoidance, from the brand through a mix of the relevant neurotransmitters.

The airline mechanic promises to do a thorough job, checking and rechecking the aircraft to make sure it's safe—that's the promise of airlines in general. The promise of Southwest Airlines is that the customer will get a low fare. Restaurants promise to provide fresh food made in clean environments; the promise of a Michelin-starred restaurant is that it will give you food of a quality that is above a fairly high bar. Often, there are legal repercussions that bind people to fulfil these promises, but more often than not, promises and vows are maintained based on the individual's own moral and ethical code; the contract is implicit rather than explicit. We have an unspoken contract with the people we live and work with, that they will do what they say they'll do. We have similar agreements with companies, products and services. And with brands.

At the heart of branding, therefore, is the promise that is made by the organization to the customer. The brand promise tells the audiences who the brand is, what it believes in, and what unique value it provides. The ability to fulfil its promises at every stage of the relationship is the defining factor for most organizations' success or failure. When promises are broken, the reputation of the organization is called into question, and the brand suffers. When brand promises are kept, audiences respond with loyalty and affection.

The simple act of getting a soda out of a vending machine is an exercise in brand promise. The vending machine offers many drink options to choose from, but more than likely, our drink selection will be based on prior experiences with a specific product. We have an expectation of an experience when we make our selection, much of which has been established through the decision-making steps of awareness, interest, desire and satisfaction. Interestingly, the things that influence our decision-making process have little to do with the product or service. Much of our experience with a product or service is created through the associations that we've made with the product through advertising, brand identity and the environment in which the product is experienced.[208]

Dubai promises luxury. A part of this promise comes to visitors from 1999, with the opening of the Burj Al Arab, often referred to as the only seven-star hotel in the world. The sail-shaped hotel became an instant symbol of excessive luxury, sending the implicit message that the standard for all hotels in Dubai is luxury. In 2007, the emirate reinforced its positioning strategy by building the Burj Khalifa, the tallest tower in the world, which houses the first and only hotel designed by Giorgio Armani. Even the police force has embraced the luxury brand, acquiring a Lamborghini Aventador worth US $4,50,000 to complement its fleet of police cars. These actions speak louder than words. Dubai didn't inherit an Eiffel Tower, but the emirate was able to create a brand advantage based on its value proposition of luxury. This brand promise didn't come out of nowhere. It was rooted in the prevailing brand image of overindulgent sheikhs in the Middle East.[209]

Consider, also, the controversy of forced deboarding of an elderly passenger on a United flight. This poor customer service incident elicited anger from millions globally. The outrage only grew after the CEO's comments defending the airline crew's actions. On subsequent interaction with United, our anterior insula would fire up, increasing its risk perception. Following this event, United stocks dropped sharply, by $1.4 billion.[210] United had to pay a heavy price for forgetting their brand promise of making 'every flight a positive experience for customers'.[211] The decrease in dopamine made the airline lose a couple of notches as a choice on a given route for many potential flyers. This incident was a forewarning to all companies to re-evaluate their staff alignment with the brand's promise.

## Brand Transcends Product

Brands are a stable asset. Products might fail, companies are bought and sold, technologies change on a daily basis, but strong brands carry on through all these changes. Brands are the most sustainable asset of any organization, and when aligned with the overall strategy of the organization, they can function as the central organizing principle for the organization's decision-making.

Moreover, people don't have relationships with products, they are loyal to brands. In a firm's strategy, brands have a purpose that people can get behind. Brands can inspire millions of people to join a community. Brands can rally people for or against something. Products are one-dimensional in a social media-enabled world, whereas brands are like Russian dolls, with many layers, tenets and beliefs that can create great followings of people who find them relevant. Brands can activate a passionate group of people to do something like changing the world—once the mirroring effect (Brain Operating Principle [BOP] #5) goes above a certain scale. Products that have not developed into brands can't really do that.[212]

In the face of the economic and cultural challenges brought about by the SARS-CoV-2 pandemic, it's worth noting that powerful brands do better in tough times compared to unbranded products. They provide certainty in a time of uncertainty. Paradoxically, because people have been shaken out of their usual pattern of behaviour, and are being exposed to new products, they can be persuaded to try new things.

Brands outlive product cycles. And in challenging times, like a pandemic-induced time, there are still great brands being built. Brand owners still recognize opportunity and their brands will thrive in the years ahead. Brands such as H&M of Sweden, or Tesla, a great car brand, which started out as products a few years ago, now enjoy a growing global customer base.

Furthermore, brands can exist independently of the product.

Steve Jobs died on 11 October 2011.[213] But to this day, his name is synonymous with Apple. To this day, even years after his death, people still remember him. The brand he created for himself has far outlived his physical being. Lambretta started as a scooter brand in Italy. It was then licensed to Scooters India Ltd in India. When Scooters India stopped making scooters, the brand was licensed and a royalty paid on products that were using the Lambretta brand logo. The Jawa brand of motorcycles, originally a Czech brand, had a huge following in India; it has been relaunched in India by Mahindra & Mahindra in 2019, some twenty years after the original Jawa brand of motorcycle went off the roads in India. Lambretta and Jawa are a part of the procedural memory of a certain set of people, and also part of a familiar pattern (BOP#6 and BOP#3).

A timeless example that can be used to understand the advantage that a brand has over a product is that of Thums Up, a brand of cola in India, which was launched in 1977 after the withdrawal of Coca-Cola from India. The brand was later bought by Coca-Cola when it came back into India in order to compete against Pepsi. In February 2012, Thums Up was the leader in the cola segment in India, commanding approximately 42 per cent market share and an overall 15 per cent market share in the Indian aerated waters market.

This comes with an interesting story. In 1978, American cola giant Coca-Cola abandoned operations in India rather than accept a government mandated sale of 60 per cent of their equity to an Indian company. Following this, the Parle brothers, Ramesh Chauhan and Prakash Chauhan, along with then CEO Bhanu Vakil, launched Thums Up as their flagship drink, adding to their portfolio of older brands Limca (lime flavour) and Gold Spot (orange flavour). Thums Up enjoyed a near monopoly with a much stronger market share, often overshadowing domestic rivals like Campa Cola, Double Seven, Duke's and United Breweries Group's McDowell's Crush, although many small players sold well in their own markets. It was one of the major advertisers throughout the 1980s. In the mid-eighties, it faced short-lived competition from Double Cola. In 1990, when the Indian government opened the market to multinationals, Pepsi was the first to come in. Thums Up and Pepsi subsequently engaged in heavy competition for endorsements. Pepsi spokespersons included major Indian movie stars like Juhi Chawla, while Thums Up increased its spending on cricket sponsorship. Consumers were divided. In 1993, Coca-Cola re-entered India after a prolonged absence, spurring a three-way cola war with Thums Up and Pepsi. That same year, Parle sold out to Coke, and Thums Up had an 85 per cent market share in the cola space when sold. In spite of having a strong equity, the brand would lose its popularity among the core drinkers of cola falling in the age group of twelve to twenty-five years. One of the reasons for this decline was the lack of advertising.

Initially, Coca-Cola reduced its spending on advertising and production for Thums Up to pull customers to their main brand. It, however, soon realized that the customers of Thums Up would choose Pepsi over Coke, if Thums Up were to be withdrawn from the market. Coke, instead, used Thums Up as a competitor of Pepsi. The company had captured approximately 60.5 per cent share of the Indian soft drink market by this time. However, it realized that if it were to withdraw Thums Up, it would be left with only 28.72 per cent of the market (according to a report by NGO Finance & Trade in India). The year 1996 was a crucial one and a turning point for the Indian cola industry due to the Cricket World Cup. In the absence of Thums Up, most of its fans switched to Pepsi, thanks to Pepsi's aggressive marketing, which had struck a chord with Indian sentiments. That was the year when Coca-Cola finally realized that by killing Thums Up, it was serving significant market share to Pepsi on a platter.[214] Before it was too late, Coca-Cola relaunched Thums Up as a manly drink, building on its previous reputation as a more power-packed drink as compared to other colas. The intent was to make it into an 'adult' drink that would appeal to young consumers. 'Grow up to Thums Up' was a campaign that arguably was an important contributor to the increase in the brand's market share and equity.[215]

The contents of the bottle of Thums Up were easily replaced by a competitor, but the brand Thums Up itself could not be uprooted easily. It provided a combination of familiarity (serotonin—BOP#3), excitement (dopamine—BOP#4) and affiliation (oxytocin and/or vasopressin—BOP#5), which helped it stay relevant to its target customers. For a few years, the product (the aerated drink) was not present in the market; however, the brand continued to reside in the minds of customers. And when the product came back, people flocked back to the brand. The brand continued to exist independent of the product for quite a few years. It is now known that the brain reacts to the soft drink brand independent of the taste.[216] It is now amply clear that once a brand has embedded itself in the brains of its customers, it can linger there for a very long time, even in the absence of the product that generated the brand in the first place.

## Brands in the Era of Individualism

Brands matter increasingly because societies are moving towards increasing individualism. Even in the North American and Western European societies, till the 1960s, where the person would have different kinds of experiences; the self was bounded by birth, location, occupation and social class. While the rigid social stratification of medieval times had gone in form, it still survived in spirit till well into the twentieth century—to be a clerk, for example, meant a certain type of behaviour, dress and material ownership patterns. Today's greater freedom of individuals to express who they are and to vary that over time means that people have begun to construct their identities out of available symbolic resources to weave a coherent account of who they are.[217] An increasingly important 'available symbolic resource' includes the brands that an individual consumes. While individualism is an established fact in developed countries, it is now becoming a stronger phenomenon in emerging markets and collectivist societies like Japan, China and India.[218] The advertisement[219] of Bajaj Pulsar, a popular motorcycle model in India, acknowledges this growing appeal of individualism and shows two riders on their bikes. The bikers go on to perform dangerous stunts against the backdrop of narrow, bustling city streets. At the end of the ad, the voiceover signs off with its tagline 'Distinctly ahead', indicating it is for those who are daring, adventurous and risk-takers.

Human brains are wired to connect to other entities—whether people, animals or objects (Brain Operating Principle [BOP] #5: mirroring). With the decline of connections to other individuals in society, those connections are coming from pets and, yes, brands as well. As individuality becomes increasingly important in consumer decisions, the consumer evaluates brands based on how the brand affects and serves them as an individual, beyond its functional value. Earlier, people would be loyal to the brands which seemed consistent with their preferences, outlook and choices, but now, they look to brands even to provide them with a new identity.[220] Many times, they change the way they appear to conform with a brand they swear by. As a consequence, the value that customers are looking for is also evolving to incorporate a greater proportion of intangible value. The intangible value requirements include, for example, requirements such as a product being green, a company being a good social citizen; these along with other factors such as usage lead to a 'bonding' and 'relationship' that a customer has with a brand—the feeling that 'this brand is a part of my life'.

The increasing proportion of intangibility in the value that firms provide is manifested in the increasing ratio of market capitalization of listed firms to their book value. The ratio of market capitalization to book value for listed firms has increased over time for listed firms in the US, UK and India, for example.[221] Intangible assets permit the company to earn cash flows in excess of the return on tangible assets; they augment the earning power of a firm's tangible assets. Patents, trademarks, franchises, R&D and brands are considered intangible assets that have value. For a sample of fifteen firms, between 30 and 151 per cent of the firm's replacement value came from the brand; and across twenty different industries, the brand equity value ranged from 25 to 95 per cent of the intangible value of the firm.[222]

Brands have intangible value in the mind of the customer and on the balance sheets of firms. Since brands are intangible and in the mind of the customer, what is the nature of this intangible value? How does it manifest for the firm? Keller[223] defined customer-based brand equity as the differential effect of brand knowledge on consumer response to the marketing of the brand. A brand is said to have positive (or negative) customer-based brand equity if consumers react more (or less) favourably to an element of the marketing mix for the brand than they do to the same marketing mix element when it is attributed to a fictitiously named or unnamed version of the product or service. When a customer develops knowledge about a brand, he forms associative networks in his brain related to the brand. Brand associations can be measured in terms of their favourability, strength, and how they are congruent to and overlap with one's sense of self. The stronger the brand associations in one's memory, the stronger the customer-based brand equity. Building brand equity requires creating a familiar brand name and a positive brand image—that is, favourable, strong and unique brand associations. The strength of customer-based brand equity can be measured through elements of brand image and awareness, and through the impact of brand knowledge on consumer response to elements of the marketing mix.

Many companies put the value of their brand on their balance sheet. British consumer goods firm Reckitt Benckiser Group, makers of Dettol and Disprin, bought Ahmedabad-based Paras Pharmaceuticals for Rs 3260 crore ($726 million) in a move that shocked rival bidders. Some analysts said that this price was too steep and wasn't in line with the industry standards, which was around four times the market capitalization of Paras. This valuation was around thirty times Paras Pharma's earnings before interest, taxes, depreciation and amortization (EBITDA) that year, and roughly around 8.1 times its sales.[224] The firm felt that the price was not unreasonable because most Paras products were among the top brands in their category. Reckitt factored in the growth potential of India's fast-growing market. This price was not solely for Paras, but also for the estimated cost of recreating the brands in the Indian market. Reckitt Benckiser bought Paras Pharmaceuticals for Rs 32 billion—paying a premium of 300 per cent over the market capitalization of the firm. It reasoned that was about the investment it would have to make in order to recreate the brands that Paras had created in India: Moov, Krack, etc. The premium paid was for the brand value.[225] Brands, thus, provide economic value.

The value of organizations is divided into two areas, intangible and tangible assets, with brands being intangible assets. A study of organizations showed that over a thirty-year period between 1975 and 2003, the overall corporate value of intangible assets increased from 17 to 80 per cent. The magazine *Businessweek* has concluded that brands account for more than one-third of shareholder value. And this value stems from the neural imprints that a brand had created among its customers. This leaves us with the conclusion that the value of most businesses comes from intangible assets, brands being the most prominent of these assets.[226]

Or consider the value of a brand to a non-profit like Red Cross and the importance of their brand in attracting donations and volunteers. Because of their financial impact, brands are a unique organizational asset. Brands play a key role in attracting employees, partners and, most importantly, audiences, to an organization. Brands help cut through the clutter of the marketplace, creating awareness for organizations and helping them attract and develop the mutually beneficial relationships with customers, suppliers and the public that they need to reach their goals.[227]

## Brands as Decision Heuristics

As consumers are exposed to more products and brands, brands become the heuristic that consumers use to choose and decide which products to use. We saw in Chapter 2 how consumers tend to be cognitive misers. Indeed, the human brain is wired to conserve energy; it does not like to think too much. It is constantly seeking ways to minimize effort (BOP#2). Brands offer a way to use heuristics, which save energy. In short, your brand is the way your customer perceives you using mental shortcuts.

Many small organizations and start-ups neglect spending the necessary time thinking about their brand in this broad sense and the impact it has on their business.[228] In the near term, entrepreneurs and the founding team are the brand to their customers, investors and employees. It is the personality of the entrepreneur and the relationships that they have built with other stakeholders that has left the first neurophysiological imprint in the minds of customers.

Neuroscience helps to diagnose steps that need to be taken to make the brand emotionally more meaningful and push the brand deeper into the unconscious. It helps in assessing where a brand is positioned in the brand ladder. Essentially, the brand should be using System 1 processing only as a rule: the consumer is no longer deliberately thinking about the brand as a choice, but tends to choose a brand in a product category as an automatic choice. System 2, which involves more deliberate thinking, should be employed only as an exception. The goal of all branding, is therefore, to move a consumer to a place where the firm's brand becomes an automatic choice.

Neurally speaking, a brand should engage with the gain-responsive network, including regions previously shown to be associated with the anticipation and receipt of monetary rewards—the dorsal and ventral striatum, VMPFC, ventrolateral PFC, anterior cingulate cortex (ACC), OFC, and dopaminergic midbrain regions[229]—these areas should become more active in anticipation of a positively rewarding experience and then again during and after the brand interaction.

In the previous few sections, we tried to make sense of why brands matter at all and how concepts like brand relationships, brand love and brand personality can help steer an increasingly individualistic consumer in this era of consumerism towards a brand. And now we will discuss perhaps the first step a brand should take when declaring itself, whether establishing itself for the first time or reassessing its role in the consumer's life, to make it penetrate deeper into their life.

## In Summary

Brands are a combination of identifier, functionality, affect, relationships, promise, experiences; they are the sum total of the conscious and unconscious memories that have been created in the mind of a customer through the interactions that they have had with the firm's product, people and processes. These interactions create a mix of neurotransmitters in the brain of the customer that is better than that of the competition and that better mix of the neurotransmitters is what the customer wants. Brands are vital because of increasing individualism that leads consumers to want to relate to objects and, therefore, an increasing proportion of the value of firms is coming from intangible value. Brands are the principal source of intangible value for a firm, as reflected in the increasing market cap to book ratio for most firms. The challenge for firms is to build long-term, sustainable brands that are built on a deep emotional connect with the customer, given that customers are using brands increasingly as a decision heuristic. The deep emotional connect and the automatic decision heuristics get wired into the brains of customers and this is the objective that marketers can aspire to.

Now that we have a sense of how the brain works and takes decisions in the context of brands, what brands are and why brands matter to the brain, we explore how to build a brand in the next chapter.

# Chapter 5

# Diagnosing the Nature of Your Brand and Steps to Building a Brand

Snapple was a juice drink that came out of New York, which grew to sales of $640 million by 1993, from $4 million ten years earlier. It was a quirky, fun, parties-and-parade drink that consumers loved. Buyers would pay and come to hang out at events organized by Snapple. Snapple was not a cola and it was not a 'should drink' beverage. Snapple stood for a playful exuberance, an expression of a vivid sensuality (personal authenticity), and a mix-and-match ethos. People not only felt good about buying Snapple but also considered it to be an authentic partner that was different from a Coke or other similar drinks. And similar kinds of people bought Snapple. Buying Snapple enabled people to feel part of a group. Snapple was about adding a little whimsy to the humdrum and the everyday. In short, consumers co-created the brand with the firm; the brand appeared to be in the relationship stage (along the dimensions of brand partner quality and love and passion). Arguably, buying and consuming Snapple and participating in Snapple events gave people a dopamine spike and an increase in serotonin levels. And then, after Quaker Oats purchased Snapple, the brand went off the boil. Could a diagnostic have prevented the decrease in the popularity of Snapple?

To keep interest in a brand alive, change is also required. Change is required because Brain Operating Principle (BOP) #4 means that for the brand to keep providing the dopamine spike, it needs to change in some fashion to keep the interest levels high.

In a different product context, the year 2010 brought us iPhone 4. With 2012 came iPhone 5, iPhone 6 in 2014, iPhone 7 in 2016, iPhone 8 in 2017, iPhone X in 2018, and iPhone 13 in 2021. The only constant factor through all these years? Apple. A brand arguably outlives a product. A brand sets the tone for its products for many years to come. What were the changes? Steve Jobs passed away. The number of releases of the underlying product in each generation proliferated. Other product brands were launched, such as OnePlus and Redmi. While Apple as a brand continues to enjoy the loyalty of many customers and did not fall off the cliff like Snapple, its brand has declined relative to what it was. How does one diagnose this?

The time-tested fan tradition of camping out all night to buy the new iPhone or the new Harry Potter book is one that astonishes many. Many of us sitting at home watching video clips of this shake our heads, unable to understand this mindless frenzy. After all, how can it be worth spending a night out on the cold pavement surrounded by strangers when you can easily get one if you only wait a bit longer? How can people worship a product with such devotion? What do these early adopters get out of it (other than the product, of course)? The answer to these lies rooted deep in neuroscience. As does the behaviour at the other end of the spectrum. The Nirma and Ghadi brand detergents in India are bought primarily for their functionality, with the promise that they will wash clothes well at a reasonably low price. And yet, they also influence the brain strongly, albeit some different parts (as well as some common parts) as compared to Apple.

Snapple, Apple, Harry Potter, Nirma and Ghadi use different ways to keep their consumers satisfied and at times, even wanting for more. While functionality seems to work for the detergent companies, the provision of a sense of belonging works for Snapple. The devotion commanded by Apple and Harry Potter is partly because of their popularity as a risk-free investment and partly because of the anticipated dopamine spurge (BOP#4) from owning a novelty and the curiosity about the said novelty. So given these examples, how does one build a brand in a more efficient and effective way using the insights now available about how the brain works and the way it takes decisions? At the same time, we will try to see why the branding tactics exploited by the aforementioned companies work the way they do. When you're looking to create a brand, there's always a checklist of dos and don'ts. Here, you won't find the complete list. What you will find, however, is an aggregation that will enable you to diagnose and take some steps to build a strong, long-lasting brand by leveraging neuroscience.

Even leading brands have only just begun to tap into the marketing power of neuroscience. So whether you are a new player still trying to gain a foothold, or you are a veteran in the market, it is a level playing field. It is still anyone's game. Neuroscience, if leveraged in the right manner, might just be that differentiator that sets you apart from the rest. The very first question one must ask is, 'Where is the brand in the mind of your customer?' We can use the following table as an illustrative first step to help diagnose where one's brand is in the mind of the customer.[230]

**Table 1: Diagnosing Status of Brand Relationship**

| Questions | Identity | Function | Affect | Brand Relationship |
|---|---|---|---|---|
| Does my brand engage the customer's emotions? | | | ✓ | |
| Does the customer consider my brand a companion? | | | | ✓ |
| Is my brand bought by the customer primarily for its functionality? | | ✓ | | |
| Is my brand thinking on behalf of the customer? | | | | ✓ |
| Is my brand just another name in the herd? | ✓ | ✓ | | |
| Is my brand linked to the customer's aspirations? | | | ✓ | |
| Is there a strong brand community that exists around my brand? | | | | ✓ |
| Is my brand promise converting into the brand relationship lived by the consumers? | | | | ✓ |

| Am I able to create passion through my brand? | | | | ✓ |
|---|---|---|---|---|
| Is my brand able to nurture the consumer at the levels of body, mind and soul? | | | | ✓ |
| How much of the brand is co-created by the customer? | | | ✓ | ✓ |

Once you have answered these questions, you will have a fair estimate of where the brand is in the minds of the consumers. For example, if most of the answers lead you to an 'affect' level, you know that the brand requires effort to put it on the 'relationship' rung to convert the consumer's fleeting yet positive experiences into a long-term commitment.[231]

At the relationship level, the brand is more likely to become the unconscious, automatic choice of the customer—a much desired goal, the holy grail, the brand nirvana, of any brand manager, or indeed that of any CEO. The table above provides the first step in the process. There will be a couple of more steps in the diagnosis.

Once we have a diagnosis, we can then take the next steps on the way to building the brand. A preliminary diagnosis could involve articulating the relationship by asking whether the brand has an emotional or a functional appeal and if it falls in line with the consumers' aspirations. If the firm's employees can feel the passion created through the brand, it becomes easier to align them to create a seamless consumer experience. When the brand thinks on behalf of the consumers and is considered a companion, it is able to create pleasant experiences for the consumers. If the brand delivers upon its promise and is co-created by the consumers, it could be involved in a ritualistic consumption. If your brand is thought of as a companion for all types of times, is not just another name in the herd, and if there exists a community about it, the brand is well on its way to creating in-groups and out-groups. Further, if the co-created consumer experience delivers upon its promise by reflecting consumer aspirations, it holds the potential to change the behaviour of its consumers.

One would need to determine if the affinity with the brand is for the functionality of the product or if the relationship is developed with the brand primarily on the basis of emotion and affect. A person may use a particular phone purely for its functionality and not share a relationship with brand. One needs to ask this: Is the brand a fun brand? Is it for hedonistic people who love life? Does it strike a chord with its customers? Does it make the purchaser feel good about themselves? These are some of the aspects that capture the love, passion and intimacy of brand relationships.

Edelweiss is a Rs 3674.86 crore ($549 million)[232] boutique financial services firm based out of Mumbai. It started life in the wholesale banking space and over the years, spread into retail financial services like investment, life insurance and advisory. Over the past decades, it has sought to create a brand image that is professional, expert and an enabler to achieve one's financial goals. In a brand tracking study conducted among retail customers,[233] Edelweiss was perceived as being a cub or a puppy; innovative, knowledgeable, aggressive, progressive, international, different and prestigious. There seemed to be a distance—a power hierarchy between the customer and the brand. For instance, in comparison with its competitors, who were considered to be friendly, Edelweiss was perceived to be more formal, needing the customer to take an appointment before a meeting. Unlike other respondents, employees perceived the company as being a cheetah—a symbol of speed and precision. Edelweiss was perceived as being more trustworthy and providing better advice than the competition. However, there was no evidence that retail customers had any 'relationship' with the Edelweiss brand. There was simply aided and unaided brand recall and a reputation of the brand as innovative, knowledgeable, aggressive, progressive, international, different and prestigious. This goes to show the clear divide between providing functionality and cultivating a brand relationship.

Surely, functionality is where it all starts. Yet, even the highest functionality will be rendered useless if customers aren't aware of it. To take it from there, one climbs the ladder from unawareness to customer loyalty—from brand recognition to developing brand relationship. The brand ladder concept[234] has its origins in the early eighties, when both marketing researchers and practitioners sought ways of moving beyond the practice of marketing products by features.[235] The brand ladder is generally known to connect product and brand attributes to the personal and social factors of customers' lifestyles. It helps in delivering premium customer experience to its adopters.

So what are the different ways to building and managing a brand relationship with the customer? How can a firm migrate its customers up the ladder so that a greater proportion of the value comes from affect and relationships? Below, we outline the key steps that firms need to execute to develop and sustain strong brand relationships.

**Step 1: The first step is to articulate the nature of the brand and the relationship that the brand can have with the customer.** Like any relationship, the root of a brand relationship draws on whether the brand is based on beliefs and values that underpin its existence. Powerful brands have an underlying raison d'être, a belief, a foundation of intangibility that underpins their existence and acts like a bulwark. Brand beliefs are almost like a cause—one that makes people rally behind brands. The cause is underpinned with belief but does not stop there. The aim is to somehow win hearts and minds; to get into the nucleus accumbens, the amygdala, the ventral striatum, the basal ganglia; to be the brand that provides the combination of dopamine, serotonin, oxytocin, acetylcholine that makes it the automatic choice. A strong brand belief married to a holistic and continually updated understanding, communicated with energy and imagination and backed by the delivery—by walking the talk—makes for a compelling brand belief in the mind of the customer and is able to provide the increase in the relevant neurotransmitters. The creation story of the brand can also become a part of the brand's belief and the values that it espouses.

One of the applications of neuroscience that has received a lot of attention in marketing is its ability to understand individual differences at multiple biological levels. It helps in understanding when different individuals employ different choice strategies. Neuroscience has portrayed the ability to identify neural markers that correspond to individual traits. In other words, despite the fact that consumer behaviours are heterogenous, neuroscience can illuminate the lesser-known fact that biological traits that engender those differences likely exist at many points (e.g. genes, hormones, brain regions) in the neurobiological mechanisms pertaining to decision-making. Isolating and identifying different components of that mechanistic heterogeneity would facilitate broader predictions in marketing.[236] A powerful brand undergirded by a set of values, beliefs and other intangibles acts as the glue that is able to bring together different people through a common pattern that appeals across these categories (Brain Operating Principle [BOP] #3) and the effect of WOM, what others are doing and a sense of community (BOP#5).

When a customer evaluates a brand or buys a product, they determine if they like the product and its price. This is commonly referred to as preference measures. A customer's preferences vary and are largely influenced by context; the context may include the mood, the personality that is induced by the environment, etc. These resulting variations in cognitive and neural processes affect choice. fMRI studies have depicted regions of the brain such as the orbitofrontal cortex (OFC) and the ventromedial prefrontal cortex (VMPC) that constantly encode various measures of individual opinions (e.g., the willingness to pay). Neuroscience uses these studies to map brain activity in regard to preference measures.

Attributes such as emotions, memory, social comparisons and previous actions are known to affect consumer choices. Neuroscience studies attempt to understand how choice processes are modulated by various contextual changes, be they external (e.g., framing of a problem that changes the base from which a dopamine change causes an effect) or internal (e.g., mood, memory that results from changes in dopamine and serotonin). It facilitates an understanding of how and when preferences change or how they deviate from the norm. This can be used for predictions or how changes in behaviour might be encouraged or discouraged. The evoked emotions and memories flow from the brand values and beliefs.

Consider Camper shoes, a family business working out of the Mediterranean island of Majorca. Camper values slowness; it abhors the trend towards speed in modern life as exemplified by brands like McDonalds and Nike. Although Camper is a brand with global reach, the traditional Majorcan way of life provides the design inspiration for many of its shoes. Some take their shape from ancient Mediterranean ships, from a slower way of life. Others are inspired by the name: Camper means 'peasant' in Catalan and it is hard to think of a more earthy name. The qualities of a peasant way of life—austerity, simplicity and discretion—are reflected in the design. Many of the designs are classics that are produced year after year, with only subtle enhancements, which runs counter to fashion's usual seasonal U-turns. Another belief element was provided by the firm's chief designer Marti Guixe in 2003 with the motto emblazoned on some Camper bags: the English translation is 'Don't buy them if you don't need them'. A customer's desire for simplicity, or the need to be seen to be simple, may well be leveraged by the firm, which believes in and lives its simplicity to get the consumer to put Camper in their brand portfolio. It becomes an emblem of simplicity, an integral part of their life, illustrating the application of Brain Operating Principle (BOP) #3 (pattern of simplicity), BOP#4 (contrast from everyone else, who changes too quickly) and BOP#5 (a set of people behaving similarly in adopting simple shoes), all built around common values.

Amul, a butter and cheese brand in India, is built around a mascot, a small girl, the vision of a 'child who is impish and lovable': to quote the brand's tagline, 'utterly, butterly delicious'. The semiotic significance of the moppet derives from an Indian mythological character, Krishna, who was known for his penchant for butter. Further, Bal Krishna epitomizes the innocent naughtiness that endears a child to any onlooker. In that context, the Amul mascot girl can be thought of as representing Bal Krishna. The brand is built around a playful, innocent, naughty attitude that plays on the mythological knowledge and imagination of the customers. The result? With the help of an extensive distribution outlets reach, Amul now holds more than 90 per cent market share in the organized butter market.[237]

As individualism advances in all societies and consumers draw more on brands to construct their selves, the role of brand belief and values becomes more central to the brand relationship. Who, what, why and how are important features of any brand relationship. The age, gender, ideology, etc., of the 'who' or the consumer base can provide tons of information required for branding campaigns. For example, a neuroanatomy study has shown that as we get older, our tolerance for risk-taking diminishes because of a decrease in the grey matter in the right posterior parietal cortex (rPPC) region of our brains. The grey matter volume of rPPC has been found to correspond to the variation in risk preference and its decrease and therefore, indicates an increased aversion towards risk.[238] A behaviour study also indicated that adolescents have a tendency to be more risk-averse in cases where risks were clearly stated.[239] Companies wanting to lure adolescents or older people, therefore, could focus their resources on making their consumer experience as pleasant as possible, thereby allowing the consumers to view the risk-free experience for what it is: something to keep coming back to. A neuro approach would, therefore, also help identify those customers who are more/less risk-averse and, therefore, help to identify customers outside the traditional segment for the brand. This sameness in the customer at the brain level, which cuts across differences that may be wide but superficial, is the reason that Ford Mustang buyers included older people in the USA in the 1960s, even though the demographic target was young people. It the reason that Mahindra Scorpio buyers in India in the 2010s included powerful local politicians and contractors who also wanted to feel macho and powerful, and whose identities matched the values being espoused by the brand for the original intended target audience that was different.

The dorsal medial prefrontal cortex has been shown to facilitate expression of both 'social identities' (that is, the sense of belonging) and 'personal identities'.[240] Further, our ventromedial prefrontal cortex is the hub of morality and decision-making, and brings together cognitive and emotional processes to guide social behaviour.[241] Something that would go against our moral values would therefore create friction if options were to be considered. If employees are able to relate to or seem to have moral values similar to the corporation's, it would make decision-making easier. Clothing companies like Victoria's Secret, Zara and H&M regularly face a backlash because of a plethora of reasons: exclusion of coloured models from fashion shows, not producing clothes in the plus-size category, not acknowledging the different body shapes of women according to their ethnicity (despite the fact that the three companies have a huge consumer base worldwide), environmental and labour-related issues, etc. What these companies perhaps needed to do was to redefine their manufacturing and their image according to their consumer base. The increasing awareness among people about these issues has sometimes driven both consumers and employees away from these companies if they don't find the brands reflecting the same principles that the customer subscribes to.

It is interesting to note here that women and men have different neural regions corresponding to 'trust'.[242] A study focusing on online purchasing behaviour found that women utilize the following regions more than men do: dorsal ACC, thalamus, striatum and fusiform gyrus light up when women evaluate trustworthy offers, and dorsal ACC and DLPFC activate in men. Untrustworthy offers, on the other hand, activate completely different regions in both women and men. They concluded that overall, women employ more limbic structures (functions include emotions, memory, learning) than men while evaluating trustworthiness. Women also comprehend more information than men while making purchase decisions. This evidence supports the general assumption that women are more emotionally driven during purchasing decisions and often look at more aspects of a product than men. Note that ad campaigns of women-centric industries like cosmetics, feminine hygiene products, contraceptives, fashion, etc., often bank on these drives. Even FMCG companies, whose products are consumed by anyone and everyone, end up having women-centric campaigns because they realize the reality that women are responsible for most FMCG-related purchasing decisions in a typical household. In the Indian scenario, advertisements about personal finance, banking and four-wheeler automobiles mostly revolve around a male protagonist in scenarios that also speak to the viewers' emotions and to the rationale of engaging with these brands. For example, a car-related commercial is likely to emphasize not only the mileage and the performance of the engine, but also directly or indirectly discuss the topic of pride or the macho-ness related to buying that brand.

Decoding the personalities of the target base is important to understand what drives them towards a brand, to create a match with their values. A good start could be with the Big Five Personality Traits, namely, conscientiousness, extraversion, neuroticism, agreeableness and openness to experience. Our individuality could be attributed to variations in these traits. A neuroscientific personality study[243] indicates how these traits were represented by the amount of volume of certain regions of the brain.

Conscientiousness encompasses behaviours like industriousness, orderliness, self-discipline and a lack of impulsivity, distractibility and disorganization, primarily reflected in the ability of having some sort of control on their own selves, and an understanding of inhibition to achieve non-immediate goals.[244] It has been found to be positively associated with volume in the middle frontal gyrus in the left lateral PFC, a region identified to be associated with self-regulation, working memory and execution of planned actions. Office supplies brands and even furniture brands like Ikea, for example, would appeal to this organized side of their consumers. Appealing to the conscientiousness or the middle frontal gyrus in the left lateral PFC could truly point customers to the functionality of the product. The values and beliefs of a certain type of brand would gel more closely with this kind of person; the pattern would fit better (Brain Operating Principle [BOP] #3).

Extraversion is strongly linked to the experience or the promise of reward and is expressed as a number of traits like assertiveness, sociality and talkativeness.[245] Often manifested in social behaviour due to our human tendency to associate reward with social acceptance, belongingness and affection, it was found to be associated with volume of medial orbitofrontal cortex, a region often associated with the evaluation of rewards. One could associate the adventurous and social type of people with extraversion. Travel, sports apparel and equipment, dirt bikes and race cars, and leisure brands appeal to our extraversion through their brand experience.

Neuroticism is linked to negative emotions like anxiety, self-consciousness and irritability.[246] Its biological reflection in the brain is highly associated with threats, punishments and conflicts, as can be seen with its association with regions like the hippocampus (negative association), mid-cingulate cortex (positive association) and dorsomedial PFC (negative association). Reduced volume in the hippocampus is associated with stress and depression[247] and the mid-cingulate cortex is often associated with the detection of errors[248] and response to both physical and emotional pain.[249] Smaller volumes of the dorsomedial prefrontal cortex (DMPFC) indicates a tendency to view the self negatively. The financial and medical sectors bank on our anxiety and anticipation of punishment by building a brand that assures consumers of the brand's integrity and dependability in case of instability. The key driver would be (Brain Operating Principle) BOP#3 and BOP#5 from the requirement of a pattern of dependability and integrity and what others are doing.

Agreeableness encompasses altruistic behaviours and it is positively expressed through traits like cooperation, compassion and politeness. Neuroanatomically speaking, it is negatively associated with volume of posterior left superior temporal sulcus, which is activated during the interpretation of others' actions and positively with volume of posterior cingulate cortex,[250] hypothesized to play a role in modern forms of theory of mind.[251] Marketing campaigns for donations towards the well-being of the poor, people in danger because of tyranny or disease, or towards climate change, would require them to concur with a person's agreeableness. Stimulate the posterior cingulate cortex to motivate potential donors with images, statistics or reports of related causes.

Openness and intellect encompasses traits like imagination, intellectual engagement and aesthetic interest.[252] One region was found to be associated with regions of the parietal cortex involved in working memory and attention. A prominent portion of the technological industry projects its merchandise as a tool to make great presentations, innovate and express creativity and directly appeal to the intellectual and the innovator within us.

Each of these personality traits, when present above a certain level, therefore, could correspond to a segment (that can now be identified from online behaviour), and brands can align their values and beliefs to appeal more closely to the relevant segment. Mountain Dew, therefore, would appeal more to people who are extraverted and open to experience, to people who have a larger medial orbitofrontal cortex and larger relevant sections of the parietal cortex, people who are primarily dopamine- and norepinephrine-driven (BOP#1, BOP#4).

**Step 2: The firm should align internal company processes, capabilities and people so that it helps to build the articulated brand relationship.** Perhaps the most successful example of this alignment on a large scale is provided by Southwest Airlines, the low-cost airline that has had a brand promise of being the low-fare airline since its launch in 1973. That builds relationships with customers on the basis of low fares, fun and reliability and is an integral part of the life of many flyers. Every aspect of the firm's internal processes is geared to deliver on the brand promise and to build and maintain the relationship. The firm, for a very long time, has flown only one type of aircraft, the Boeing 737, since this reduces maintenance costs. Flying to secondary airports saves on landing charges. Not interlining baggage with other airlines and not providing meals saves on time and costs. Selling most tickets directly saves up to 10 per cent of the costs of delivering ticket prices. Flexible union contracts enable baggage handlers to help check-in people, improving the turnaround time at the gates, enabling the plane to leave faster, keeping the planes in the air for longer, increasing asset utilization and decreasing costs. Having five to seven people (of which only two or three may be directly working with the new hire) independently interview new hires makes for a certain kind of hire—one who sings announcements on planes and tries to make the plane ride a fun experience. Hiring similar people in this way plays on the mirroring proclivity (Brain Operating Principle [BOP] #5)—more easily achievable once a certain scale is in place, a scale that was put in place in the first fifteen years of the existence of the airline by the founder Herb Kelleher and his team.

Amul's (the largest dairy cooperative in India) creative team is dedicated and engaged in constantly building creative quotes for the moppet, releasing new witty themes for customers every few days. The frequent release of the cartoons ensures that people are constantly exposed to the brand and the witty caricatures. Amul has given the brief for the advertising campaign to Dacunha Associates, where the account has been for more than forty years. Management continuity on both sides has ensured that the core of the market positioning and the brain markers sought to be influenced has remained in place. People see both continuity and familiarity with the same character (BOP#3) and the change and newness with the absolutely current spoof (BOP#4).

Wawa, a convenience store chain in the north-east of the US, has a careful and rigorous hiring practice that includes personality assessments. New employees are given far more and in-depth training than is standard in the mass retail industry. Wawa instils in them pride in the products offered, particularly in its private label. Individual attention to customers makes regular patrons feel a part of a community. Wawa believes in keeping employees informed of company goals and letting them know how their individual efforts have an impact on company performance. Research in the UK with over 350 managers confirms that intellectual and emotional buy-in of the employees is critical in improving the performance of a brand.[253]

Aligning employees of a company with its ideologies would make every employee a vessel of the brand, therefore providing the consumers with an immersive branding experience. Research has shown that utility, identity and values are the three grounds on which one can align people.[254]

1. A utility-based approach is often grounded in the motivation to incur change so as to please the people in control of the reward or punishments, in a corporate environment—this could be the firing of people or attaining a promotion.

2. An identity-based approach focuses on how a company allows its employees the expression of their identity. Whether it is a personal identification (identification with a leader) or social identification (the sense of belonging), whatever accentuates an employee's identity in a social group would motivate them to go through with a brand's ideology.
3. A value-based approach banks heavily on emotional motivations vis-à-vis acceptance of corporate moves that are in line with a person's values.

While the first motivation works as an obvious ultimatum of sorts in a corporate scenario, the anticipation of a reward has been shown to induce activity in the nucleus accumbens, where an interplay of dopamine and serotonin would take care of the rest.[255] In the hubbub of life, we incessantly search for our identity. And we are looking to match our environment with our set of values—millennials, especially are known to do this. The organization design, therefore, should enable the match.

While actions having the aforementioned components have the potential to neurally motivate people to follow their leaders, research has also shown[256] that activity in frontopolar cortex (FPC) is related to increased willingness to exert cognitive or physical effort for rewards and counteract the devaluation of reward at high-effort levels. Through an anodal transcranial direct current stimulation (tDCS) experiment, it was also concluded that FPC plays a role computing whether the required cost (monetary payoff, freedom or effort) is worth the reward. In fact, another study concluded that FPC[257] is activated more strongly in entrepreneurs (with venture experience) while they make decisions, as compared to managers (with no venture experience), indicating that the formers' circuits are more tuned to making exploratory choices. In effect, if you allow your employees to be more entrepreneurial by empowering them to make their own decisions, even a large corporation would be able to allow for a better employee experience, while at the same time furthering its brand ideologies. Thus, a company that would like to establish a brand reputation for being innovative should empower employees.

In an interview published on forbes.com,[258] Robert Reiss asked top CEOs to comment on their leadership style. Here are a few excerpts from their responses.

> '. . . establish a clear vision and then empower the team to lead the company's future growth.'
>
> —Michel Doukeris, president and CEO, Anheuser-Busch

> '. . . getting the player to believe that greatness already exists inside of them . . .'
>
> —Vincent Bo Jackson, president and CEO, Bo Jackson Signature Foods

> '. . . and all driving and reinforcing accepted values and behaviours (culture).'
>
> —Lawrence Calcano, CEO, iCapital Network

> '. . . bring out the best in each . . .'
>
> —General David Petraeus, chairman, KKR Global Institute

'... and stepping back to let them do their best work ...'
—John Seifert, chief executive worldwide,
The Ogilvy Group

Here are quotes by leading Indians in industry:

'I want people to excel at what they are doing
so that they can aspire to be me in the future.'
—Indra Nooyi, former CEO of PepsiCo

'Leaders need to inspire optimism, creativity,
shared commitment and growth through
times good and bad.'
—Satya Nadella, CEO, Microsoft, in his memoir *Hit Refresh: The Quest to Rediscover Microsoft's Soul and Imagine a Better Future for Everyone*

'It is important for your teammates and associates
to find inspiration and encouragement
while working with you.'
—Upasana Taku, co-founder, MobiKwik[259]

All show an undeniable pattern (BOP#3) about 'empowering' employees to make their own decisions, but within a larger group (BOP#5).

**Step 3: The third step to building brand relationships is to construct experiences around the brand and its usage by the customer.** The masters in this category of constructing brand relationships are firms like The Body Shop, which have built brand communities. Members of these communities have lifestyle choices and activities built around the brand that enable brand relationship development along the dimensions of intimacy, love and passion, interdependence and commitment. For example, as mentioned earlier, in the process of consumption, Harley-Davidson owners also start entertaining each other and socialize, making consumption a socializing tool. The experience of socialization helps the brand develop relationships on the dimensions of interdependence and intimacy. This happens online on fora like Facebook, Amazon, Flipkart and Instagram, where brands like mCaffeine, an online Direct to Consumer brand, are selling coffee-based personal care products.

Evidence from neuroscience also suggests that brands always play a role for consumers; that consumer decisions have an emotion-related dimension. For preferred brands, deemed a 'rational choice', there was still a significant response in the right ventral striatum, the reward centre of the brain that is connected to emotions,[260] an important underpinning of brand value. Evidence also suggests a strong affective memory component through hippocampus and VLPFC activation for a preferred brand.[261]

Ride-sharing app Uber is a fine paradigm of a brand that learnt the importance of creating customer experience around its usage and got better at its storytelling. 'We're usually known as a saviour to your night out,' Uber's UK marketing and business development lead, Rachael Pettit, told *Marketing Week*. 'Yet there are so many other reasons to use Uber. We really do connect you with your city, shops, work and airport.' The company's 'Get there with Uber' campaign features various creatives of real drivers and riders, as opposed to actors, to show how customers and employees really use the app.

The riders and drivers were photographed and interviewed in a bid to 'inspire' potential customers and employees through their real stories and experiences of using Uber.[262] People now are all about sharing, specifically in a sharing economy. Unlike some of the older generations, people now are not as much into cars, but they are into convenience, and Uber leverages this. Uber has encompassed both of these trends into its service and branding strategy and makes it incredibly easy to find a ride and pay for it using its smartphone app; the technology on the platform enables the experience. Uber has also done a great job marketing to millennials. For example, #UberKITTENS was a campaign that Uber ran on National Cat Day. Using the Uber app, you could have kittens delivered to your house![263] Uber knew their target market very well and focused on providing convenience while creating experiences that provided a large delta from the previous experience of riding a cab (BOP#4).

'Don't go there. Live there.' exhorts Airbnb, the vacation rentals brand, promoting living vicariously like a local at a tourist destination: 'Don't go to Paris. Don't tour Paris, and please don't do Paris. Live in Paris.' According to data from Airbnb, 86 per cent of its users pick the platform because they want to live more like a local. That insight of living, being a part of a narrative (BOP#3), rather than visiting, inspired the brand. It wanted to push back against the modern tourism industry and capture the idea that people shouldn't simply go to a new place; they should live there, even if only for one night. It also released guidebooks which are fuelled and filled by locals, not tourists. Unlike some competitors, the Airbnb guidebooks allow future visitors to get a taste of what day-to-day life is like for people who actually live in the city.

While a travel website built on tourist response might tell you to go to Fisherman's Wharf, a local would tell you that the true San Francisco experience is an afternoon in Dolores Park.

At Butterfield & Robinson, a destination experience company, travel is just a vehicle for providing an experience that builds relationships with clients who come back again and again. For example, after an afternoon hiking up the walls of the Grand Canyon, exhausted Butterfield & Robinson travellers were greeted with a celebratory bottle of champagne. Standing on the rim, overlooking the vastness of the Grand Canyon and resting their sore muscles, the hikers clinked their glasses and smiled. Such experiences build deep bonds with customers who measure their relationship with the firm in terms of the number of times they have gone out with the firm. Customers are passionate about the brand experience and form lasting friendships on these trips. What is important to Butterfield & Robinson is not the number of trips that customers make, but the quality of the experience provided—like watching the sunrise fish catch in Vietnam or enjoying a private dinner party at a Czarist palace serenaded by a choir. These experiences create new levels of contrasts and dopamine spikes each time (Brain Operating Principle [BOP] #4), and make it less and less of a conscious choice, with less energy consumption, when choosing the next time (BOP#2). The experience itself creates a pattern in the mind of the customer over time (BOP#3).

Tversky, Thaler and Kahneman have shown that people are risk-seeking when choosing between monetary losses and risk-averse when choosing between monetary gains.[264] However, a recent study noted that people are risk-averse towards negative experiences and risk-seeking when it comes to positive experiences.[265] A direct implication for branding strategists could be that consumers are willing to take a chance on your brand if experience is a significant part of the brand. If they have heard positive reviews or been referred to a brand by others, consumers are willing to engage with that brand and give it a chance to woo them. Therefore, a brand should aim at creating good, new and innovative experiences around itself. The challenge, therefore, is to construct new experiences around the brand that keep providing the dopamine spikes to the customer and keep reducing their incentive to look for an alternative.

To put it all together, the process of constructing experiences around a brand brings together a lot of what we have already discussed. In Chapter 4, we talked about the nature of brand relationships and the neural basis of brand love. We discussed that relationships are often based on intimacy, passion, love, interdependence or commitment. We also discussed brand promise, which could comprise building a sense of trust, and we saw in Step 1 how different people process trust. In the same step, we discussed how a company could use findings from neuroscience about decision-making in different people on the basis of gender, age or personality. Bringing together these findings would indicate which region of the brain must we target.

For example, consider the brand experience of anywhr.co, a service company that curates a personalized travel plan for you with an element of surprise: you only learn your destination when you reach the airport to depart! The premise of the entire experience is about inviting two kinds of people—those who are a little adventurous at heart, willing to wing it, and those who wish they were spontaneous and a little more laid-back. Appealing to the extraversion trait, it appeals to the medial orbitofrontal cortex of our brains. Next, an element of surprise surrounds every communication the company has with you. It builds up your anticipation through emails conveying what to pack, and any essentials one must carry—leaving you guessing the destination for weeks before the actual trip. Dopamine helps our brain process the anticipation of reward in the nucleus accumbens. And finally, an envelope with a very vintage wax seal arrives—only to be opened on the day of travel—laying out the name of the destination, currency and a detailed itinerary. The thrill induces a second wave of dopamine. The brand promise delivers and the travellers' understanding of their personal identity matches their experience at every moment.

A brand that has a passionate following allows the consumer to be swamped with a feeling of belongingness, assuring them that although they are not 'too different from others', they are positively different from a number of others who are not that brand's consumers (BOP#3 and BOP#5). In Step 5, we discuss in depth how this feeling is translated neurally and how in-groups can further a brand's agenda.

Another way to create brand experience would be to build an immersive environment, one that works perfectly when its every element has the brand's tag. Consider the leisure industry. Growing at a fast pace, Nike and Adidas are leading the industry, with more and more people adopting their sports apparel into their daily routines. The Nike swoosh appearing on these clothes—on the jacket, the T-shirt, the shoes, the trousers and the shorts—has become something that the wearer could use as a part of every experience.

**Step 4: The fourth step to build a brand is to connect your brand with rituals.** As consumers grow older, cognition-based relationships start to become more important.[266] The affect basis of the relationship becomes the table stakes for continuing the relationship. Making a brand a part of ritualistic actions by the consumer makes the brand more connected with the consumer and strengthens the brand relationship. The brand becomes less dependent on the vagaries of affect because it is now ingrained in the rituals and habits of the consumer; it becomes embedded in the unconscious of the customer. By ritualizing Amul as the one-stop shop for breakfast and Maggi as the go-to hot snack that is easy to prepare, the brands have associated themselves with these rituals.

What are rituals? Rituals are repeated interactions that people have in their daily lives with other people, events or products. Driving your car to work can be a ritual act. Dentist appointments are rituals. Simply stopping at Starbucks for a cup of morning coffee is a ritual. Date night, the fourth of July, Diwali—the festival of lights, the Chrysanthemum viewing week and graduation ceremonies are all rituals. Rituals are active engagements that can be imbued with meaning; they can become touchpoints for the brand that can be made more pleasant, engaging and more fun. Rituals are ingrained habits and lead to automatic behaviours that arise from the basal ganglia.[267]

In the hubbub of modern life, rituals can often be overlooked or understated; but they are no less important today than they were in earlier times. What begins as a one-time event gradually becomes susceptible to context cues, promoting the formation of habits. Habits reflect associative learning and the formation of context-response associations in procedural memory. Once habits form, the perception of the context automatically brings the response to mind, and people often carry out that response. Colgate is a habit for many people associated with brushing teeth around the world. Maruti Suzuki is a habit for many older Indians and Zomato is becoming a habit for younger Indians. As habits strengthen, they gradually become independent of the incentive value of their consequences, and neural activation shifts from associative towards sensorimotor cortico-striatal brain regions.[268]

Consider Cadbury chocolates in India where, traditionally, festive and auspicious occasions are marked by ritual gifting and consumption of sweets like barfi, rasgulla and laddoo. It is customary for Indians to share sweets on occasions of joy, and these traditional sweets are deeply ingrained in the traditions for those occasions and the relationships that go with them. Cadbury attempted to associate chocolates with the ritual of gift giving with the slogan 'Kuch Meetha Ho Jaaye'. Furthermore, Cadbury Dairy Milk coined 'Shubh Aarambh', drawing from the Indian New Year or Ugadi, when it is customary for everyone to eat sweets to start the new year on a sweet note. On your graduation day, your first day of work or the beginning of a new relationship, Dairy Milk now cleverly finds its place habitually.

Think of Lego bricks. For children between the ages of two and nine, making any of the 900 million possible combinations from the eight different types of Lego bricks is a ritual of growing up that is almost taken for granted by most parents. Toy buyers and retail guests going to Lego headquarters are taken through rooms that recreate the time when the middle-aged buyers would have used Lego themselves. Today, the Lego ritual includes hundreds of websites and chat rooms as well as 'The Brick Testament' by the Reverend Brendon Smith (a site 'in no way sponsored, authorized or endorsed by the company'). Today, Lego works with these fans to build relationships.

Rituals are a form of habit that have a contextual, emotional or even cultural aspect; they represent the epitome of BOP#3. And hence, it could be theorized that most of the circuitry involved in habit formation, in the basal ganglia, propagation and maintenance would be responsible for the rituals too. In Chapter 3, we discussed how habits influence decision-making by making them more unconscious, related to emotions and automatic.

There are three stages of consumer habits regarding product usage, namely, concept formation, attainment and utilization.[269] For a brand to become a part of consumers' lives in the form of rituals, it could go through three similar stages. Concept formation would involve getting introduced to the brand ideology and experience, and an indulgence in the brand involving slow decision-making—a matching of the beliefs and value of the brand with that of the customer. Concept attainment would encompass medium-paced decision-making based on brand concepts and getting acquainted with the brand. Concept utilization, the final stage, would be achieved when brand information has been successfully assimilated with fast and automatic retrieval. A gradual shift from System 2 to System 1-based decision-making happens.

Just as it is with habits, rituals have an acquisition phase and evidence has suggested the basal ganglia sub-circuits participate during this process of acquisition of habits, procedures and repetitive behaviours. The basal ganglia circuit is engaged in iteratively evaluating contexts, selecting actions and chunking representations of actions. The chunking process has been hypothesized to simplify the process of retrieving them as an entity once a ritual has been formulated.[270] In the initial stages of habit formation, they are not automatic. However, this goal-oriented behaviour becomes more automated as we engage in it repetitively.

The loop of rituals, much like a reinforcement learning paradigm, is governed by its three components: cue, action and reward. The early stages of habit acquisition engage the limbic system, the midbrain-ventral striatal reward system, i.e., the dorsal striatum, the neocortex, and motor structures such as the cerebellum.[271] Based upon theories that put reinforcement learning and habit learning side-by-side, studies on monkeys have shown that positive reward prediction error-computing regions encompassing dopamine neurons, midbrain substantia nigra pars compacta and the ventral tegmental area (VTA),[272] [273] fire up during habit learning.

Gradually, habits would undertake an automatic circuit for retrieval and execution. Rapid memory retrieval facilitated by involvement of affect would suggest that if a habit is somehow associated with positive emotions, it could make the entire experience more rewarding through engagement of dopamine neurons. Through explicit association with major or trivial events in a person's life, a brand can attempt to establish a positive and emotional presence in a ritualistic manner to gain and keep a customer.

**Step 5: The fifth step to building brand relationships is to create in-groups and out-groups, the yin of believers and the yang of non-believers, the faithful and the pagans.**

Defining your pagans is helpful in defining who your brand is. Apple Computer twisted IBM's famous 'Think' mandate by encouraging people to 'Think Different'. A Starbucks drinker knows the difference between a tall and a grande. People who drink Starbucks in the morning are probably not going to care to have a Nescafé Instant.

The belief systems of the in-group come with their own invented lexicon and practices that the firm can help to develop. Maintaining these groups of faithfuls and pagans is also central to sustaining the brand relationships. When Wayne Rooney was reported to be considering moving from Manchester United (a valuable soccer club in England) to Manchester City, he received death threats—such was the passion of the Man U fans. Such a sharp definition of believers and others helps maintain believers and sustains the brand relationship over time; we consider other ways to sustain the brand relationship below.

Since the 1930s, Marvel and DC Comics have had a friendly rivalry, stemming from the comic book pages and now extending to the big screen. DC boasts of Superman, Batman, Flash and others while Marvel parades its Iron Man, Hulk and Captain America, among others. Their movie adaptations, such as *The Dark Knight* (DC), *The Avengers* (Marvel), and *Guardians of the Galaxy* (also Marvel), have broken box office records.[274] This has created a divide in the comic fanbase, with both DC and Marvel commanding enviable fanbases. Needless to say, the rivalry between the fans of the two franchises is quite intense. If you go around praising any particular one of the two franchises, you can be sure that you'll ruffle a few feathers. DC and Marvel's rivalry has been a relatively friendly one, with very little tension between the companies (Marvel has often referred to DC as the 'Distinguished Competition').[275] Competition is good and both companies realize that.

Humans have an emotional desire to 'belong'. It can be considered to be a manifestation of Brain Operating Principle (BOP) #5. 'Belongingness' is considered vital for human survival. Humans are uniquely social creatures in that we get most of what we need for survival from our social groups rather than from the natural environment. And therefore, the sense of belonging to a group is deeply coded in our brains as more than just a positive experience; mirroring and social confirmation (BOP#5) are the mechanisms that help to achieve that goal. It has been recognized as something that creates meaning in life.[276] It also goes beyond that. We would rather be a part of a group that follows a social norm that would otherwise seem absurd rather than being left alone. This phenomenon, called social conformity, has been tested in social environments multiple times. A basic example of this is the Asch experiment. When questioned by the examiner, subjects often agree that the line on the left is equal to line 1 or 2 on the right, if it is given as the majority opinions of the 'other' participants.

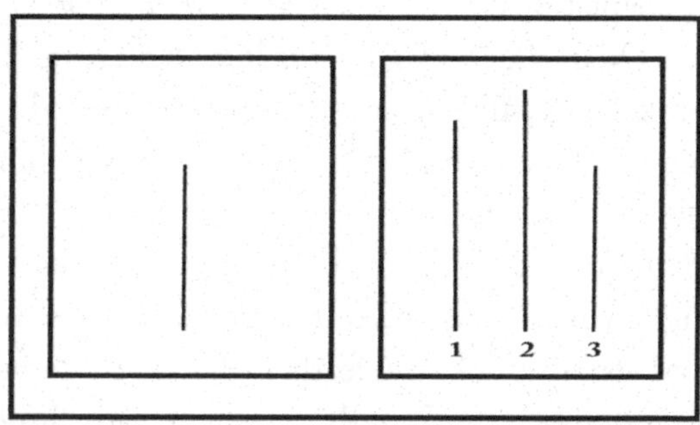

A number of neuroscientific studies have highlighted the similarity between the neural encoding of reinforcement and that of social conformity. A study[277] showed that a conflict within a group activates the rostral cingulate zone (RCZ) and deactivates the nucleus accumbens (NAc), both of which are known to be involved in calculating prediction errors. The activation of RCZ also indicates a need for adjustments that a person needs to make in order to resolve the conflict. Stronger deactivation of NAc was observed in cases when conformity followed than in cases when it didn't, following a conflict, indicating a stronger calculation of prediction error. In both the regions, RCZ and NAc, we think that there are certain neurons in the brain called dopaminergic neurons that regulate the reinforcement of social conformity—a BOP#5 activity that reduces prediction errors and increases belongingness.

In these in-groups, reciprocity can be an important norm of behaviour. When treated kindly, humans would often reciprocate that act to achieve a collaborative aim. It is observed that while making decisions, consensus groups exhibit higher behavioural trust, which is driven by reciprocity expectations, than individuals.[278] Neuroscientists have demonstrated that the striatum is engaged in deciding whether to reciprocate or not, even in encoding abstract feelings such as those achieved by mutual cooperation.[279]

Look back at all those times you have changed your opinion about a particular kind of wine the moment you heard the price. Popular social norm dictates that the pricier the wine, the better it is supposed to taste. And it does! Multiple studies[280,281] have reported increased taste perceptions in light of subjective knowledge about the wine such as price and origin of wine. In one such famous study, Plassman[282] showed how the knowledge of the price of the wine affects the expectancy of the flavour by changing activity in the medial prefrontal cortex (mPFC), a region of the brain that has shown to be related to behavioural pleasantness ratings for properties like odour, taste and music, even when the price of wine is varied and the wine is kept constant.

A new term, 'informational gerrymandering', was coined in a recent paper, highlighting how just the wrongful perception of a 'majority' political alignment can sway a perfectly divided group of people into one that votes majority after gaining knowledge of only their neighbours' affiliations.[283] People sway to the side which looks like the 'best', socially acceptable side.

In short, we humans like to be part of a social group and tend to conform to social norms, even in the absence of observers. However, our social behaviour isn't limited to just being in any group. Once part of a group, we tend to stick to our guns. We form what are called in-groups and out-groups.

A 2009 study[284] replicated a small in-group study conducted in 1971[285] inside an fMRI scanner. It concluded that there exists a pertinent in-group bias, *even among strangers who had been randomly assigned a group.* The scans showed increased activation in the dorsal medial prefrontal cortex, posterior anterior cingulate cortex, tempoparietal junction and precuneus when participants were engaged in social categorization and showed in-group favouritism. The former is often related to our 'social identities' (that is, the sense of belonging) and when we think about our 'personal identities' or personal attributes.[286] The posterior anterior cingulate cortex activation is related to social comparison, that again leads to an increased positive association with the in-group. The latter two are involved in self–other differentiation and episodic memory retrieval.

Creating in-groups and out-groups with respect to brands could, therefore, invoke a feeling in consumers of positivity towards the brand and towards themselves as its consumers, and at the same time, re-emphasize the differentiation between people who do consume as 'us' and people who don't as 'them'. It has also been shown that we empathize with in-group members and that we perceive their actions differently.[287] Hence, if a brand's in-group include a consumer's idols (celebrity, best friend, a critic), their actions could be easily perceived as 'best' (we identify with the actions of our in-group), thereby reinforcing our faith in the brand.

Mirror neurons (BOP#5), therefore, play an important role in furthering in-groups, and could act as a strong recruiting agent for a brand-related in-group. We have a tendency to mirror behaviours deemed 'plausible', 'unique' or 'efficient', whichever suits our personal taste. Scientists believe them to play a role in the die-hard fandom sports teams enjoy.[288] This is why graphic visuals portraying what it could mean to own a brand's commodity could prove important. A leather jacket-wearing, tough-looking woman riding a motorbike on mountainous roads sends a strong signal to all those women who want to do something that looks 'intimidating'; it would motivate them to direct their attention to the brand too!

Is there a sequence to the steps that have been outlined? Which ones should one focus on more? Both these questions would, of course, need to be examined in the specific context of particular firms and brands that raise the question!

In summary, therefore, firms that follow these five steps in an appropriate manner will be able to use neuroscientific principles in addition to existing ideas to enhance the creation and development of brands. Once a brand has built itself up to a certain level of awareness, liking and loyalty in the market, perhaps, has reached a level of emotional loyalty, even a habit, with a set of customers, the challenge is to sustain it over time, to keep it fresh and to even rejuvenate it at times. This forms the subject of the next chapter.

# Chapter 6

# Sustaining and Rejuvenating a Brand

Once a brand has built some traction in the market, the challenge is to sustain it, to draw a stream of revenue from it for the firm and to keep it fresh and rejuvenated over time. How does one accomplish this?

In this chapter, we outline steps for sustaining and rejuvenating a brand. What can a firm do to keep a brand firmly implanted in the brain of the customer so that there is a steady cash flow from the brand sales? How does one keep a brand 'fresh' over time—and in case the brand has wilted somewhat over time, how does one reinvigorate the brand in the brain of the customer?

**Step 1:** Brands exist in the brain. Once the brand is established in the brain, it is associated with a pattern (BOP#3). This pattern needs to be nurtured and strengthened in the mind of the customer. The first step, therefore, to sustaining (or rejuvenating) a brand is to periodically match the belief and values in execution terms. These actions by the firm need to recapitulate and strengthen the earlier pattern that exists in the mind of the customer (and therefore, satisfy brain objectives [BOP#2 and BOP#3] of reducing the energy required by the customer to choose the brand—and simultaneously increase the energy required to consider other brands).

Consider a situation where the earlier pattern has atrophied in the brain of customers. The Cooperative Bank in the UK, whose roots go back to the cooperative movement in the UK in the nineteenth century, started to help mill workers get out of 'bonded labour' from the mill owners who paid them a pittance and then got back the money by selling them sub-standard goods. The bank's roots lay in ethical and humanitarian practices—in helping its customers get a fair deal. By 1990, the Cooperative Bank found itself in a tiny niche with its market share of current accounts falling from 2.7 to 2.1 per cent in the five years leading up to 1991. Along with this decline, there was a decline in the quality of customers. In a market where everyone chased the same young, professional, high-value customer, the Cooperative Bank was left with the older, poorer, low-margin end of the spectrum. The bank was seen as old-fashioned, working class and not providing full service.

Cooperative turned things around by focusing on its roots, which had to do with ethical investment practices—partly a result of the stance that the bank had taken, in recent memory, against investment in apartheid South Africa and a vaguely remembered concept of humanitarian roots of the cooperative movement. The Cooperative team concluded that growing commercialism under Thatcher's Britain, with its perceived rapaciousness, had created a space for an image of an ethical bank that customers could relate to and build a relationship with on the dimensions of intimacy, brand partner quality and commitment.

The bank proceeded to define being an ethical bank as 'responsible sourcing and distribution of funds'. More importantly, it asked its customers to define what ethical banking and investing meant and as a consequence, it stopped serving customers like tobacco firms, industries that exploited animals and oppressive regimes. It closed several accounts. The Cooperative Bank then had an intensive training programme for its employees to help them explain to present and potential customers what ethical investing was all about. And then it started an advertising campaign underlining its ethical banking practices. The bank's 1993 annual report showed a return to profits for the first time in three years. Retail customer deposits grew from £1 billion in 1993 to 10 billion in 2003.[289]

Fostering a feeling of trust in customers can prove invaluable to a brand in the long run. The feeling of trust is furthered by the involvement of oxytocin (the hormone associated with love, bonding and other such social behaviour). Research has shown that an increase in oxytocin is related to increased trust.[290] Walking the talk and making good on brand promises alleviates the perception of risk involved in allying with the brand. More than 90 per cent of information is processed subconsciously (below controlled awareness) by human brains; this information greatly influences the decision-making process.[291] Responses to risky situations result in part from direct emotional influences, including feelings such as worry, fear, dread or anxiety. Research shows that emotional reactions to risky situations often diverge from cognitive evaluations of risk severity.[292] When such departures occur, the emotional reactions often exert a dominating influence on behaviour and frequently produce behaviour that does not appear to be adaptive.[293] The activation of the anterior insula switches us to a risk-limiting strategy.[294] This can have a destructive influence on our perception of the brand and negate any positive growth.

Sustaining a brand is about increasing the level of perceived risk (activate the anterior insula) of changing away from the brand. Rejuvenating the brand is about providing that small bit of change (dopamine) that increases the excitement of being with the brand; it is about increasing the attachment levels with the brand (increasing the oxytocin).

**Step 2:** The second step is to reinforce and/or rejuvenate the brand relationship by capturing elements of contemporary consumer experience with the brand that build and nurture relationships, and then sharing these with present and potential customers through appropriate marketing communication messages.

We know that people are more risk-averse towards negative experiences such as disgusting foods—but more risk-seeking for positive experiences. This is because reference points may be determined not by neutral values but rather by extreme values (e.g., the best dessert and the worst dentist visit).[295] People asked to recall *typical* instances of past experiences in positive and negative domains, in fact, recall the *most extreme* positive and negative experiences they have had in those domains, leading them to be ready to take more risks, with a lower activation of the anterior insula, for a positive experience, and be less ready to take risks with a negative experience.

A contemporary customer experience provides variety and contrast from the earlier images of the brand (Brain Operating Principle [BOP] #4) while remaining consistent with the earlier pattern (BOP#3). Consumers need to be reminded about why they love the brand and they need to be given a dollop of dopamine to keep them interested.

Parle-G is one of the oldest cookie brands in India, with a history dating back more than fifty years. Its brand positioning is on taste and health: '*Swaad bhare, shakti bhare* (full of taste and strength/energy)'. It is a part of the everyday life of a wide cross-section of the middle and bottom populace of pyramid India, and shows brand relationship dimensions of brand partner quality, commitment and intimacy. The brand faced fierce competition and a declining brand loyalty in the first and second decade of the twenty-first century. While sticking to the core message, and keeping the core position of taste and energy, Parle-G tailored its message by increasing its granularity. For mothers, it came up with the message 'Parle-G—G for Genius'; which mother did not aspire to have her child move to a genius status? Sounds far-fetched? It worked in a relatively low-income country where parental aspirations for children are the driving force behind many business transactions and relationships. For those wanting to buy Indian, it portrayed itself as Hindustan's *taakat* (the country's strength). It reminded people of why they had chosen to have Parle-G as a part of their lives in a way that resonated and renewed the commitment and intimacy on the part of the customer. All of these interventions created the dopamine spikes on top of the existing patterns in the mind of the customer. They enabled the customer to imagine the experience in their minds in a contemporary way.

Heinz is an iconic brand in the US with high levels of brand commitment and interdependence. In 1999, faced with generic store brands and competition, Heinz decided to do something to re-excite their consumers (provide more dopamine!) and maintain their relationship with customers. With the help of their advertising agency, Heinz came up with messages like '14 billion French fries can't be wrong', and 'Quiet please, tomatoes meeting inside'. Based on contemporary consumer experience with the brand, the hundred-year-old brand found a new way to engage consumers in a fun way and reminded them about how and why they loved the brand.

The trick is to weave your brand into your customer's life. Is the brand I am buying just like me? Does it match my aspirational self? Creating this junction between self and the brand is important. Becoming a part of an individual's identity requires telling the right story that they can connect to. Triggering memories of the brand as a beloved addition to one's life, the firm can cement its bond with its customer. Episodic memory brings forth vivid experiences from a person's memory store. Reliving happy experiences thanks to the brand's communication can form favourable associations in the customer's mind. While 'love at first sight' may seem alluring, the key to long-term success is the acceptance of the 'invitation to dance' and the gradual development of the relationship.

**Step 3:** As customers move to a time and place where experiences matter more than products, the brand needs to pay attention to providing rewarding experiences to its customers. This will translate into accurate and fast recognition of the brand at a later time by creating shortcuts to impulse decisions. It will embed the brand more deeply in the unconscious memory of the customer. An aspirational goal for a brand is to become the unconscious automatic choice in its category and the customer no longer expends energy choosing in that category (BOP#2).

Memory is an essential component in the development of customers' attitudes. When thinking of a new dish we ate recently, we may not recall its name or how it tasted. What is not memorable is not remembered. The 'recordability' of an experience depends on its affective component, in particular on its arousal dimension. 'What happened' and 'how it felt' are integral parts of recording of experience.[296] Emotional stimuli are better recognized than neutral stimuli and people tend to remember them rather than just having a vague recollection. The power of arousal steers attention to the prominent stimuli and encodes information as worth retaining. Arousal marks the importance not only explicitly via conscious experience but also implicitly by stimulating the adrenergic hormones which trigger responses in the amygdala. The more active the amygdala, the stronger the long-term memory consolidation.

Hero, an entry-level everyday 100–150cc motorcycle brand in India, has deep roots in rural India, where an emphasis on its sturdy quality leads to an experience that is of a reliable and durable product—one that the buyer can depend on.

Interactivity is the other basis for embedding a brand experience in the mind of the customer. An experimental investigation into the role of interaction in user experience with a controlled manipulation of interactivity features (e.g., avatars, interactive video) on a university information website showed that the interactive version had better affect and hedonic ratings, even though its perceived usability was worse.[297]

Consolidation of information in the long-term memory is a gradual process and is subject to emotional influences after the initial recording took place. In this regard, the added arousal contributes to the previously marked information. Consider, for example, that experiential gifts produce greater improvements in relationship strength than material gifts, regardless of whether the gift giver and recipient consume the gift together. The relationship improvements that recipients derive from experiential gifts stem from the intensity of emotion that is evoked when they consume the gifts, rather than when the gifts are received. Extending this to the realm of brands, therefore, leads us to the conclusion that brands that are able to provide positive valanced experiences that have an emotional connect will do better.[298]

By aligning the brand communication and experience, the firm can even modify the original sensory experience and enhance the qualitative ratings of even the pretty lousy perceived taste of a fruit juice. Overall, the emerging picture is of a tight correlation between the external world of stimuli and its behavioural meaning on the one hand, and the resulting internal representations on the other hand, at all possible timescales: the reflection of the macrocosmos in the microcosmos. In other words, experiences of the external world are embedded in the neuronal structure of the brain. Experiences create a different synaptic structure and new memories. The firm can, thus, create new memories around the brand!

**Step 4:** By connecting the brand in an emotionally meaningful way to the culture and deeply felt nuances of a country's life, a brand can dive right into the collective of that culture and become a part of the life of the people in that market/country; the brand can vault a couple of rungs up the brand ladder and build a relationship. It can evoke oxytocin and vasopressin, those powerful emotional bond-creating neurotransmitters. Gillette was always a niche brand in the men's shaving market in South Africa, associated more with white males in the country till they ran the campaign that connected to the reality of how many black men grew up in South Africa without their fathers; they were raised by their mothers and grandmothers. Launched on Women's Day in South Africa, the deeply moving and authentic video became the highest viewed YouTube video in South African history and was cited by the president of the country; it is unprecedented for a private brand to be cited by the leader of a country.[299]

**Step 5:** Firms have to be prepared to pivot when black swan events, such as the Great Recession of 2008–09 and the COVID-19 pandemic of 2020–22, occur. Events like these increase the level of fear in consumers. Serotonin levels drop. There is anxiousness about jobs, income and in the case of a pandemic, there is a perceived threat to life. In these situations, brands need to build reassurance in their overall architecture. This would require changes that can be small or quite large. The degree of change in the foundation of the brand relationship may be small (a luxury retailer like Burberry) or large (an airline like Emirates). The Burberry retail stores, which are set up to showcase the Burberry design and chic to provide a sense of excitement and exclusivity

(BOP#4), will remain largely the same and be able to maintain the brand relationships. But Emirates (and indeed most, if not all airlines) would need to change the product offering considerably. Emirates, for example, now offers a COVID-19 test for flyers. BOP#1, the need for security, has taken precedence and this need would have to be assuaged at multiple levels for Emirates to maintain its existing brand relationships across customers.

## How do Brand Relationships Exist and What Kind of Brand Relationships Can You Build?

Research and other evidence on brand relationships indicate the following:

**First**, brand relationships exist across income strata, but there are product category effects and income effects.[300] Consumers are more likely to form brand relationships with products that they use more frequently and are dependent on for functional or emotional reasons. Consumers who are above a certain consumption threshold (in terms of the variety and quantity of products and brands consumed) are more likely to develop brand relationships. Some data suggests that the higher the income, the stronger the strength of a brand relationship. On the other hand, many owners of Hero CD100 Dawn, the entry-level Indian motorcycle, also display evidence of brand relationship along the dimension of brand partner quality and interdependence.[301] The brand has established patterns of behaviour in the customer. Also, the role of family in brand usage is greater than the role of peers in the Indian context, which is not the case in developed countries. But if the consumer has developed a strong relationship with the brand, it is highly unlikely that they will switch, even despite a strong familial influence.

**Second**, age and gender have a significant influence on the nature of the brand relationship that is established. Across countries, young consumers, and teenagers in particular, have strong relationships with their brands. Younger consumers tend to establish stronger affect-based brand relationships as compared to older consumers. Our research indicates that the age group thirteen to nineteen is higher on the affect dimension than young adults (twenty to twenty-five years); as they go through a transition phase, they construct their identities out of available symbolic resources in order to weave a coherent definition of who they are as they grow more independent of their parents. The older group develops strong brand relationships also, but they are relatively more rational about their relationships with brands. In older people, the excitation of the amygdala tends to happen at a much higher level in response to an arousing stimulus; lower levels of amygdala arousal mean that the responses are more 'rational' and less 'emotional.'[302] Therefore, appeals need to utilize less energy consumption (BOP#2) from the required cognitive effort in a way that still provides credible information.

McDonald's is still the most visited restaurant for the millennial demographic in India, according to analysts at Morgan Stanley. For college students who are on a budget and want to grab a quick bite with friends, McDonald's is the go-to place. It also occasionally rolls out promotions offering discounts to students. The brand has been introducing more fresh ingredients and customizable burgers tailored to Indian taste, for example, to compete with fast casual brands.[303] Students don't just go there for the food, they go there for the fun times they share with their friends over the burgers.

Price, while a sensitive factor in many Indian customer segments, is not the primary driver of purchase. Consider Nike. Its apparel doesn't come cheap. Data shows that millennials believe exercise is essential for health, while their parents only focused on diet, and Nike is the go-to brand, holding 62 per cent of the athletic shoe market. 'Increased activity leads to increased athletic apparel and footwear spending,' the analysts write. 'We see athletic footwear and apparel as more than a fashion trend.'[304] Nike with its clever campaigns capturing the imagination and aspirations of the youth with its 'Just do it' tag, appeals to its customers forming a part of their very identity. It becomes embedded in the emotional unconscious of the customer leading to an increase in the probability of purchase.

Hero MotoCorp targeted young women for the brand's scooter, Hero Pleasure, with its brand message 'Why should boys have all the fun?' It depicted girls riding a Hero Pleasure in the sun and rain, underlining the message of girls having fun and challenging misogynistic views favouring only boys. Its brand communication transcended functional mobility. This is in stark contrast to its communications in the two-wheeler segment aimed at men. Here, its primary focus leans more towards highlighting the functional utility of the bikes, while also portraying manliness.

**Third**, brand relationship development is a function of opportunities in the 'market'. A politician, for example, utilizes opportunities to build awareness of themselves and simultaneously connects on a relationship basis with his constituents. In August 2010, when more than 30 miners were trapped 700 metres below the ground in a mine in Chile in South America, one official on the surface increasingly finding himself in the spotlight was Laurence Golborne, the Mining Minister. He had interacted warmly with the miners' families, crying and laughing with them as he spent the nights and days at the mine. One family even asked him to preside over a religious wedding planned between one miner and his long-time partner after the rescue was completed. According to a private polling firm, Adimark, Golborne's public recognition factor shot up 24 points to 91 percent since the disaster.[305] Laurence Golborne built a strong enough relationship of his personal brand with the Chilean voters during this time. He became a recognized pattern (BOP#3) in the mind of many constituents.

Consider also the event of demonetization in India in November 2016, when the government, overnight, removed 86 per cent of the cash in circulation as currency notes. In a matter of a few hours, people with Rs 500 and 1000 notes had worthless pieces of paper that they had to deposit in the bank to have any hope of getting back the value. While the demonetization scheme sent many businesses into crisis, and caused some hardship to many individuals, several brands seized this opportunity to reposition themselves. With the ban on Rs 500 and 1000 notes, players in the electronic transactions field, like Paytm and FreeCharge, took full advantage of the wind blowing in their sails. A mere three minutes after the news became public, Paytm, a payments company based out of Delhi, wasted no time in taking to Twitter with its witty message: 'We have got two words for you: Paytm karo' (Use Paytm [to make payments]).' What a fascinating use of pattern and contrast (BOP#3 and BOP#4) simultaneously to give the brand a boost. By mid-2021, Paytm had more than 140 million users.

While this was breaking news in India, all the way across the globe, a monumental election was taking place in the US in November 2016. Uber announced free rides to and from polls in Florida, Pennsylvania and other places. While the immediate effects of this brand message were geographically limited, the news the offer was based on had global consequences. With the whole world talking about the elections, Uber was clever in its positioning, urging citizens to exercise their right to vote.

Opportunities in the market, triggered by one-off events, are frequently a chance for a brand to provide dollops of excitement to the customer and to the brand (BOP#4).

**Fourth,** in many instances, the desire for a brand leads to significant changes in the consumer's behaviour. For instance, when consumers develop relationships with the luxury/high-end brands they are ready to change themselves to suit the brand requirements. A consumer who wears a Rolex watch changes himself to suit the brand requirement, his appearance, the way he carries himself. This, as we know, has been called the Diderot Effect after the French philosopher. The effect was first described in Diderot's essay 'Regrets on Parting with My Old Dressing Gown'. Here, he narrates how the gift of a beautiful scarlet dressing gown leads to unexpected results, eventually plunging him into debt.

Initially pleased with the gift, Diderot came to rue his new garment. Compared to his elegant new dressing gown, the rest of his possessions began to seem tawdry and he became dissatisfied that they did not live up to the elegance and style of his new possession. The contrast was glaring. He replaced his old straw chair, for example, with an armchair covered in Moroccan leather; his old desk was replaced with an expensive new writing table; his former, beloved prints were replaced with more costly prints, and so on. 'I was absolute master of my old dressing gown,' Diderot writes, 'but I have become a slave to my new one . . . Beware of the contamination of sudden wealth. The poor man may take his ease without thinking of appearances, but the rich man is always under a strain.'[306] In this instance, the purchase of the gown triggered a change in the pattern; the new gown became the keystone for an entirely new pattern, building on an unconscious desire in the philosopher's mind.

The gown provided the initial trigger dopamine to Diderot (BOP#4: the contrast effect). The underlying desire for a pattern (BOP#3) then took over, driven by the salience of the gown, somewhere in the recesses of Diderot's brain.

**Fifth**, in many brand relationships, there is a strong brand community[307] of users that provide a sense of mirroring (BOP#5); a significant part of the brand relationship benefits comes from the brand community-based activities and the emotional benefits generated. Among American Harley Davidson consumers, for example, there exists a hierarchy based on the status of the bikers. They reinforce the ethos and values with the community and show a ritualistic pattern in their usage. The individuals who are a part of the subculture – their identity, motives and level of commitment evolve in patterns that are linked to the product and its usage. [308] Fellow riders develop relationships with others who have similar values and perspectives, indicating the co-construction of the Harley–Davidson brand experience. In this process of consumption, consumers also start entertaining each other and socialize thus, making consumption a socializing tool and the brand a symbol of that socialization.[309] In many of these cases, the brand relationship appears to exist along all the dimensions of brand relationship.

Sixth, sustaining a brand also means that the manager needs to increase the perceived risk of buying another brand. It turns out that mood is a significant predictor of the level of risk that a person takes. Au, Chan, Wang and Vertinsky[310] reason that context determines good mood, which will lead to overconfidence, greater optimism and greater risk-taking. Under well-defined situations, good mood should lead to lower risk-taking; in contrast with unknown probabilities, good mood may lead to greater risk-taking because of perceptions of more control. Au et al.[311] found that participants in a good mood were less accurate in their decision-making, lost money and took unnecessary risks. Sadness implies loss or a sense of something missing, which should prompt people to seek rewards or replacements, while anxiety signals uncertainty and a lack of control, which should prompt people to reduce uncertainty and be risk-averse.[312] In three experiments involving gambling or job choice decisions, participants who were sad sought high-risk/high-reward alternatives while those who were anxious sought low-risk/low-reward options.

The goal of brand management is to form enduring brand relationships with the customer. Some commentators also call this process 'brand engagement', a term loosely used to describe the process of forming an attachment (emotional and rational) between a person and a brand. What makes the topic complex is that brand engagement is partly created by institutions and organizations, but is equally created by the perceptions, attitudes, beliefs and behaviours of customers that these institutions and organizations are interacting with. From the organizational perspective, the goal of brand engagement and building brand relationships is to generate brand awareness, purchase, use and, most importantly, loyalty. Brand loyalty is critical because the cost of acquiring a new customer is often many times that of retaining a customer.

In the next section, we look at how to build a brand by using brand extensions. When will brand extensions work? Can they be used to sustain, extend and/or rejuvenate a brand?

## Brand Extension—Meaning, Advantages and Disadvantages

Brand extension is the use of an established brand name in new product categories. This new category to which the brand is extended can be related or unrelated to the existing product categories. A renowned/successful brand helps an organization to launch products in new categories more easily. For instance, the Nike brand's core product is shoes. But it is now extended to sunglasses, soccer balls, basketballs and golf equipment. An existing brand that gives rise to a brand extension is referred to as a parent brand. If the customers of the new business have values and aspirations synchronizing with/matching those of the core business, and if these values and aspirations are embodied in the brand, it is likely to be accepted by customers in the new business.

Brand extension is used frequently by a firm to take advantage of the brand equity that has already been established by the firm and is leveraged to launch new products. In most of these cases, the brand extension is part of the overall pattern that is associated with the brand in the brain of the customer (BOP#3). It is also a low-cost way for the firm to launch a new product and to reach new sub-segments. Nike is associated with sports and physical activity. And most, if not all, of the other products with the Nike name are related to sports and/or physical activity.

Brand extensions have the potential to both enhance the liking of the brand extension and induce positive spillover effects on the parent brand. Such dual outcomes enhance the brand's growth potential also. Three factors endemic to any brand extension decision (brand reputation, brand extension fit, brand extension benefit innovativeness) jointly impact the positive outcomes that can result from the brand extension.

For strong reputation brands, these dual outcomes are maximized when the brand extension is low in fit and offers innovative benefits because low fit motivates consumers to process innovative brand extension information more deeply—they become curious, invoking BOP#4. For weak reputation brands, the positive effects of the brand extensions are maximized when the brand extension is high in fit and offers innovative benefits because high fit strengthens consumers' trust in the weak brand's ability to deliver promoted benefits, leveraging BOP#3. The results suggest two distinct brand growth strategies for strong and weak reputation brands.[313]

Extending a brand outside its core product category can, thus, be beneficial sometimes.

Instances where a brand extension outside of the core category has been a success are:

i. The Tata Group in India was initially just a steel and truck company. It now transcends the category with a brand that is built on trust and ethical behaviour and includes products like software, salt, chemicals, real estate, cars, watches, gold jewellery, consumer electronics, retail and capital equipment. The basis of the trust, caring and ethical behaviour is the behaviour of the Tata leadership across time. For example, every employee who had injuries or had a death in the family from the terrorist attack on the Taj Hotel in Mumbai in November 2008 was personally attended to by Ratan Tata and taken care of financially for life. Another instance is where the Tata Group used the services of unemployed German engineers in the immediate aftermath of the Second World War, which helped build skills among the Tata Motors workforce. At that time, the Tatas were able to provide only employment and subsistence-level wages due to paucity of funds. Twenty years later, these employees, who had since returned to Germany, got letters asking them where the remaining payment to them should be remitted from their earlier employment. Such a gesture was, of course, totally unexpected, a contrast (BOP#4) to contractual business operations, since there was no contract. On the back of such value-based actions, the basis of the Tata brand pattern has shifted to emotion based on trust, caring and ethical behaviour rather than from the functional benefit provided by the product. Arguably, the values of J.R.D. Tata and Ratan Tata that spanned almost seventy-five years imbue the group and are an underpinning of the brand.

ii. The Honda Motor Company of Japan, now present worldwide, transcends the automotive category and is found in other categories such as boats, lawnmowers and mobile generators. The brand extension is built around the attribution and halo effect that flow out of BOP#3, which motivates a person to fit the pattern of competency in engines in cars to all other categories of the product. Here, the brand is still built around the functional benefit rather than the emotional benefit.

We know that consumer evaluations of brand extensions are affected by two distinct types of brand reputation: a reputation for social responsibility built through commitments to societal obligations, and a reputation for ability developed by delivering quality offerings. While the two reputation types equivalently influence high-fit brand extensions, a reputation for social responsibility (vs ability) leads to more favourable responses towards low-fit brand extensions by inducing a desire to support and help the company that has acted to benefit consumers.[314] This is where the Tata brand scores as it has a reputation for social responsibility.

Furthermore, the facilitative effect of social responsibility on low-fit brand extension evaluations is more prominent among consumers who value close relationships and care for one another's well-being (i.e., those with high communal orientation).

Where brand extension has not been able to move from the product category-based pattern to an emotion-based pattern, or has not been able to include the new product in the pattern, it has failed, as in the following instances.

i. In case of the new Coke, Coca-Cola has forgotten what the core brand was meant to stand for. It thought that taste was the only factor that consumers cared about. It was wrong; the shift from the pattern was a stretch too far for the consumer. The money and time spent on research on the new Coca-Cola could not measure up to the strong emotional connect with the original Coca-Cola.
ii. Rasna Ltd is among the famous fruit-based beverage companies in India. But when it tried to move away from its niche, it didn't have much success. When it experimented with the fizzy fruit drink Oranjolt, the brand bombed even before it could take off. Oranjolt was a fruit drink in which carbonates were used as preservatives. It didn't work out because it was out of synchronization (did not fit the pattern [BOP#3]) with retail practices. Oranjolt needed to be refrigerated and it also faced quality problems. It had a shelf life of three–four weeks, while other soft drinks had an assured life of five months. Importantly, the new brand simply did not fit the pattern of the Rasna brand.

Brand extensions are also about how they satisfy the customer from an emotional standpoint. One dimension of emotion is the feeling of control that brands provide to customers. Research shows that 'when people cannot rely on feelings of control to thwart the fear of randomness, they find a sense of order and structure in their environment in other ways. For example, people seek order and structure by supporting powerful external systems, including the government and god.'[315] Under feelings of low control, people also look for structure in the aesthetic elements of their immediate environment.[316] Product designs and pictures that had strong boundaries were preferred by people with feelings of low control over other designs and pictures that did not have strong boundaries. Shelves that had clear boundaries were preferred over shelves that did not. It is almost as if people are looking to maintain tight mental boundaries in consumption options as a means of providing structure and order to their lives. The tight boundaries provide structure, groups, patterns (Brain Operating Principle #3).

Brands are categories[317] (and, therefore, part of a pattern in the mind), and people's perceptions of what fits within a given category are highly flexible. When feelings of control are low, people have an enhanced desire for structure. They therefore mentally erect narrower cognitive boundaries that dictate the space in which a brand belongs (e.g., the attributes, benefits and other associations that fit with the brand). Accordingly, when feelings of control are low, people's lower perceptions of fit for questionable extensions will lead directly to lower overall evaluations for the extensions. Notably, there is no expectation that feelings of control will influence attitudes towards good-fitting extensions—that is, extensions that do not stretch a brand outside its accepted boundaries. In such cases, people with low control will accept the fit of the extensions because structure is still maintained.[318]

Although fit is indeed a critical driver of brand extension evaluations, it is not a reflection of only people's reactions to a product's characteristics. It is also a reflection of their need for structure in general. It suggests that psychological state is an important consideration in brand extension decisions.

In a similar vein to brand extension are instances of co-branding, which is the utilization of two or more brands to name a new product.

As described in *Co-Branding: The Science of Alliance*:[319] 'The term "co-branding" is used to encompass a wide range of marketing activity involving the use of two (and sometimes more) brands. Thus co-branding could be considered to include sponsorships, where Marlboro lends it name to Ferrari or accountants Ernst and Young support the Monet exhibition.'

The ingredient brands help each other achieve their aims. The overall synchronization between the brand pair and the new product has to be kept in mind. An example of co-branding is when Citibank and MTV launched a co-branded debit card. With this card, customers can avail benefits at specific outlets called MTV Citibank Club. However, whether it benefits the brands that are forming the alliance is debatable. There is some evidence that where there is complementarity in the products representing the brands, then there may be a positive evaluation.[320] Complementarity completes the pattern in the mind (BOP#3) and is therefore likely to lead to a more positive evaluation. However, it has to be a complement in the mind of the customer.

In light of the demonetization scheme that came into effect in India, many electronic transaction companies sought to co-brand with other companies dealing with payments. Paytm co-branded with Uber, delivering discounted offerings to customers who chose to use this service.

Co-branding can be done through ingredient branding, where one uses a well-known brand as an element in the production of another brand. This deals with creation of brand equity for materials and parts that are contained within other products. The ingredient/constituent brand is subordinate to the primary brand. For instance, Dell computers has a co-branding strategy with Intel processors. The brands that are ingredients are usually the company's biggest buyers or present suppliers. The ingredient brand should be unique. It should either be a major brand or should be protected by a patent. Well-conceptualized and executed ingredient co-branding can lead to better quality products, superior promotions, more access to distribution channels and greater profits. The seller of the ingredient brand enjoys long-term customer relations. The brand manufacturer benefits from having a competitive advantage and the retailer can benefit from promotional help from the ingredient brand.

Complementarity, utility, criticality, relative strength in the ecosystem of the product and the customer and contribution to the 'whole' by the ingredient brand influence the degree of success of the ingredient brand. The more integrated the ingredient brand along multiple parameters into the whole—that which the brain of the customer can see as a 'whole' (BOP#3)—the greater the success.

When two brands collectively offer a distinct product or service that could not be possible individually, we call it composite branding, e.g., Slimfast by Godiva. The success of composite branding depends upon the favourability of the ingredient brands and also upon the extent of complementarities between them. When co-branding is attempted, the target customer segment and their thought process will influence success enormously. Slimfast Chocolate by Godiva offers a contrast (BOP#4) that can attract attention. However, the message also has to be credible.

Co-branding has various advantages, such as risk-sharing, generation of royalty income, more sales income, greater customer trust in the product, wide scope due to joint advertising, technological benefits, better product image by association with another renowned brand, and greater access to new sources of finance. But co-branding is not free from limitations. Co-branding may fail when the two products have different markets and are entirely different. If there is a difference in the visions and the missions of the two companies, then composite branding may also fail. Co-branding may affect partner brands in an adverse manner. If the customers associate any adverse experience with a constituent brand, then it may damage the total brand equity.[321]

Co-branding can also involve joining with another company to penetrate a market or to take out competition. For instance, as Uber ramped up its business globally with more money, four of its regional rivals joined hands in a bid for more scale and service continuity. Lyft in the US, Didi Kuaidi in China, Ola in India and GrabTaxi in South-east Asia have now inked a strategic partnership to work together on technology and services. This began with the customers of each company being able to use their local apps to order transportation when they travelled to the other markets in the network, starting Q1 2016.[322]

Other examples include the marketing of Gillette M3 Power shaving equipment (which requires batteries) with Duracell batteries (both brands owned by Procter & Gamble). Co-branding can be between an organization and a product also. An example of co-branding between a charity and a manufacturer is the association of Sephora and Operation Smile. Sephora markets a product carrying the logo of the charity, the consumer is encouraged to associate the two brands, and a portion of the proceeds benefit the charity.

In a nutshell, brand extensions and co-branding work when the patterns are strengthened (BOP#3) and, simultaneously, there is an addition of some change, excitement, variety, new benefit to the product/service on offer (BOP#4). The greater the number of other people that a customer sees with the brand extensions, or the more a key influencer is associated with the brand (BOP#5), the higher the probability of success of the brand extension or the co-branding.

In Chapters 5 and 6, we have examined the construction and management of a brand over time with examples and related it to particular situations where firms can use the different ideas. In the next chapter, we look at how to construct and manage brands in an increasingly digital world. This is becoming increasingly important in any case, and the advent of the pandemic triggered by COVID-19 has accelerated the process.

# Chapter 7

# Neuroscience and Building, Sustaining and Rejuvenating Brands on Social Media

The days when newspapers, magazines, radios and televisions would form a key source (apart from word of mouth) of customer knowledge of the outside world, of what the celebrities are doing this Christmas, of the state assembly elections coming up, of which trend is in again, are either already gone or on the way out. The Internet and social media are becoming a key source of information, and customers (especially millennials and Gen Z customers) then discuss this information not over a cuppa coffee or at a dinner party in a fancy restaurant, but mostly online. Their brand perceptions, attitudes and choices are also influenced by what they see online.

The incessant desire of an average human being to be connected (Brain Operating Principle [BOP] #5) has found a new manifestation in the use of social media platforms—from sharing personal news and remaining updated about our neighbours to sharing political and national news and articles, to connecting with brands and products and mirroring the behaviour of other people online. The quick clicks and swipes have enabled an increasingly individualistic person to manage a relationship with his/her fundamentally evolutionary property of 'being social', albeit a virtual one. The provision of features like the 'share', 'like', 'comment', 'watch later', and emojis like 'heart', 'wink,' and 'smiley' to respond to a post, along with features like 'add to your story', trigger an emotional response in our brains.

Our responses are influenced by the personality, the culture of the customer and often, the mood of the customer. Successful brands have attempted to leverage these emotional drives of the more than 4.5 billion people who are on social media as of 2021! In the previous chapters, we have already seen how branding techniques often acknowledge the way our brain operates and responds during decision-making and in this chapter, we will learn how brands can use the popularity of social media to promote themselves using insights from neuroscience. By publishing meticulously planned video ad campaigns and sharing time-worthy content, brands have succeeded in promoting brand information without making the users fully aware of their active participation! We will also learn about the neuroscientific basis and consequences of brands' activities.

Social media is becoming ubiquitous. The average person has five social media accounts and spends around an hour and forty minutes browsing these networks every day, accounting for 28 per cent of the total time spent on the Internet.[323]

In the US, 74 per cent of the adults who use the Internet, use social networking sites such as Facebook, Twitter, LinkedIn, Pinterest and Instagram. Facebook alone, one of the world's most popular social networking sites, has over 2.4 billion regular users,[324] or roughly three out of every ten humans on the planet. It is a terrific absorber of audiences' time and attention: 114 billion minutes a month in the US alone, on desktop PCs and smartphones. By comparison, Instagram commands 8 billion minutes a month, and Twitter just 5.3 billion. Facebook attracts roughly seven times the engagement that Twitter does, when looking at both smartphone and PC usage, in per user terms.[325] This widespread use of social media generates a massive amount of data. There are almost two billion people using social media worldwide, generating more than 1 billion Facebook posts, 400 million tweets, uploading twelve years' worth of videos to YouTube and making 3,00,000 edits to Wikipedia in just one single day. As Internet access around the world increases steadily, so will the number of social media users.

It is now possible to use the data that is available on social media to gain novel insights about customers' social cognitive processes, profiles and the neural systems that support them. Facebook has already established a neuroscience centre to understand consumer behaviour using methods like eye tracking, skin response, heart rate and facial expression. It intends to learn what users view in their news feeds, what catches their attention, what escapes their notice and what urges them to click on a link.[326]

People have an innate need to connect to others, to mirror others (BOP#5). On social media, they connect with others and also manage their reputation. Finding ways to fulfil our need to belong to a social group is important for the well-being of our brains—the brain feels good and secure when it connects to others (BOP#1 and BOP#5). Brands are also present on social media in a big way. Living as part of an interconnected group enhances physical survival and security by providing a heightened a sense of security and belonging (BOP#3). Groups increase the potential to not only survive, but also thrive; strong social bonds enhance psychological well-being and protect individuals from feelings of loneliness and depression.[327] Close-knit WhatsApp groups consisting of friends from the same school or college are manifestations of the desire to connect. Many studies have tried to measure our dependency on social media for this 'bond' by measuring the extent of our uneasiness when we are not being able to use our phones.[328] This feeling of anxiety arises due to the fear of missing out on a pleasant experience that others are indulging in—in short, FOMO, 'fear of missing out', and it has been recognized as a major driver of social media addiction.[329]

Social media thus provides a platform for people to satisfy their fundamental social drives. Specifically, social media allows us to connect with others and groom our reputation via at least five key behaviours:

i. Users broadcast information (e.g., text, pictures, links, videos, etc.). Users can share information that is personal (e.g., vacation photos),[330] or they can propagate information that is not self-referential in nature (e.g., posting an article about top vacation spots).
ii. Users receive feedback on broadcasted information. For example, a user might have pictures of a vacation

that she would like to share with others. She uploads pictures to social media and then other users provide feedback by commenting on the pictures and/or providing a signal of approval (e.g., a 'like' or 'favourite', depending on the social media platform). This reciprocity works in the opposite direction as well. Both gets dollops of dopamine for their effort (BOP#1).

iii. Users observe information broadcast by others.
iv. Users provide feedback on others' posts. For example, a user might see a picture of a friend's vacation, 'like' the picture on Facebook, and then comment on how much fun the vacation looked. Feedback is usually visible to the user's network or, in some cases, the public.
v. Users engage in social comparison by contrasting their own broadcasts and feedback to others,[331] such as through the number of likes received. This social comparison is not limited to posts and feedback; descriptive information in a user's profile may also be used for social comparison, such as online social network size, relationship status and age, for example.[332]

All these activities tap into processes and constructs like emotional state, personality, social conformity, and how people manage their self-presentation and social connections and, therefore, provide the building blocks for constructing detailed profiles of users.

While the maximum number of people are on Facebook, there are now a substantial number of people on other social media platforms, like Twitter, Instagram, Pinterest, Tinder, WhatsApp, Baidu, Hike, etc., as well. A study commissioned by Facebook examined how consumers' brains responded to the site as well as to Yahoo's and The *New York Times's* homepages. NeuroFocus, the Berkeley, California, firm that executed the study, found that of the three, Facebook scored highest on attention, emotional engagement and memory retention;[333] [334] of course, this result is partly driven by the scale of the numbers present on the platform.

Part of the reason for the high emotional engagement on Facebook is 'faces'. The face is a window to the emotions. Since childhood, we are trained to read people's faces to discern emotion, and that such information is key to survival. And our response to others' emotions itself is an emotional one. Every post, photo or video we come across while scanning our newsfeed stimulates an emotional response. Thus, every like, share and comment is an emotional response, one that reflects a part of our true self, all thanks to the 'faces' that feature as the primary object in posts on Facebook.

Cambridge Analytica (CA) infamously utilized this to influence the US presidential elections of 2016. It tried to figure out Facebook users' personalities by assessing their likes, dislikes, shares, posts, etc., to understand how an eligible voter would be voting in the presidential elections, by exploiting the fact that there is a strong connection between personality and political leaning. It subtly tried to influence users' decisions by ensuring that sponsored ads and news articles glorifying the Republicans would appear frequently on those users' feeds who, according to their analysis, would be voting against them. Additionally, it sponsored news articles that brought the shortcomings of the opposing candidates to the fore.

This technique of highly personalized, targeted advertising helped CA to influence the user's political choice.[335] The case of Cambridge Analytica has shown that it is possible to figure out people's preferences through their Facebook activity. And therefore, it acts as evidence for the claim that our social media activity is a reflection of our thoughts, personality and emotions.

Social media provides a platform where the modern human can attempt to satisfy basic social needs via the previously mentioned five key behaviours. These behaviours rely primarily on three domains: social cognition (i.e., mentalizing), self-referential cognition and social reward processing.[336]

**Mentalizing network:** Using social media requires us to think about the mental states and motivations of other users: to mentalize. For example, before and after a social media user broadcasts information, they may think about how their audience will respond. When providing feedback on another user's posts, a user may think about how this specific user may react upon receiving this feedback. Finally, when viewing information and feedback broadcast by others, a user may think about the other user's motivations for posting this information. Much of this happens unconsciously as people engage online and mirror one another's actions. The quick feedback loop online provides spurts of dopamine that the brain loves.

Neuroimaging studies of offline social behaviours have demonstrated that thinking about others' thoughts, feelings and intentions reliably recruits a network of brain regions, including the dorsomedial prefrontal cortex (DMPFC), bilateral temporoparietal junction (TPJ), anterior temporal lobes (ATL), inferior frontal gyri (IFG) and posterior cingulate cortex/precuneus (PCC). Recent studies have directly linked activity in these regions to sharing information[337, 338] and receiving others' shared information.[339] These regions, implicated in offline information sharing and receipt, as well as in mentalizing more broadly, likely also help us to process the social thoughts and behaviours elicited by social media.[340]

**People use social media to post information about themselves:** They share their own current subjective experience, recent past or opinions.[341] As such, social media use involves a great deal of self-referential thought: thinking about oneself may prompt a user to broadcast those thoughts, and broadcasting one's thoughts may provoke further self-referential thought. Receiving feedback may induce reflected self-appraisals, and social comparison likewise requires users to think about their own behaviour in relation to other users. Neuroimaging studies have also demonstrated that self-referential thought involves a network of midline cortical regions, specifically the medial prefrontal cortex (MPFC) and PCC.[342] Recent studies have also linked activity in the MPFC to the self-referential component of sharing information about the self (i.e., self-disclosure).[343] Online social media use that involves self-referential thought should likewise recruit this network of brain regions involved in thinking about the self. Self-referential thought is both conscious and unconscious.

**Social rewards:** It is to be noted that social media provides users with a consistent supply of social rewards with each and every suggestion of social connection or reputation enhancement. For example, Facebook users can receive positive feedback in the form of a 'like,' or social connections in the form of a 'friend' request. Even minimalistic cues of social success such as these may activate our brain's reward system with a dollop of dopamine and keep us coming back to Facebook (or Instagram or Twitter) for more.

Social rewards activate a network of brain regions, including the ventromedial prefrontal cortex (VMPFC), ventral striatum and ventral tegmental area. For example, sharing of information with others activates the VMPFC and ventral striatum, as does receiving positive social feedback (e.g., getting cues that others understand you, agree with you, like you or think highly of you). Providing others with these same social rewards (e.g., giving a 'like' on Facebook) may be akin to other types of prosocial behaviour, which also activate the reward system (e.g., donating to charity). Reading others' posts may likewise elicit reward activity, because receiving information elicits curiosity, a feeling associated with activity in the ventral striatum. Finally, the ventral striatum may underlie social comparison, with research showing that activity in this region reflects the comparison between one's own obtained reward and another person's, rather than the absolute level of one's own reward. These regions, implicated in offline information sharing and receipt, giving and receiving feedback, and reward processing more broadly, likely also process the rewards endowed by social media.[344] Rewards provide dopamine and other desired neurotransmitters (BOP#1) through the interaction.

In addition to the above networks, in using social media, one must attend to stimuli, make decisions and execute motor movements, among countless other behaviours. These implicate other brain systems in social media use, such as the frontoparietal attention network, the executive function network and the motor system, respectively.

Neuroscientists can take two approaches when using social media in research. They can take advantage of similarities between online and offline social behaviours, using measures from social media as a proxy for offline behaviours. Alternately, they can capitalize on differences between the online and offline world, investigating behaviours unique to the online environment.

In the next part of this chapter, we will see how the brain operating principles and decision-making processes discussed in Chapters 2 and 3 illustrate the ideas by looking at some of the brand-building and maintenance steps in Chapters 5 and 6. Brands can use these steps, in addition to contemporary research, to devise branding techniques for social media platforms, to build, sustain and rejuvenate brands, given the ubiquity and importance of these platforms.

*The most powerful brands are those that get into the unconscious and have an emotional meaning so that the brand almost becomes a habit—a part of a person's life. A person feels something is missing from their life without the brand. It becomes a part of a person's identity.*

What are some social media actions that increase the probability of getting one's brand into the customer's unconscious? In Chapter 2, we discussed that the brain is an energy guzzler. It tries to conserve energy and become more efficient. To do this, the brain has a tendency to push things into the unconscious to conserve energy (BOP#2). And it remembers things that have an emotional meaning attached to them. Building a powerful brand requires a deliberate effort to move one's brand into the unconscious of the customer.

Alibaba's 'To the Greatness of Small' advertisement[345] does exactly this. It could well have been called 'The Story of Our Lives', for it appears relatable to the viewers on a deeply personal level. It addresses the fact that we often feel small in this vast, rapidly changing world, that 99 per cent of the people feel they are small, and then the narrator goes on to state that 'small can be calculated but not ignored', celebrating the power of small. The ad demands little from the viewer, cognitively speaking, as its pretext addresses something that is deeply ingrained in us at an unconscious level and is, quite literally, a part of the viewer's life! It appeals to the David vs Goliath pattern (BOP#3) in all of us. Additionally, the subtle positivity we feel after watching the commercial enhances the company's connection with our emotions and therefore, makes the brand information more automatically accessible.

Samsung's service advertisement on YouTube,[346] first aired on 16 December 2016, which was the most watched YouTube video globally in 2017, with more than 200 million views, exemplifies the use of brain operating principles to get into the customer's unconscious. The advertisement has a story plot (the pattern—BOP#3) that the viewer follows unconsciously (a hero, the service technician, has a goal, faces obstacles, like the tree on the road, the sheep, crossing a river and difficult mountain roads, but overcomes them and achieves his goal at the end); it uses contrasts (BOP#4) through the unexpectedness of a blind girl opening the door, of blind students 'watching' a TV programme, and the singer on the programme being a friend of the viewer. It deploys conscious and unconscious emotion through the use of blind children and music that gently pushes the viewer along. The emotional engagement reduces the use of deliberate focus and attention, reducing energy consumption (BOP#2). The positive affect, the pattern and contrast provide the spikes in relevant neurotransmitters (BOP#1). Over a three-year period, more than 90 per cent of over 500 participants in various sessions where the advertisement has been shown as a part of neuroscience and consumer behaviour sessions have loved the advertisement.

Emotions play a vital role in our decision-making process. We assign our brand loyalty and respond positively to advertisements that strike an emotional chord with us. We look for brands that resonate with us.[347] These emotions are also critical and very much in play, in the way we behave on any social media platform, the way we respond to brands reaching out to us on social media. Using the brand continuously over time then leads to the development of the habit of using the brand. The brand then becomes a part of one's life.

*Neuroscience helps to assess where a brand is in the brand ladder. Essentially, the brand should have a reached a level at which the person is using System 1 processing only as a rule, reducing energy consumption. System 2 processing should be occurring only as an exception.*

Dove seeks to further its brand image, caring for the real beauty of women and their confidence and focusing on inner beauty more than superficial beauty, through each of its ad campaigns. 'Real Beauty Sketches' is one of its many famous campaigns that recorded 163 million views on YouTube. It features a US Federal Bureau of Investigation (FBI)-trained forensic artist drawing two sketches of each of the subjects; the first on the basis of the subject's description of their own face and the second on the basis of a stranger's description of the subject. The latter sketch ends up portraying a more pleasant, more beautiful person and is more accurate than the first sketch. The ad shows that how a woman perceives her own beauty is critical to her happiness. For women viewers, the subjects' thoughts are a reflection of their own thoughts and therefore, the ad touches the audience on an emotional and personal level. Time and again, Dove's commercials emphasize such personal and emotional feelings and their consistent efforts weave the brand into the viewer's emotional memories and unconsciousness, making retrieval of brand information easier and more automatic. Thanks to this emotional connect, the audience automatically find themselves preferring Dove over other products on many subsequent interactions with the brand. 'Real Beauty Sketches' won accolades and worldwide acceptance, nothing short of a positive consequence one can expect out of trying to make both meaningful and viral content.

Through this social media campaign, Dove has managed to move deeper into the affect-related territory of the brand ladder. And with many women, one can say that Dove is now in the relationship territory—that Dove has managed to establish a relationship based on a touch that is real, a touch that enables women to draw a contrast (BOP#4) between how they feel about themselves and how others look at them, the positive contrast providing a positive emotional valence that makes the connect between Dove and its customer deeper and longer lasting. The brand's communication on social media has propagated through online networks and is arguably now more System 1 based.

Remember that a brand carries a particular 'emotional positioning'. Virality is the new mantra that every brand strives to achieve on social media that helps to drive the brand deeper into the unconscious. People need to learn about the brand's presence. Virality may be the new popular term on the block, but it needs to be implemented right. An advertisement going viral, while getting the brand noticed, does not necessarily imply that it is helpful in building a brand. A successful viral ad is able to push brand-related decisions to System 1, which we talked about in Chapter 2, and make decision-making a seamless and automatic process. Repeated virality, therefore, needs to have a consistent emotional position. A series of campaigns that keeps the user consistently emotionally engaged may fare far better than one campaign that turns heads and creates buzz but dies soon after.

Consider the example of the Ice Bucket Challenge. ALS Association in the US and Motor Neuron Disease Association in the UK led the ALS Ice Bucket Challenge in 2014, with the aim of increasing awareness about ALS[348] and encouraging donations towards research into ALS. They invited people to film themselves as they poured a bucket of ice on themselves and to nominate others to do the same challenge. The challenge followed a pyramid scheme for nominating people, went viral, and ended up raising $220 million in 2014. However, despite the noble intentions of creating awareness and raising funds for ALS, when some organizations tried to revive the challenge in the summer of the next year, it didn't fare as well as it had in 2014! *The contrast (BOP#4) and interest that it had generated in the first year did not happen in the second year as there was now a level of unconscious familiarity, one that wasn't particularly emotional or demanding a repetition.* This was not a brand building exercise but a 'sale', and the same contrast will not generate the sale again. The brand ladder did not really come into play at all.

As mentioned earlier, using social media requires us to think about the mental states and motivations of other users: to mentalize.

Before and after a social media user shares any content, they may think about how the people in their circle will respond. When they share brand content that resonates with their identity, they do so because they are sure of eliciting a similar response from a part of their circle. The anticipated dopamine surge resulting from the positive feedback from their circle and an enhanced reputation for sharing such content drives them to share. This activates the brain's reward network and makes us keep coming back for more. If this is done with repeated frequency, the brand gets pushed deeper into the unconscious and we automatically find ourselves doing this out of habit. Reading the brand's posts may likewise elicit reward activity, because receiving information elicits curiosity, a feeling associated with activity in the ventral striatum. We will find ourselves operating on autopilot upon encountering the brand again. We become the goodwill ambassadors for the brand and ardent supporters without even realizing it when we reach the brand relationship stage or have brand affect above a certain level. When viewing information and feedback broadcasted by others, a user may think about the other users' motivations for posting this information.

*Brands should work hard online to create in-groups and out-groups. In a sense, powerful brands are like a religious group, with strong affiliations just like religious groups.*

Online rivalry between two brands can often end up helping them in the long term. Brands can create content that *invokes a sense of belonging to their bands in the viewers.*

Consider the 'Get a Mac' campaign by Apple Inc and Microsoft's nimble reply 'I am a PC'. 'Get a Mac' features a geeky-looking guy in formal wear representing PC and a suave young guy in jeans and T-shirt representing Mac on short humorous journeys to discuss PC's problems and how Mac doesn't seem to have them! 'I am a PC' features various actors, and even Bill Gates, saying 'I am a PC'. It illustrates how PC users come in all shapes and sizes, from one that wears glasses to one that wears jeans to one that designs jeans to one that designs buildings! The ad, therefore, strikes a chord with PC users and illustrates how these users are elite and, at the same time, different from other groups, the yin and the yang, the in-group of one set of users versus the out-group of the other set of users—that is so much a part of sustaining and rejuvenating brands. The unconscious association a PC or a Mac user has developed over time with Microsoft or Apple has enabled a personification process that lasts for a lifetime. And both the ads only amplify it, quite literally, by anthropomorphizing computers; we relate more to humans.

Another example of a rivalry that has helped to build a brand is the one between two YouTube Channels: PewDiePie and T-Series. In an attempt to claim the title of the 'most subscribed channel on YouTube' the two channels appealed to their fan following to hit 'subscribe' and spread the word. PewDiePie's fans took it upon themselves to see that the channel gets the support it deserves. They did everything from placing posters to playing Kjellberg's diss track against T-Series. One YouTuber launched an advertising campaign where they bought every single billboard, radio spot and local TV spot available in support of PewDiePie's channel. One fan hacked into 50,000 printers and printed a message on the paper in support of PewDiePie and against T-Series. T-Series, on the other hand, has a huge Indian following. It uploads multiple music videos every day and after PewDiePie's appeal, Indians started hitting 'subscribe' to ensure that an Indian channel became the number one on YouTube. Both the channels amassed a huge number of supporters ready to rally behind them, and eventually reached more than a 100 million subscribers online. T-Series, however, emerged as the winner at the showdown. The two brands have become such a big a part of their fans' life that it seemed normal for them to stand up for something as intangible and inanimate as YouTube channels. Sometimes, rival brands even tweet snarky comments about the rival and the followers of each brand then comment about their brands' tweet and the competing brands' tweet in a competitive way, amplifying the emotions of both sets of customers and keeping them engaged through actions of support that buttress group feelings—leveraging BOP#5 and BOP#3.

In April 2016, the e-commerce giant Amazon launched a quirky digital-driven campaign, 'We Indians', that celebrated the unique traits of Indians, part of an effort by Amazon to fit into the pattern of being Indian (BOP#3)—in this case, that Indians tend to want stuff quickly when buying retail.[349] Simultaneously, a series of films sought to address our major concerns about online shopping (to reduce the perceived risk of shopping online). Each of the videos captured our distinct quirks and tied it back to the brand: a woman crossing the road using her hand as a stop signal, a man booking himself a seat on a crowded bus by dropping a handkerchief from the window, and many more. Visuals and contests helped amplify the buzz on social media. Everyone laughed along and shared the content which appealed to their 'Indian-ness'.

*What Alibaba, Samsung and Amazon harnessed was the power of unconscious emotional association and the brain operating principles we discussed in Chapter 3. The two rivalries both depended on an emotional connection that the brands assumed they had with their customers. The personification process Apple and Microsoft have gone through made the campaigns successful, pushing the brands even further into the deep unconscious. The astute use of brain operating principles in the online space keeps the customer engaged.*

*Actions that increase memorability (surprise, comfort, emotional meaning, emotional connection with others, repetition, smells that evoke fond memories) on social media platforms all help to increase the strength of the brand.*

Brands get established because they get deeply embedded in memory—in the emotions of the person. Through the repetitive exposure of the brand, there needs to be consistency. It needs to not only evoke emotions but also take care to do so in a particular way.

Emotions obviously have an impact on sharing and discussion, but different emotions result in different types of discussion. The question of interest is: which emotions impact sharing, and how can different emotions elicit different reactions from the audience?

Emotions such as inspiration, happiness and amusement often lead people to broadcast the information to others through Facebook shares and tweets. Emotions correlated with dominance are most important in broadcasting, partly because people feel in control when they feel inspired.

For the launch of its compact sedan Figo Aspire, Ford started a pre-launch campaign called 'What Drives You?' The objective was to discover the aspirations driving modern India, much like the new sedan that reflects the needs of the young consumer. And to discover what young India aspires to, Ford roped in Farhan Akhtar as an anchor to present passionate stories of real-life achievers, which included the founder of RedBus.in and the co-founders of Happilyunmarried.com, among others. Each of them shared their story in a drive-by interview with Farhan while he drove a Figo Aspire. And with the unfolding of each of their stories, we feel inspired, our minds get the feeling of being rewarded (BOP#1) through mirroring (BOP#5) and patterns in the scenarios being shown in the advertisement (BOP#3), and a positive neural bond is formed with Figo.

When people encounter emotions that make them feel out of control, such as anger, sadness and fear, they are more likely to 'narrowcast' the information by engaging in discussion in comments, or sharing with smaller groups of other users. Arousal is most important when it comes to narrowcasting.

Why does a particular advertisement or online post go viral? Why does one post get thousands of retweets/shares while others strive to get noticed? Why does one video get shared incessantly while there are plenty of others which don't? While creating emotional content is the main undertone in sustenance of the social media presence of the brand, play with the curiosity of the users to get them started in the first place.

If a firm wants its customers to share its content or read its blog, one way to do so may actually be to tell them not to.

Tempt them with a titbit. Ask them a topical question that leads to the only answer: your product.

Inspiring curiosity lights up the pleasure centres of our brains. Carnegie Mellon professor George Loewenstein's Information Gap Theory illustrates this fact perfectly. When we experience a 'gap' between the known and the unknown, our brains tend to fill it, like yours just did. In effect, the brain creates a pattern—because it is a pattern-making engine, after all (BOP#3).

Curiosity may have killed the cat, but it inspires action in humans.[350]

Kia Motors's 'Magical Inspirations' successfully translates the brand ideology of focusing on design into a YouTube video advertisement,[351] and at the same time piques the curiosity of the viewers. The viewer is hooked to the ad as soon as the astronaut comes on the screen, among a sea of graceful and precise ballerinas. Next, footballers, a singing bird, a tiger and some bugs feature in the ad as a designer looks at the scenario, seemingly assessing the activity of an absurd-looking group with keen interest. There is a sense of expectation that is built. Finally, as a cloud clears, literally, we see a meticulously designed red Kia car emerging from it and the voice-over says, 'What happens when magical inspirations come together? You get stunning Kia designs.' And in that one moment, our curiosity is fed and queries answered! It all falls into place. It is the absurdity of the sequence in the ad that increases its memorability quotient because of the constant surprises (contrasts—BOP#4) that keep on springing up at the viewer.

Good news travels faster. In traditional media, good news is no news. But social media has generated new rules of engagement. Neuroscientists and psychologists are finding that online readers also share positive, feel-good posts over tales of destruction and woe, and that includes the sharing of customer service experiences.

The same finding applies to online video. When senior research associate Karen Nelson-Field of the Ehrenberg-Bass Institute for Marketing Science studied video-sharing habits, she found that a strong positive reaction is 30 per cent more likely to get a share than negative responses like anger or shock. Creating posts that exhilarate also make viewers better remember your brand.

Michelob Ultra and Ikea took it to a completely new level. Both the brands exploited autonomous sensory meridian response (ASMR) principles to explicitly invoke pleasant, relaxing feelings in the viewers. While there are those who deny that gentle whispers, crackle or accents are soothing to them, there are millions out there who feel a sensation in their scalp and down their bodies when they hear such soothing sounds. Michelob Ultra's Super Bowl commercial starring Zoe Kravitz uses whispered narrations, the sound of the bottle of beer opening, its sound against the wood of the table top, and the fizz of the beer to invoke soothing feelings. These are all information inputs that are much more likely to go into the unconscious of the individual.

Ikea's 'Oddly Ikea' was a part of their 'back to college' campaign and the ad portrayed something a college-goer actually goes through on a daily basis: a person setting up their dorm room. The actor's hands feature in the ad, touching and sliding against the bed covers and duvets, arranging the hangers in her cupboard, sliding perfect fitting boxes in and out of the shelves and so on as the sound generated from these actions is amplified for the viewer to listen to. The actor does this as she narrates everything she is doing in a soothing tone and asks the viewer to really listen to the sounds. Despite the fact that ASMR fans make up a small segment of Ikea's vast consumer base, Ikea made these videos for this small audience, which implicitly sent the message that it cares for every small segment of its consumers. The result? Ikea's back to college sales were up by 27 per cent that year as against the previous year![352]

Another way to go about it would be to do it differently. That new car smell. A new puppy. The latest iPhone. Studies show that when you expose us to something new, our brains reward us with a booster shot of the feel-good chemical dopamine. It's no wonder we seek out novelty. Even the word 'new' motivates and engages us. So can new uses of colours, images and words.

Our brains feel good when we encounter originality, and that includes chomping down on innovative content. Since the web is the be-all-and-end-all of cutting-edge information and material goods, with every reboot and click comes the hope of some new treasure and/or creative thought. Keep your audience in that constant state of anticipation between your communication campaigns.

Stories are in a class of triggers all their own. They activate the subconscious, emotional area of the brain, which is the main influence in our decision-making. Because stories stimulate areas in our brains that are connected with our senses and memories, they have the magical quality of creating bodily responses, as if what we read is happening in real time. Move your audience by telling a riveting, buzzworthy story that motivates the desired action. Stories are patterns that we latch on to immediately; they can incorporate surprise, emotion, emotional meaning, comfort, etc., to engage with the customer.

In 2014, Always, a feminine hygiene brand, launched the 'Like a Girl' campaign that reached millions of views worldwide, solely because of its brazen move to reinvent the perception of the phrase 'Like a Girl'. The ad performs well on many levels. One, the premise of the story it narrates, 'a girl's confidence plummets during puberty', is easily relatable to its women viewership of the age group of ten to twenty years on a personal, and therefore emotional and unconscious, level. It may not be an understatement to claim that it evokes some memories of the viewer having experienced the plummet. Two, the questions the director asks her subjects evoke contrasting responses in six to nine-year-old girls and in twelve to fifteen-year-olds. While the former put in all their energy to illustrate their skills, the latter act as if they are responding to 'run/throw/fight like you can't', which clearly reflected that they took the phrase 'like a girl' as an insult. This serves as a shock to the viewer. Three, the ad follows an age-old pattern—raising the problem, addressing the perceptions, confronting the reality, the process of reasoning—to finally arrive at a stereotype-breaking change, i.e., the solution! The pattern of a story (BOP#3)! Such storylines are easy to follow and fit into a pattern that our brains are on the lookout for because they serve as shortcuts. And a subtle connection between a positive feeling induced because of the solution ('I do so-and-so like a girl because I am a girl! And I am not ashamed of it') and Always is instantly made, the emotional connection and comfort is there, increasing the memorability of the ad, and therefore, the brand.

Ariel India's 'Share the load' and Paisabazaar's 'The Wedding Speech' ad campaigns illustrate originality in another way. Both focus on shedding light on a different point of view of already acknowledged issues. 'Share the load' encourages Indians to teach their sons to lend a hand in household chores now that we actively encourage our daughters to study, have a career and become independent, so that these daughters can have a life post-office hours too! The 'Wedding Speech' primarily features a groom and his dumb brother where the former is putting into words the latter's actions as he delivers the wedding speech. The dumb brother goes on to thank the groom for not being pitiful or overly patient with him or treating him any differently than a brother would treat another brother. He thanks him for not considering his 'special ableness' as a limit to his capacities and for believing in his skills and finally, for giving him good advice about his career decisions. It is this new perspective, of following the life of the caregiver of a specially abled person, that lends the ad the originality it portrays, and it is quite successful in creating a strong and emotional connection in the viewers' brains between 'good advice' and Paisabazaar, a BFSI (banking, financial services and insurance) company.

Moreover, both the ads connect with the viewer in many subtle ways. 'Share the load' makes the viewer remember some instances of, say, the sister being taught basic household chores and the brother not being asked to help out, or of all the times a mother exclaims 'your brother doesn't know a thing about work'—an emotionally meaningful connect for many. Among Indians, such instances aren't uncommon. The second ad has a high surprise and contrast quotient—one, the fact that the brother was dumb was unexpected. Two, the speech taking off as a rant against his brother and turning out to be his expression of gratitude towards his brother was equally unanticipated. These instances make these ads relatively hard to forget, having fed the viewer's appetite for originality and presented them with memorable responses at the same time.

Discover. Explore. Share. Join. Find. Our brains assign importance to action words. What does it do with the passive ones? It tends to filter them out. Passive words sit static on screens, but words that convey activity, movement and emotion titillate our brains, and are much more likely to engage and call us to action. So wield action words and wield them well.

For memorability, whether the story is sad or it enrages users, there is no one simple answer to what combination makes it work for your brand. Align these with your brand's story. However, this knowledge can provide significant direction to any content marketer or online marketing professional, as it paints a picture of how the interplay of emotions affects users. Conflicting positions should be avoided at all costs as this may increase the risk perceived by your followers.

*Usability features of a product that provide a better touch interface and improve ease of use, so that one can use a product without having to think, make a brand stronger. These make the product and/or the process of using the brand fall into a pattern that makes it easier for the brain to adopt (BOP#3) and reduces energy consumption (BOP#2). With familiarity comes reduced risk. Include this message in your communication.*

Visual features of the product that evoke fond emotions, memories or surprise in an effective way help to create memories and therefore brands. The element of contrast makes the brand interesting by creating dopamine spurts in the brain.

Breaking the Maggi brick of noodles into two over a pan of boiling water is a very easy doable/usable thing and evokes your own experiences and memories.

Maggi has made a successful comeback since the ban in 2015. In April 2016, it launched a YouTube video series called #NothingLikeMaggi, that played on nostalgia. The mom, the hostel guys, the papa who only knows to cook Maggi, returned from history to remind viewers that there's 'nothing like Maggi'.[353] The ad, the jingle, the setting was carefully chosen for each of the three films that celebrated the good old spirit of Maggi, the familiar 'two minutes' and people bonding. It reinforced the pattern (BOP#3) associated with Maggi along with the positive emotions (that were perhaps largely unconscious but were then being brought into the conscious mind) in the pattern.

Misereor, a relief organization focused on creating self-help initiatives for people in Third-World countries, collaborated with Stripe to develop a creative solution to make donating a pleasant and risk-free experience. The outcome was 'the Social Swipe'. In the first move of its kind, they developed posters that allowed swiping credit cards for a fixed 2 Euro donation to Misereor. The act of swiping initiated two different kinds of visualizations:

1. Of bread being sliced and a poor person taking it.
2. Of shackles being broken—with the card acting as a knife in the first scenario and a breaker-of-chains in the second one! The poster decreased the cognitive involvement experienced during donation through an easy-to-use interface and by assuring the donors that their contribution would actually be used for a good cause through the impactful visuals. While this campaign had little to do with social media, a video

explaining the Social Swipe did, however, emphasize their campaign and helped increase the credibility of the organization.

Both Samsung and Google have repeatedly challenged Apple in a series of ads that explicitly lay out the differences between their products. For example, in some impressive ads, Google showcases how Pixel's night mode clearly triumphs over iPhone 10's and how the former's Augmented Reality Google Maps Navigation is much more fun than the plain old Maps of the latter. Samsung's 'Ingenius' ads follow an Apple genius as he tries, in vain, to counter iPhone 10 users' concerns that Samsung S9 is better than iPhone 10 in some major aspects. Both the companies have even published instruction videos illustrating the ease of switching from an iPhone to a Pixel or a Galaxy without the worry of data loss—addressing the usability concerns of the user. These ads, aimed at showcasing the comfort of switching to Pixel or Galaxy because of their superior specifications, remove a major source of friction that iPhone users face when they desire a switch, making upgrading to a new phone even easier! The unconscious comfort and the perceived higher risk of switching that keeps customers with one brand away is being countered by a conscious cognitive reminder that the switch is actually easy with low risk (thus reducing energy consumption and anxiety arising from too large a contrast—BOP#2 and BOP#4).

Popularized through YouTube campaigns, Misereor, Samsung and Google used their ads to convey information about their easy-to-use interface to millions. While TV commercials would be the norm earlier, the Internet is what everyone resorts to for information. Try searching for 'how can I transfer my data from iPhone to Pixel' on YouTube and you will see hundreds of simple how-to videos popping-up. The companies, perhaps, decided to get ahead of the issue and release their own short, funny how-to videos. And they successfully make the process seem easy and effortless—taking less than five minutes for most transfers! This user-friendly feature of the products, along with the funny how-to videos, drastically decrease the risk perception of making a switch.

In short, if you want your brand to break its 'tough nut to crack' image, there's no better way than to reach millions through social media and convey your message directly to them. Of course, reaching people through social media is one part of the effort. One also needs to actually make the product more user friendly. Social media engagement emphasizing the product's usability decreases the perception of risk, increases association with the brand and makes following through brand decisions a smooth process.

*Any feature that reduces perceived risk, and, therefore, insula activation (as also energy consumption by the brain—BOP#2), will improve brand perception, adoption and use.*

Claims like 'We are the number 1 brand', 'Our product featured as the most recommended one by so-and-so survey', etc., are made on an almost daily basis by brands. In ads by FMCG brands like Tata Salt, Dettol, Pepsodent, etc., such claims have maintained a constant presence. For example, Tata Salt claims that it has the appropriate amount of iodine while its competitors may not, and Dettol claims that its disinfectants can kill 99.9 per cent germs. And their effort isn't without positive consequences. These easy-to-understand statistics make their products appear risk-free and a safe option. Also, it is easy for a consumer to imagine that a lot of people must already be using these 'number one' products and therefore, these ads end up invoking a virtual informational cascade in the minds of the consumers, making their decision-making process relatively smooth and more efficient.

*Any feature or online message that reinforces the pattern relating to the brand and that provides some variety and differences to retain viewers' interest will help sustain and rejuvenate the brand.*

Companies like Coca-Cola and Fevicol embraced the trending Face App Challenge in their own creative ways to reinforce patterns (BOP#3). Fevicol has established a reputation in India of being an extremely effective adhesive that can make anything stick firmly and for a long time. The Fevicol advertisement, for example, shows that an egg fixed with the adhesive won't crack, even after application of a lot of force that might be enough to break much stronger material;[354] the sheer absurdity of someone hammering an egg which does not break sticks in the mind.

Coca-Cola has tried to show why it has remained a favourite for the past hundred years or so. People didn't seem to mind online poster-cum-ads because of the explicit humour in the content and the fact that it was based on an already socially acceptable and relatable trend. It fits the pattern and reinforces the familiarity and comfort that customers have with the brand. For some brands, COVID-19 disrupted the pattern. For example, famous restaurant brands listed in Michelin's guide need to reach out again to build and reinforce the brand, which has an overlay of fear now. Profiling customers would help to nuance the message that these restaurants would need to send out. It is possible to do dual brand personality-based messaging,[355] so that both risk-averse and risk-seeking customers, for example, are addressed simultaneously and more online WOM is created.

*Social media is about connecting to others. It is about mirroring (BOP#5). The brand manager needs to leverage this as much as possible by building the context for the brand. Without relevant context, a brand may get ignored.*

In 2007, the Washington Post conducted an experiment. They had one of the best musicians in the world play one of the most expensive instruments in the world (a $3.5 million Stradivarius violin) on a subway platform during morning rush hour. Most people simply ignored him, and 'the final haul for his forty-three minutes of playing was $32.17. Yes, some people gave pennies.'[356] There were no tuxedos or playbills or expensive tickets. No sold-out concert halls or rave reviews from critics. Just some of the best music in the world but, without the social cues to the quality of the performance, nobody noticed. So even if you're the best writer in the world, writing on a world-class web platform, with a ground-breaking design, without social proof, you'll be very lonely. This book is being published by Penguin Random House and so, presumably, will fare somewhat better. Social proof is the idea that people rely on the reaction of others to make decisions, and we assume that others (individuals and especially groups) know more about the choice than we do. When social proof starts to accumulate, you have an informational cascade.

The premotor cortex is a part of the frontal lobe of our brain. It is responsible for mental planning of movement and sensory guidance of motion. When you hook up a test subject to a brain-scanning machine (like an fMRI or EEG), you'll see this region of the brain activates when the subject performs some sort of action. Scientists studying monkeys in the 1980s and 1990s found that a percentage of the neurons in the premotor cortex also lit up when the monkeys watched another monkey or a person perform a task. The scientists called these cells mirror neurons, and evidence has since been found that indicates that humans also have these empathic neurons, and they don't reflect motion only: they've been found to mirror other frontal lobe functions like sensations and emotions. These neurons make up the mirror neuron system that we discussed in Chapter 2 and their concept puts a neuroscientific framework around the socio-evolutionary theories of informational cascades. The selection pressures in favour of imitation may now be seen as having influenced the development of specialized mental hardware for copying others.

Consider two restaurants and a group of people on the street outside deciding which one to eat at. The most well-informed individuals (those with higher precision in making these types of decisions) will decide first and everyone will see some people start to line up outside one restaurant. If the others know this person is of higher precision (and even if they don't), a few people will follow their lead and join the line. Each new person who lines up outside the restaurant sends a signal to the rest of the group (and in particular, to their friends and family) that this is the restaurant to pick. The more people who follow the signal, the stronger it gets and you have a viral effect or an informational cascade or herd behaviour—the outcome of mirror neuron systems having their logical effect.

In the online world, these informational cascades are built by customer reviews of products and brands, by influencers commenting on brands and products on blogs, by the tweets of influencers, and by the posts of regulars on platforms like Facebook, by a succession of moves that provide a 'neurotransmitter dollop' to each succeeding person that joins the cascade.

In applying this knowledge to viral marketing and social media, we must remember that at its simplest, viral content is nothing more than bits of mental source code that say 'Copy me!' From a functional point of view, the act of spreading a piece of content to your friends (after the initial 'seeds' spread it) is an imitative one. Someone sends you an email or WhatsApp forward, and you turn around and do the same thing. Your friend retweets a post, you imitate that gesture and do the same. A friend follows a page on Facebook; chances are you'll do exactly that. When we see others doing something, we copy that and we reduce our own risk.

What this means for marketers is that one of the best viral 'calls to action' is to allow the reader to see other people doing what you want them to do. Social proof is a sort of indirect or implied effect that results from this. It may also indicate that we should seed our online campaigns in ways that reflect how we want them to spread. Looking to 'go viral'? Create content that optimizes the message you want broadcasted in such a way that it activates these imitative brain cells.

A firm should prioritize delivering consistent communication to its group of followers, who will in turn function as its trusted brand ambassadors; overspending heftily on trying to get the attention of new users to whom you are a risky bet. Retaining a customer requires less effort than attracting a new customer. Engaging this group of followers emotionally becomes the most important task.

Rapid mirroring will make a social media post go viral quickly. Psy's 'Gangnam Style' video went viral online, as did Dove's 'Real Women' campaign, as many people identified with the characters in the message (matched the pattern in the mind) and with the message (provided good dollops of oxytocin). For a social media post to achieve rapid mirroring, therefore, requires a careful design that matches stimuli that will achieve the dopamine, serotonin and/or oxytocin spikes in the target customer with the set of stimuli in the social media message and platform. In a COVID-19-influenced world, the content for mirroring would, of course, be related to COVID-19-related issues—safety, health, feelings of loss of control due to not being able to do the activities that one normally did . . . One's normal pattern of activity and brand usage was disrupted, the pattern (BOP#3) was broken—violently, one may add—and the brands that were and are able to help in the creation of new patterns using the online medium will do well.

*Social media offers opportunities to build contrasts (BOP#4) at scale and speed to support a brand because the information that provides the opportunity to build the contrast is rapidly available.*

In 2019, an incident involving Bollywood actor Rahul Bose being charged Rs 442 (US $6) for two bananas, an exorbitant sum in India, at a JW Marriott Hotel became trending news on social media. And soon enough, companies like OYO, IRCTC, Pizza Hut and Reliance Smart piggybacked on the trend and released posters of how much one could get from their companies for Rs 442. For example, OYO Rooms' Instagram post quipped, 'Don't slip, for 442 you can get a whole room' and Reliance Smart's proclaimed that for 442, you could get a couple dozen bananas at their store! Much liked and talked about, the companies successfully managed to create content that marketed their brand without getting ignored as 'just another advertisement'. They may have even urged users to check out their websites to see if their claims were, in fact, true!

Repeating such actions, whether offline or online, by latching on to trending items on social media provides a new tool to get attention through a new contrast (BOP#4) that still has the power to draw attention and get into memory. Note that the ability of this stimulus to get continued attention declines quite rapidly. As a tactic, therefore, one would need to continuously come up with newer such 'trending hooks' that the brand can ride on the coattails of. Perhaps the best example of riding on the coattails of a trend to sustain a brand comes from Amul, the dairy brand in India that uses spoofs of contemporary events using a familiar mascot to provide the effort on both BOP#4 and BOP#3 (in this case, however, the effort is mainly offline; the interesting question is when, and if, the effort should shift online).

*Social media offers a very large canvas for a brand to showcase and share its values and beliefs with customers. What does the brand stand for? And how is that allegiance to a value/belief/position expressed by the brand in purchase or use (BOP#1)?*

It is important that a brand has something to say not because it wants to say something, but because it has something to say; and what it says to the customer has to appeal at a fundamental level in terms of rewards, security, avoiding pain, etc. (BOP#1); this requires a set of values and beliefs that the brand stands for.

Old Spice decided to break its original pattern of targeting its male customer and acknowledged that women shop for men 60 per cent of the times the men need body wash. The result? One of its most famous moves, albeit a risky one, was its 'The man your man could smell like' ad campaign. Aimed exclusively at women, the incredibly humorous, and therefore demanding low-cognitive capacities, ad features a very handsome man in a rapidly changing background setting—from that of a bathroom to a boat to a horse on a beach—telling women viewers that if they wanted their man to smell like him, they should go for Old Spice body wash, and this is said twice in the 30-second ad![357] Very explicitly, this provided the viewers with the only answer to the question 'What should a man smell like?' The ad quickly grabbed people's attention, thanks to its surprising, contrasting scenes (BOP#4) that were also funny and related to a primal instinct (mating, which maps on to BOP#1). Its YouTube channel quickly climbed the charts and became the all-time most viewed branded channel; in the first three months of 2010, Old Spice captured 75 per cent of all conversations in the category, most of which were generated by women! What came after the ad became an unexpected part of the campaign. The company shot 186 video responses to the questions fans and celebrities had posted about Old Spice on Facebook, Twitter and Reddit. These video responses were aimed at building a personal relationship with their fans and it turned out to be one of the fastest growing and most interactive campaigns.[358] If it wasn't for social media, this second leg of the campaign would not have helped make the brand as popular as it did on an individual level. With this entire campaign, the company set a new tone for its branding, a new pattern for its newly recognized audience.

Consider also TED videos. TED is considered an organization that only invites people with original and good thoughts to share them on an international platform. Therefore, TED and TEDx videos are something one can share online without having second thoughts, without an otherwise involved apprehension about the responses of one's social circle. Its risk-free content is an excellent example of something that makes the process of sharing and talking about it easier and less stressful. Sharing TED videos would also let one's social circle know that one is an intellectual intrigued by scientific and philosophical discussions, thereby improving one's social reputation. It is TED's brand image, along with the anticipated reward, that pushes related decision-making to the unconscious and persuades the viewer using System 1 to decide to attend a talk rather than go through an evaluation process using System 2.

WWF, the World Wildlife Fund, is another organization that creates impactful and impressive content in a bid to encourage people to save wildlife. Its minimalist and yet direct posters convey the message of the organization with clear intent. In a recent poster series, it used elements from our daily experiences with our PCs and laptops to send across messages related to plastic usage. An enlarged picture of a plastic straw in oceanic water featured in a YouTube-like interface, where the words 'you can skip this in 300 years' were written in one corner. Another one featured an extremely polluted beach in the background and a dialogue box exclaimed that it was preparing to delete and that '1000 years (are) remaining (for this action to be completed)'. This kind of imagery captivates the viewer because it presents contrasting elements that invoke memories related to usage of PCs and YouTube, which in today's world are a constant part of our lives. This directness leaves a strong and emotional impact on our brains. It is also easier to rally behind the idea of 'clean environment' when the brain is engaged with these forms of contrasts and, therefore, sharing such posters online is a relatively risk-free decision.

Social causes, perceptions and stereotypes are an excellent resource for a brand to utilize. Their emotion-driven followers can be influenced to associate, share and talk about a brand. Even those who aren't particularly sympathetic towards them generate conversations in an effort to look worldly, internationally aware and sympathetic. Content incorporating these principles has the potential to 'go viral' by feeding off the feeling of FOMO. However, a brand attempting such a feat should a take a leaf out of Dove's book and understand that a consistent brand image is an essential feature of any ad campaign; a brand must learn how to balance the two for long-lasting gain.

In summary, therefore, social media provides another platform for the implementation of the brain operating principles and the decision-making processes of customers. The difference, of course, is that the scale and speed of action and reaction is higher and that the time scales of neurotransmitter feedback in humans is shorter, leading to a higher probability of the right set of stimuli creating stronger brands in a shorter time. An interesting questions that arises, therefore, is whether one can actually create long-lived brands in a shorter time period using the faster cycle time of interaction on social media to more deeply imprint the brain through neurotransmitters. Would these brands then stand the test of time like Amul?

Or IBM? Or Absolut? Or Toyota? Or would social media which is primarily about communication a less stronger way to construct a brand as compared to the experience of using a brand? The balance of evidence suggests that ultimately it is the 'experience' of the customer with the product or service—the complete customer journey from search, evaluation, purchase, consumption, WOM, service encounter, etc., that determines the strength of the brand. To the extent that these are all online, it will be online that will drive the brand in the brain. To the extent that the experience is mostly offline, that will drive the strength of the brand in the brain and online will merely be a way to reach and engage the customer.

Regardless of how a brand is built, they do have an economic value. Indeed, increasingly, a large proportion of the value of a firm comes from brands. Our next step is to understand the economic value of the brands that one has created—the subject of the next chapter.

# Chapter 8

# How the Brand in the Customer's Brain Leads to Brand Value for the Firm

*'If this business were split up, I would give you the land and bricks and mortar, and I would take the brands and trademarks, and I would fare better than you,'*
—John Stuart, chairman of Quaker, in 1900

In this chapter, we examine the rationale for brand valuation, the various approaches to the valuation of the brand and analyse the link between what happens in people's brains, their perceptions of brands, and the valuation that we ascribe to brands as a consequence of the perceptions in people's brains. We also assess what may happen to these brain chemicals and the valuations in the light of COVID-19.

## Why Brand Valuation

Increasingly, CEOs are placing more emphasis on their companies' brands in investor communications. Many more annual report column inches are now dedicated to discussing an organization's commitment to its brand. Numerous companies take their brands seriously enough to report their value over time to investors. Brand assets today are often the most important assets that a firm possesses, which account for about one-third of the value of Fortune 500 companies. Many argue that the brand is a strategic asset of the company, and brand equity needs to be '. . . leveraged within business processes to provide sustainable competitive advantage.'[359]

The brand also continues to be a key driver of acquisition premiums in mergers and acquisitions. Often, it is the latent potential of the brand that is driving this premium through its ability to enter new markets and extend into adjacent categories. A broad skill set, combining market research, brand and business strategy, together with business case modelling, is required to quantify the latent financial potential of the target brand. Brand valuation methodology can also be used to complement other traditional techniques for setting royalty rates for brands. By identifying the value created by a brand for its business, combined with an evaluation of the relative bargaining power of the parties involved, we can determine the proportion of brand value that should be paid out as a royalty rate in return for the right to exploit the brand.

For most of the twentieth century, tangible assets were regarded as the main source of business value. These included manufacturing assets, land and buildings or financial assets such as receivables and investments. The market was aware of intangibles, but their specific value remained unclear and was not specifically quantified. Brands, technology, patents and employees were always at the heart of corporate success, but rarely explicitly valued.

However, towards the late 1980s, the constant increase in the difference between a company's book value and its stock market valuation, as also steep increases in premiums over and above the stock market value paid in mergers and acquisitions, gained recognition.

'Rowntree was an English confectionery business based in York. Rowntree developed the Kit Kat, Smarties and Aero brands in the 1930s. Throughout much of the nineteenth and twentieth centuries, it was one of the big three confectionery manufacturers in the United Kingdom, alongside Cadbury and Fry. In 1988, Rowntree accepted a whopping £2.55 billion buyout offer from Nestlé.'[360]

In the same year, British conglomerate Grand Metropolitan PLC cut a deal to buy Pillsbury Co. for $5.7 billion. This acquisition was just one of the many huge takeovers that rocked Wall Street that year.[361] These transactions accounted for goodwill on the balance sheet. With this came a stellar shift in the understanding of creation of shareholder value. Today, it is possible to argue that, in general, the majority of business value is derived from intangibles. Brands (along with intellectual property and management capability) constitute these intangibles. Management attention to these assets has certainly increased substantially.

The brand is a special intangible that is the most important asset in many businesses. This is because of the economic impact that brands have. They influence the choices of customers, employees, investors and government authorities. Even non-profit organizations have started embracing the brand as a key asset for obtaining donations, sponsorships and volunteers.

Some CEOs are willing to make these critical brand strategy decisions based on qualitative strategic analysis and intuition. The majority, however, are looking for a business case that goes further. They want to understand the likely overall financial impact on the business over time, covering a range of alternative scenarios. In addition to a detailed breakdown of the expected costs to deliver, a rounded business case will also quantify the expected impact on the top line through the modelling of key revenue drivers (these will vary based on the business, but could include customer acquisition, churn, price premiums, share of wallet, frequency of purchase/visit, average basket size and so on) and on profit margins from any operational changes required to deliver the new strategy. Finally, sophisticated techniques such as Monte Carlo simulation may be employed, running thousands of possible permutations in order to estimate the most likely outcome.

By bringing together market, brand, competitor and financial data, the brand valuation model is the ideal framework within which such business case modelling can be conducted. As global competition becomes tougher and many competitive advantages, such as technology, become more short-lived, the brand's contribution to shareholder value will only increase. Brands are one of the few business assets that can provide long-term competitive advantage. Companies as diverse as Samsung, Philips, Hyundai and AXA, among many others, have used brand valuation to help them refocus their businesses on their brands, motivate management, create an economic rationale for branding decisions and investments, and make the business case for change.

There is a strong correlation between brand value and brand strength.[362] Brand strength analysis is the key diagnostic tool to measure brand performance and better understand the reasons behind its strengths and weaknesses, both internally and externally. It supports strategic brand management by prioritizing areas of the highest impact for managers.

For the brand manager or the brand owner, a brand strength analysis is of special interest because it offers a robust, evidence-based and data-driven methodology to manage and govern the brand across markets. A brand strength analysis:

- Enables constructive dialogue about the business by creating a common language for discussion of brand performance. By introducing a common set of metrics across the organization, it ensures that different parts of the organization begin to view the brand through the same lens.
- Provides global and local managers with an actionable tool to make informed marketing decisions, empowering management with insights to implement brand strategy. Since brand strength is always relative to the competition in that specific market, it allows local managers their individual market-level insights to tailor specific tactics. On the other hand, it provides the corporate office a high level 'dashboard' detailing the relative strengths and weaknesses in the brand at a more strategic level.

- Allows responsibility for performance on the different factors that contribute to brand strength to be allocated to functions across the business, building engagement and a sense of responsibility for the brand across the organization.

When the role of brand and brand strength analysis are connected to the brand value, they provide a framework for resource allocation and prioritization based on the opportunities expected to have the greatest impact on brand and business value. During the late 1990s and well into the 2000s, under the leadership of CMO Eric Kim and his team, Samsung set itself the target of increasing the valuation of its brand to a number that was higher than that of Sony and used that goal to drive internal organizational changes and increase the firm's market orientation. Ultimately, everything we do as brand managers is best considered through a value-creation lens. Considerable investments are made in brands and it is important to determine if these actions are creating value for our customers and, in turn, our shareholders. Brand valuation methodology seeks to determine, in both customer and financial terms, the contribution of the brand to business results.

*There is also evidence that companies that promote their brands more heavily than others in their categories tend to be the more innovative players in their categories.* Studies have shown that less branded businesses launch fewer products, invest significantly less in development and have fewer product advantages than their branded counterparts. Almost half of the 'non-branded' sample spent nothing on product R&D compared with less than a quarter of the 'branded' sample.

The pressing need to keep brands relevant encourages companies to invest in R&D to push out better products.

For example, Amazon is investing heavily in its drone delivery technology to make same-day deliveries a reality. Companies like Google, Uber and Tesla are investing millions in their R&D towards self-driving cars. In 2015, amid much criticism, Apple announced the release of the new iPhone 7, which changed the way headphones were used—it removed the headphone jack on the phone and introduced AirPods, the wireless earphones, the first of their kind for a phone.

Given the direct link between brand value and both sales and share price, the potential costs of behaving unethically far outweigh any benefits. Nike, a company once criticized for the employment practices of some of its suppliers in developing countries, now posts results of external audits and interviews with factory workers at www.nikebiz.com. The more honest companies are in admitting the gap they have to bridge in terms of ethical behaviour, the more credible they will seem. Airtel is introducing the 'Open Network' initiative in India captioned 'Because you have a lot to say. And we have nothing to hide' in order to reassure customers about their concerns on connectivity problems through sharing of relevant data. One can check their coverage signal strength and report network issues to the company. Providing real-time details of the network range fluctuations, the operating towers, data consumption info, etc., India's second largest telecommunications provider stepped up to enhance customer satisfaction. The concern of multinational companies is understandable, considering that a 5 per cent drop in sales could result in a loss of brand value exceeding $1 billion. It is clearly in their economic interests to build strong brands that have an ethical orientation.

Many brand metrics are available, and some, with the right application together with other tools and approaches, can link the brand to long-term financial value creation and this, along with its many other applications, makes brand valuation a versatile strategic tool for business.

A study by Interbrand in association with JP Morgan concluded that, on average, brands account for more than one-third of shareholder value. McDonald's brand used to account for more than 70 per cent of shareholder value. The Coca-Cola brand alone accounts for 51 per cent of the stock market value of the Coca-Cola Company. Figure 1 below captures this rising proportion of intangible value for NYSE 100 and BSE 30 companies over time.

**Figure 1**

| Countries | 1977 | 2018 |
|---|---|---|
| USA | 95% | 20% |
| India | 98% | 50% |

**Book Value as a Percentage(%) of Market Cap**

***Source:*** *Author's compilation based on BSE 30 and NYSE 100*

Studies by academics from Harvard and the University of South Carolina, and by Interbrand, of the companies featured in the Best Global Brands league table, indicate that companies with strong brands outperform the market.

Leading companies have focused their management efforts on intangible assets. For example, the Ford Motor Company reduced its physical asset base in favour of investing in intangible assets. In the past few years, it has spent well over

$12 billion to acquire prestigious brand names such as Jaguar, Aston Martin, Volvo and Land Rover. Samsung, a leading electronics group, invests heavily in its intangibles, spending about 7.5 per cent of annual revenues on R&D and another 5 per cent on communications. In packaged consumer goods, companies spend up to 25–40 per cent of annual revenues on marketing support.

In terms of accounting standards, the UK, Australia and New Zealand have been leading the way by allowing acquired brands to appear on the balance sheet and providing detailed guidelines on how to deal with acquired goodwill. The principal stipulations of all these accounting standards are that acquired goodwill needs to be capitalized on the balance sheet and amortized according to its useful life. However, intangible assets such as brands that can claim infinite life do not have to be subjected to amortization. Instead, companies need to perform annual impairment tests. If the value is the same or higher than the initial valuation, the asset value on the balance sheet remains the same. If the impairment value is lower, the asset needs to be written down to the lower value. Recommended valuation methods are discounted cash flow (DCF) and market value approaches. The valuations need to be performed on the business unit (or subsidiary) that generates the revenues and profit.

The economic value of brands to their owners is now widely accepted. How is this value calculated? Also, how does the brain's propensity to go for and relate to brands create this economic value for firms?

Unlike other assets such as stocks, bonds, commodities and real estate, there is no active market in brands that would provide 'comparable' values. To arrive at an authoritative and valid approach, a number of brand evaluation models have been developed.

## Approaches to Brand Valuation

There are five primary categories of approaches to brand valuation.

The first category of methods is based on the actual present cash flows of a firm, with decisions on what part of the cash flow is attributable to a brand, combined with a multiplier that is related to discounting future cash flows. These methods are also called indicator methods (or earnings split methods) and include approaches by Interbrand, AC Nielsen, Brand Finance, Brand Rating and Semion.

Simon and Sullivan (1993)[363] build on these to provide a more robust method in this category by clearing delineating the non-brand factors that are a part of the firm's intangible assets, such as management skills, distribution infrastructure and intellectual property—separate from the brand value.[364] Simon and Sullivan presented a technique for estimating a firm's brand equity that is based on the financial market value of the firm. Brand equity is defined as the incremental cash flows which accrue to branded products over unbranded products. The estimation technique extracts the value of brand equity from the value of the firm's other assets. The result is an estimate of brand equity which is based on the financial market valuation of the firm's future cash flows. The methodology has three important features:

1. Brand equity is treated as an asset of the firm and the methodology objectively separates brand equity from the other assets of the firm.
2. Brand equity is measured in a forward-looking perspective, since the market value of the firm's traded securities reflect an unbiased estimate of future cash flows.
3. The value of a firm's brands changes as new information becomes available in the market.

This technique is useful for two purposes. First, the macro approach assigns an objective value to a company's brands and relates this value to the determinants of brand equity. Second, the micro approach isolates changes in brand equity at the individual brand level by measuring the response of brand equity to major marketing decisions. The macro approach estimates brand equity at the firm level. Firm-level estimates of brand equity are of interest because they allow a firm to compare the effectiveness of its portfolio of marketing policies to others in the industry. One drawback of this approach is that it does not provide estimates of brand equity at the individual brand level. The micro approach isolates brand equity at the individual brand level by measuring the response of brand equity to major marketing decisions. Since the value of a firm's securities changes as new information hits the market, the estimate of firm-level brand equity adapts to marketing decisions, such as new product introductions and major advertising campaigns. A change in firm-level brand equity, which is prompted by a brand-level decision, reflects the change in the value of the underlying brand. The micro approach allows evaluating the impact of specific marketing decisions made by the firm and its competitors. The results are in accordance with what one would expect: the industries and companies with big brand names have high macro estimates of brand equity. They further substantiated the methodology by showing that micro estimates of changes in brand equity vary with marketing decisions and market conditions.

The second category of methods depends on customer attitudinal data collected through primary data collection methods that attempts to put a numerical value to customer preferences of brand-related attributes. Young and Rubicam's Brand Asset Valuation model is one such method in this category. Also included are factors such as brand awareness, advertising (share-of-voice), market penetration, level of distribution, market share, etc., that provide indicators of brand strength[365] (see Dyson, Farr and Hollis 1996 for an example).

This category of methods tries to explain, interpret and measure consumers' perceptions, which influence purchase behaviour. They include a wide range of perceptive measures such as different levels of awareness (unaided, aided, top-of-mind), knowledge, familiarity, relevance, specific image attributes, purchase consideration, preference, satisfaction and recommendation. Some models add behavioural measures such as market share and relative price.

Through statistical modelling, these measures provide an overall brand equity score. However, these approaches do not differentiate between the effects of other influential factors such as R&D and design and the brand. They, therefore, do not provide a clear link between the specific marketing indicators and the financial performance of the brand. A brand can perform strongly according to these indicators but still fail to create financial and shareholder value. Unless the brand equity indicators are integrated into an economic model, they are insufficient for assessing the economic value of brands.

Interbrand, for example, believes that four internal factors:

- clarity, commitment, governance, responsiveness and six factors that are visible externally:
- authenticity, relevance, differentiation, consistency, presence, engagement make a strong brand.

Performance on these factors is judged relative to other brands in the industry and relative to other world-class brands. The strength of the brand is inversely related to the level of risk associated with the brand's financial forecasts (a strong brand creates loyal customers and lowers risk, and vice versa). A proprietary formula is used to connect the brand strength score to a brand-specific discount rate.

There are three key components in all of their valuations: an analysis of the financial performance of the branded products or services, analysis of the role the brand plays in the purchase decision, and analysis of the competitive strength of the brand. These are preceded by a decision on segmentation and at the end of the process are brought together to enable the financial value of the brand to be calculated.

Segments are typically defined by geography, business unit, product, service or customer group. Why is segmentation important? A robust valuation requires a separate analysis of the individual parts (or segments) of a business to ensure that terms of the three key components of the brand valuation (financial performance, role of brand and brand strength) can be taken into consideration. From a brand management perspective, the insights and recommendations that result from the brand valuation exercise will be at the segment level, so it is also important that they are at an actionable level for the client's brand teams.

The number and choice of segments therefore depends on:

- The strategic priorities of the business and of the brand valuation exercise
- The level at which brand management decisions are taken
- The number of parts of the business that can be identified where financial performance, role of brand and brand strength can be isolated and analysed separately
- The availability of data

Interbrand measures the overall financial return to an organization's investors, or its 'economic profit'. Economic profit is the after-tax operating profit of the brand minus a charge for the capital used to generate the brand's revenues and margins. A brand can only exist and, therefore, create value, if it has a platform on which to do so. Depending on the brand, this platform may include, for example, manufacturing facilities, distribution channels and working capital. Interbrand, therefore, allows for a fair return on this capital before determining that the brand itself is creating value for its owner.

They build a set of financial forecasts over five years for the business, starting with revenues and ending with economic profit, which then forms the foundation of the brand valuation model. A terminal value is also created, based on the brand's expected financial performance beyond the explicit forecast period. The capital charge rate is determined by reference to the company's weighted average cost of capital.

According to this method, calculating brand value involves (a) identifying the *true brand earnings* and cash flow, and (b) capitalizing the earnings by *applying a multiple to historic earnings as a discount rate to future cash flow*.[366] The brand weights are based on both historical data, such as brand share and advertising expenditures, and individuals' judgements of other factors, such as the stability of the product category, brand stability and its international reputation. The brand equity (or brand value) is the *product of the multiplier and the average of the past three years' profits that are attributable to the brand*.[367]

In a sense, this approach merges the financial cash flow and discount rate-based approach with customer attitudes and organizational factors.

The third category of methods is cost-based and uses probable replacement costs as an indicator of brand value. The IIPEN method is representative in this category. Cost-based approaches define the value of a brand as the aggregation of all historic costs incurred or replacement costs required in bringing the brand to its current state, that is, the sum of the development costs, marketing costs, advertising and other communication costs and so on. These approaches fail because there is no direct correlation between the financial investment made and the value added by a brand. Financial investment is an important component in building brand value, provided it is effectively targeted. But if it isn't, then it won't make even a shred of difference. The investment needs to go beyond the obvious advertising and promotion and include R&D, employee training, packaging and product design, retail design and so on.

A classic example of replacement-based brand valuation is the price paid by Reckitt Benckiser when it acquired the listed firm Paras Pharmaceuticals Ltd. in India for a price of Rs 3260 crore when the market capitalization of the firm was Rs 800 crore. As explained earlier, Reckitt Benckiser calculated that it would cost them at least Rs 3250 crore if it were to try to create brands such as Moov, Itchguard, etc., from scratch in a market like India. As the seller, Darshan Patel of Paras understood that the financial markets had not priced the value of his firm based on the value of the brands to a buyer like Reckitt Benckiser and was able to negotiate and get a price in that range.

This approach has some analogical comparison with arriving at a value for a brand on the basis of something comparable. But comparability is difficult in many cases for brands as by definition they should be differentiated and thus not strictly comparable. Furthermore, the value creation of brands in the same category can be very different, even if most other aspects of the underlying business such as target groups, advertising spend, price promotions and distribution channel are similar or identical—because monetary value, as was the case with Reckitt Benckiser, is in the eyes of the buyer, just as beauty is in the eye of the beholder. Comparables can provide an interesting cross-check; however, even though they should never be solely relied on for valuing brands.

The fourth category of methods is based on licence price analogies (e.g., Arthur Andersen, KPMG) and depends on evaluation of brand revenues from a licence granted to the brand in a comparable market. In essence, this approach imagines that the firm does not own its brand but licenses it at a market rate from another firm. The net present value of the money stream from licensing is indicative of the brand value as per Tollington.[368]

The fifth category of approach to brand valuation is in the premium that the brand can command over an equivalent non-branded product. In the premium price method, the value is calculated as the net present value of future price premiums that a branded product would command over an unbranded or generic equivalent.[369] However, the primary purpose of many brands is not necessarily to obtain a price premium but rather to secure the highest level of future demand. The value generation of these brands lies in securing future volumes rather than securing a premium price. This method is flawed because there are rarely generic equivalents to which the premium price of a branded product can be compared. Today, almost everything is branded and, in some cases, store brands can be as strong as producer brands, charging the same or similar prices. The price difference between a brand and competing products can be an indicator of its strength, but it does not represent the only or the most important value contribution a brand makes to the underlying business.

The cash flow approach with some variations, which was developed in 1988, combines brand equity and financial measures, and has become the most widely recognized and accepted methodology for brand valuation. It has been used in more than 3500 brand valuations worldwide. This economic use approach is based on fundamental marketing and financial principles:

- The marketing principle relates to the commercial function that brands perform within businesses. First, brands help to generate customer demand. Customer demand translates into revenues through purchase volume, price and frequency. Second, brands secure customer demand for the long term through repurchase and loyalty. Loyalty and repurchase stem from customers that have those brands on their brains from a combination of relevant brain operating principles.
- The financial principle relates to the net present value of future expected earnings, a concept widely used in business. The brand's future earnings are identified and then discounted to a net present value using a discount rate that reflects the risk of those earnings being realized. Future cash flows are a function of whether or not customers will continue to buy that brand.

The research literature shows that, on average, a firm with more advertising repetition will have a brand that has awareness levels, choice probabilities and brand value that tend to be proportionate.[370] The key, of course, is that there is a difference between financial management and brand value management. Brand value management is a continuous process as shown below.

| | Financial | Brand Management |
|---|---|---|
| **Applications** | Investor Relations<br>Mergers and Acquisitions<br>Licensing/Royalty Rate Setting<br>Financing/Securitization<br>Tax Valuations<br>Balance Sheet Valuations | Brand Performance Management<br>Brand Portfolio Management<br>Resource Allocation<br>Brand Tracking/Dashboards<br>Return on Investment Analysis<br>Organizational Brand Engagement<br>Management KPIs |
| **Typical Frequency** | One-off | Recurring |
| **Primary Objective** | A robust value with supporting analysis | Ongoing brand management leading to insight and recommendations to grow brand value |

## How Accurate is Brand Value?

The brand-specific discount rate is used to discount brand earnings back to a present value, reflecting the likelihood that the brand will be able to withstand challenges and deliver the expected earnings into the future. This is equal to brand value. Brand valuation is undoubtedly a strong measure of a brand's performance in the market. Understandably, a number of progressive organizations around the world are employing valuation metrics in managing their brand to consistently create value.

But as the practice of brand valuation has gained ground, the number of practitioners of brand valuation have multiplied and with it, the methodologies that they employ to arrive at the brand value. What disrupts the pitch even more is that different practitioners, employing different methodologies, can arrive at differing brand values for the same brand. For the brand manager or the brand owner, the question would be: which is the 'correct' value that should be used to track performance?

The short answer is that they are all equally correct (or incorrect) because 'value' is always an opinion and hence, an estimate. This is true not just of brands, but practically every transaction that you enter into, in your daily life. Your mentally assigned 'value' to an article is only an estimate. It only becomes definite when you pay the price (and as long as that price is lower than the 'value' you estimated in your mind, you've got yourself a great deal).

And so it is with brand valuation. Different valuation methodologies (and different league tables) can assign differing value to the same brand, none more 'correct' than the other. We see similar differences in values all the time in other contexts too. Equity analysts, for example, are paid by banks and stockbrokers to predict the future share prices of stocks around the world, and the price you're willing to pay for a stock is influenced to a great deal by the value these analysts assign to those stocks. But those values can differ widely.

Valuation (of any asset or business, not just brands) is both an art and a science, based on quantitative and qualitative assessment. The science is in the measurement and the art is in the interpretation. Of course, valuing a brand is not as straightforward as valuing a tangible asset. The valuer's view on the key levers of brand value creation (in Interbrand's case, the role of the brand in driving choice and its competitive strength—brand strength) will determine what will be measured, but not every firm is looking at the same factors or giving certain factors the same weight in their methodologies. With so much variation in methodology and considering all that is open to the analyst's interpretation, differences of opinion are bound to arise. Yet, it is perfectly reasonable to expect different organizations to have their own opinions on how brands should be valued—and inevitable that people will perceive value differently.

So, if the best-known brand valuation approaches are all more or less valid, which one should you rely on? Assuming you are looking for a brand valuation to identify opportunities to unlock growth for your business, or to evaluate a potential change in brand strategy, which criteria should you use to base your choice of methodology and value on?

It is advisable to work with a holistic, forward-looking approach that takes into consideration a wide range of data sources and inputs (rather than only relying on the 'rear-view mirror' that market research delivers), considers the strength of the brand inside and outside the organization, and is capable of delivering actionable insights and a clear road map of quick wins and longer-term activities to unlock growth. In some cases, especially the financial applications of brand valuation, it helps if the methodology followed is ISO-certified and values brands using methodologies that are based on established and accepted business practices for the valuation of other assets.

The final consideration is to see how versatile the methodology is, especially in delivering value beyond the number. Because while the number itself is nice to have, what's more important for brand owners and brand managers is to know what goes into creating—and growing—that number.

*And once an approach has been arrived at, one needs to stick with that approach over time to see the direction in which the brand value are moving; the direction, speed and magnitude of movement are more important than the absolute value from a management perspective.*

Firms can follow several branding strategies to grow their brand value. In general, most firms begin with a single product and become multiproduct firms over time. In such cases, there is a brand name for the first product that most likely is related to the name of the corporation, which marketers refer to as corporate branding. As new products are added, the managers of the firm have the option to use the firm identification in the brand name and to continue the corporate branding strategy. If the initial brand name did not use the firm name and if the firm chooses different names for each new product (without the firm name), this is known as a 'house-of-brands' strategy. However, if a firm acquires another firm (or a division of another firm), the products of the acquired firm will have brand names in place; in this situation, the branding strategy of the new entity is a mixed branding strategy. Mixed branding also occurs if a firm uses corporate names for some of its products and individual names for others. In general, the type of branding strategy can be inferred from examination of all the brand names of a firm's products: we refer to this as 'manifest' branding strategy and only occasionally use that adjective herein. More importantly, the manifest strategy is a result not necessarily of deliberate brand decision-making but of other decisions that the firm may have made.

New product launches and acquisitions require decisions on branding strategy (corporate, house of brands or mixed) in order to maximize intangible value). Rao et al.[371] concluded that corporate branding strategy is more value-creating than others. While seemingly inconsistent with the idea of market segmentation, we may also attribute the result to the fact that a larger proportion of people and firms are more aware of firms than before. Rao and colleagues classified the 103 firms from which they collected data into three groups: forty business-to-consumer (B2C; mainly consumer goods companies), thirty-three business-to-business (B2B; mainly industrial goods companies), and thirty mixed. They found that corporate branding strategy had a significant effect on performance from B2C and B2B firms, but that the effect was stronger for B2B firms. Very interestingly, the house of brands strategy was not significantly impacting valuation for B2B firms, but had a significant negative impact for B2C firms. While a firm's manifest branding strategy depends on corporate decisions, such as global expansions, mergers, and which markets to compete in,[372] and one may not want to generalize completely from Rao's results, nevertheless, their study does suggest that if you are a new firm, you should focus on a corporate branding strategy rather than a house of brands approach.

As global competition becomes tougher and many competitive advantages, such as technology, become more short-lived, the brand's contribution to shareholder value will increase. The brand is one of the few assets that can provide long-term competitive advantage. The increasing value placed on intangibles through mergers and acquisitions over the past two decades has forced accounting standards to acknowledge and deal with intangible assets on the balance sheet.

Strong brands enhance business performance primarily through their influence on three key stakeholder groups: customers (current and prospective), employees and investors. They influence customer choice and create loyalty; attract, retain and motivate talent; and lower the cost of financing.

The influence of brands on current and prospective customers is a particularly significant driver of economic value. By expressing their proposition consistently across all touchpoints, brands help shape perceptions and, therefore, purchase behaviour, making products and services less substitutable. In this way, brands create demand, allowing their owners to enjoy higher returns. Strong brands also create continuity of demand into the future, thus making expected returns more likely—or less risky. Brands, therefore, create economic value by generating higher returns and growth, and by mitigating risk.

The question, therefore, is how does the nature of the relationship between the 'brand' as it exists in the brain of the customers translate into monetary value.

## From the Brand in the Brain to Valuation of the Brand

A strong brand is able to sustain demand, engender loyalty and ultimately, reduce risk for the company and its customers. How does this translate into 'economic value' reflected in the intangible value that is measured partly in the increasing price to book value ratio? In brand valuation? What is the relationship between how the brand is processed in the brain with the valuation of the brand and the profitability of a firm?

When a brand reaches a stage in the brain of the customer where it is the primary provider of desired neurotransmitters (dopamine, serotonin, acetylcholine, oxytocin, etc., or a particular combination), then the customer tends to choose that brand over other brands. Trust, in a brand, for example, is positively associated with levels of oxytocin (often associated with love, reproduction and bonding).[373] Research has shown that an increase in oxytocin is related to increased trust among people.[374] From the perspective of the brain, the choice of a brand over another brand is because the valuation on the scale in the VMPFC is higher for that brand as compared to its competitors.[375]

At the top of the brand ladder, in the relationship stage, the brand becomes an automatic choice, a habit, where the customer is no longer thinking consciously about alternatives. The delta of desired neurotransmitters given by the brand is driven by the relevant brain operating principles (BOP#1, BOP#2, BOP#3, BOP#4 and BOP#5).

A brand like Dettol, for example, is an automatic choice based on a sense of comfort and familiarity, low use of energy and the herd effect of everyone using it (BOP#2, BOP#3 and BOP#5). It has become a part of the procedural memory of many customers; they do not even think about choosing an alternative. This leads to a higher brand valuation for Dettol as a brand, and by extension, a higher intangible value for the brand owner, Reckitt Benckiser.

In such a situation, there is an almost guaranteed revenue stream for the company that is the brand owner. To the extent a firm is able to provide the brand at a cost that allows it to make a profit, therefore, a brand that is deeply embedded in the brain of its target customers is a source of cash flows, present and future. The deeper the brand is embedded in the brain, therefore, the steadier the future cash flows, contingent on the firm being able to continue to provide the product underlying the brand.

We know that cash flows have a direct correlation with the valuation of the firm in the stock markets. Therefore, embedding the brand in the brain of the customer is directly correlated with the valuation of the firm and, therefore, with the monetary value of the brand. And as we discussed earlier in the chapter, CEOs are increasingly concerned with understanding the likely overall financial impact of the brands on the business over time, covering a range of key revenue drivers (these will vary based on the business, but could include customer acquisition, churn, price premiums, share of wallet, frequency of purchase/visit, average basket size and so on), and their impact on profit margins from any operational changes required to deliver the new strategy.

Clearly, therefore, a firm has to increase the valuation of its brands in the mind of its customers, since the increase in valuation is a function of what is happening in the brains of customers. What happens in the brains of customers is a function of the customers' experiences. These experiences are a function of the actions that the firm takes to engage with customers. And customer engagement happens through the actions of the people in the organization who provide the product to the customers.

In the aftermath of the pandemic of 2020–22, the value of strong brands has grown for those that have been able to pivot with the requirements of the situation and cater to customer demand. Among sectors that have been most negatively impacted (travel, hospitality, etc.), the stronger brands are the ones that will be left standing once the dust settles. Indigo Airlines, the brand leader in India, will survive and grow as travel returns—as customers go to the brands that they feel 'safer' with. Notice that in the longer term, the pandemic will be a mere blip in the trend of brand value over time, especially if the stewards of the brand have helped keep the brand embedded in the brains of their consumers. Amul, the dairy brand of India, for example, has gained during the pandemic at the expense of lesser-known brands. While brand value calculations are awaited, Amul's revenue growth in the two years of the pandemic has been impressive.

In summary, therefore, firms should use one method to track the value of their brand(s) over time to assess their marketing performance. The more firmly a brand is embedded in the brain of the consumer (through traces in the NAc, insula, basal ganglia, unconscious memory, etc.), the greater the brand value. The aspirational goal for brand marketers would be to construct a map that shows the linkages between the activity levels of different parts of the brain and brand value!

Finally, we know that the behaviour of the people in an organization and its performance in the marketplace is a function of the organization structure.[376] Therefore, in the next chapter, we will explore the link between the organizational structure of a firm and the creation, development and sustenance of a brand.

# Chapter 9

# Organizational Structure and Design to Deliver the Brand in the Brain

A firm may have come up with a brilliant brand positioning idea; the creatives may have been developed and executed very well. The product underlying the brand may be a very good one. However, ultimately, the brand depends on the customer experience and customer experience is partly a function of the product experience and partly, also, a function of the customer's experience with the firm and their interactions with the firm—especially for service brands—but even for product brands that need after-sales service of one kind or another.

Importantly, the interactions with the customer are a function of the organizational structure and processes involved in the brand management process. The organizational structure is also a determinant of the ability of the organization to create, manage and sustain brands. 'An organizational structure defines how activities such as task allocation, coordination and supervision are directed towards the achievement of organizational aims.[377] It can also be considered as the viewing glass or perspective through which individuals see their organization and its environment.'[378] While organizational structures have developed over time from hunter–gatherer tribes to farming communities to feudal organizations to the military to the modern large corporation,[379] the twenty-first century organization in the aftermath of the pandemic of 2020–22 is changing into a more flexible, less physical structure.

Branding is an activity that requires lot of investment and commitment from organizations to ensure successful brand building, brand sustenance and brand enhancement. The companies that are getting this alignment right and adjusting as per the dynamic environment are the ones that are most successful and are most preferred by customers. On the other hand, companies that are facing challenges in aligning their internal processes appropriately towards marketing and branding are either failing to gain new market share or are unable to sustain their position in the market.

One of the greatest challenges for the effective implementation of branding strategies is achieving support across the organization in order to develop the company's corporate and product brands as key assets. In their study of financial brands, de Chernatony and Cottam[380] conclude that: 'Managers . . . need to consider internal consistency between the brand values and those of the subcultures within the organization. A problem (among the brands they studied) was a high degree of inconsistency and multiple, diverse subcultures which resulted in considerably weakened brands.' Firms need to deal with this because brand assets today are often the most important assets that a firm possesses, which account for about one-third of the value of Fortune 500 companies.[381]

In this chapter, after very briefly summarizing organizational forms, we explore the various organizational forms that have been used by firms to create, build, sustain and rejuvenate brands. We first provide examples from the organization of different firms for brand management processes. We look at different organizational forms that firms have used to roll out, sustain and rejuvenate their brands and provide some pointers on which organizational form to use when. We then link these organizational forms to brand-related actions and the impact on customers' brains.

## Organizational Forms to Support Brand Activity

The primary organizational structure forms are functional, divisional, matrix or some combination of these at different levels of aggregation and disaggregation. [382] A functional structure means that people work in different functions, such as finance, marketing, production, credit, HR, IT, R&D, etc. In marketing, there would be sub-functions such as sales, brand management, customer insights, planning, etc.; other functions would have a similar set of sub-functions. The functional form was primarily meant for organizations that had a single product and geography at a particular scale of operations. With multiple products and geographies, organizations started using a structure wherein each product or product group or geography was organized as a separate division, with each division having its set of functions. Sometimes, in a divisional organization, the different divisions shared a function. For example, most global banks tend to share IT functions across geographies. The matrix structure allowed for managers reporting across a function/division/geography.

More recently, a disaggregated organizational form is taking root. Consumers expect companies to stand for something meaningful, serve them relentlessly and better than yesterday. The increasing expectations for agility, promise and, in many sectors, D-to-C (direct-to-customer) services has led to the development of a new form of organizational structure called the Market Oriented Ecosystem (MOE).[383] Companies like Facebook, Alibaba, DiDi and Supercell are leading breakthroughs in technology and more, thanks to their ability to respond to current consumer needs quickly, recognize future consumer needs, collaborate with potential allies and provide an employee-empowering environment, among other factors. These companies have successfully adopted many features characteristic to MOE to mitigate the issue of agility and promises.

A typical MOE is structured as follows:

1. **Cells:** Small independent units of people that work on an idea and try to make it happen. In Amazon's case, they are called two-pizza teams. Every cell in Amazon accommodates only as many people as those that can comfortably eat two pizzas. The independence of the cells enables the constituents to put their curiosity to use, take up new problems to solve, respond to a demand with agility and enable innovation at a fast pace without the need to stick by what the 'superior' demands. Every game that

Supercell releases, and thousands of other ideas that it doesn't go through with, has originated from such small cells. The smallness of the cells enables agility in decision-making, be it regarding products, services, public relations or any other faction of the company. This agility enables the company to allow its brand to be relevant to the current times, and appropriately associate itself to the evolving environment.

2. **Platform:** A shared platform that enables cells to utilize tools, technology and resources to facilitate agile responses to consumer needs, without them having to develop every solution from scratch. Every code that is utilized multiple times qualifies to become an automatic and shared tool that could be provided by the platform. Cells and platforms have a non-hierarchical relationship. This shared platform could help a brand keep its core branding mission constant by building solutions related to the mission.
3. **Allies:** Potential collaborators that cells or a company as a whole can work with to develop a plausible solution, therefore eliminating the need to develop every solution from scratch. Companies may take three approaches to gain allies: buy, borrow or build. Facebook bought Instagram and WhatsApp because the decision fit its mission, which says 'People use Facebook to stay connected with friends and family, to discover what's going on in the world, and to share and express what matters to them'. Sometimes, companies may decide to venture together and develop a solution and then part ways. Tencent, the Chinese gaming, chat, platform and payments firm, often uses this way

to develop solutions along with its many collaborators like JD.com, Meituan, DiDi, 58.com and Netmarble. Building core concepts is important for a company to remain unique and different from its competitors. Apple keeps its secrets closely guarded until the very day a new product is released.

The MOE structure is essentially non-hierarchical and it encourages innovations like no other structure does. A 2005 study[384] concluded that when employees perceive an element of social injustice in management decisions, they negatively associate this with unfairness and suggest that leaders should, instead of deflecting the blame, own their mistakes to avoid the feeling of injustice from settling in for long-term. Studies have also found that the anterior insula is also activated when unfairness is perceived.[385] Free will, curiosity, creativity and independence are rewarded and these qualities make employees feel empowered and free enough to generate and work upon innovative ideas. Cognitively speaking, free will, curiosity, creativity and empowerment are important for employees to believe in themselves, and by extension, in what their company's brand stands for. We have already seen in previous chapters that employees are as much a part of the image of a brand as the product or services the company provides. They truly may become brand ambassadors of the company and hence, feel motivated enough to keep on contributing. For example, in Supercell, people are allowed to work with any team they want, catering to their needs for free will and empowerment. Employees are not the only ones who play the important part. A strong leadership, with a consistent vision and a knack for being supportive when needed and decisive at other times, is an important part of the success of an MOE. Indeed, without strong leadership, arguably, the MOE may not work as the different supercells may lack a coherence of direction and action.

From a brand's perspective, the MOE needs to remain consistent and constant, but it also needs to be responsive and representative of the changing scenario. It needs to accommodate emerging trends, and be constantly on the lookout for the changes to come. For its promise and mission to remain to relevant, it needs to be representative of current as well as future needs of consumers and be able to connect every related marketing move to its brand. Only then will customers be able to trust the brand. The agility that flows in an MOE structure helps the brand stay relevant for times to come.

Given the above, what are some current organizational structures to support brand development and sustenance? The following section provides some examples.

## The Hindustan Unilever Ltd (HUL) Brand Management Organization[386]

HUL is organized by function at the corporate level. However, marketing is the primus inter pares function and brand managers are the leaders of the pack and lead the charge for the brand that is their charge. Brand managers start as management trainees who are hired from top business schools. After a year of training, which includes a month-long rural stint, the marketing trainees move into sales roles as sales managers and area sales managers for a period of two to three years. After this, they move into brand management, beginning with the first role.

The brand management role has two parts. The first has to do with the packaging, supply chain and product specifications. In India, packaging tends to be a large role as pack sizes can vary from very small to very big. For instance, shampoos come in SKUs of 5 ml, 10 ml, 25 ml, 125 ml, 300 ml and 1 litre. The requirements are quite different in each.

The second part of the role has to do with the more traditional brand management activities such as positioning, marketing spend, liaising with creative agencies, monitoring brand performance, coordinating with manufacturing, supply chain, R&D and finance, and is a P&L role. Here, the brand manager is the leader of a team that includes all the above functions and makes decisions relating to product configuration, pricing and a mix of marketing communication activities across regions, since India is many different markets. This team formally meets at least once a month. Most tactical decisions are taken at the brand manager level. These would include seasonal promotions, schemes for the distribution channel, decisions on incentives for the distribution system, etc. The importance of distribution cannot be overemphasized—brand managers spend up to twelve days a month on the road. The area sales managers would spend close to twenty days a month on the road. The brand managers also lead teams that include people from manufacturing, finance and logistics.

Some major decisions are pushed up, such as the decision to change the grammage of Lifebuoy soap, as this is the single largest brand by unit volume for HUL. The decision to locate the third Dove soap factory for Unilever in Indonesia rather than in India was taken at the highest levels of the organization.

By the sixth to eighth year, a manager would have had exposure to sales and both the brand management roles.

After brand management, the manager can rotate back into the sales role or stay on in brand management. At the apex of the organization, the management committee has a sales head, a marketing head, a supply chain head, a manufacturing head and an R&D head. Within the management committee, there are strategic business units (SBUs); so there is a housing and personal care division (that includes detergents, soaps, etc.), a food division and so on. As of 2019, Priya Nair and Sandeep Kohli were the executive directors of home care and of beauty and personal care, respectively. The two departments contributed more than 80 per cent of the total 2018–19 turnover of Rs 37,660 crore.[387]

Salaries are largely fixed, with a variable component that goes up as one goes higher up the corporate ladder.

This structure allows HUL to make its product available in more than 7 million outlets in India. Availability is a key part of building a brand at scale in India. The marketing communications and positioning activities are also driven by the brand manager, who acts as a mini-CEO for the brand and is responsible for the growth of the brand on various parameters, including sales, brand attitude and brand value. One could argue that the HUL brand stewardship structure is a modified MOE with the brand manager as the leader.

## The Amul Brand Communication Operations

Amul, an Indian cooperative dairy company, was founded in 1946. Its Operation Flood helped revolutionize the dairy industry in the country and helped make India self-sufficient, milk-wise, leaving the then leading country, USA, behind.[388] Its brand vision to 'remunerate returns of farmers and serve the interests of consumers' has helped it build a trustworthy rapport with farmers and consumers alike.[389] The farmers are, in fact, quite happy, given the recent four-fold increase in their income in the seven years from 2011 to 2017.[390]

Its external structure is organized in a three-tier system: the village dairy cooperative societies that facilitate procurement of milk, the district milk union that acts as the processing unit and the state milk federation, which is the marketing unit. Amul management is organized in a similar hierarchical structure, with a managing director heading each unit.[391] The management reviews the performance and contributions of each of the members and a profit-sharing mechanism that supplies bonuses in proportion of the contribution is enacted. Therefore, the employees are directly in control of and are responsible for their rewards and punishments.[392]

Its internal organization could be called bureaucratic, as it is highly influenced by the bureaucracy in government organizations—its tall and narrow top authoritative structure is the only part that is responsible for important decisions. It has departments that each follow the hierarchical structure—finance, marketing, sales and purchasing, production, quality and product, store and dispatch and HR. Each of these departments has multiple levels of management—senior manager, manager, deputy manager, assistant manager and so on.[393]

Amul's branding is handled by the marketing organization, which sits above the cooperative and the district milk unions. Amul's brand approach has been very successful so far. In India, where a cartoon in a school textbook can create a political furore, the tongue-in-cheek humour brought alive by the Amul mascot has thrived now for more than fifty years. Amul and its creative partner, Dacunha Associates, have, on an ongoing basis, contracted more than 6000 billboards and hoardings pan-India. These ads first appeared in 1966[394] and continue to do so as of 2021, in an unbroken continuity of theme and presentation. Think about it! Fifty-five years of continuity and change—the mascot is the same, the message changes each time based on a contemporary event (Brain Operating Principle [BOP] #3 and BOP#4)—that continues.

Each Monday morning, the creative team meets and lists possible issues that can be spun off into ads. Topics like politics, sports and Bollywood (India's Hollywood) are perpetual favourites. A list of ten is drawn up and on average, five are pushed each week. That is an average of a hoarding every one and a half days.[395] This decision-making lies with the MD of the organization. The brand narrative is built around the creative, an extensive distribution system that has unparalleled reach and quality production that ensures that fresh milk and milk-based products are available by the morning after. Amul has made a traditional functional marketing organization work with an overlay on top of the cooperative structure beneath. It works because of strong leadership and continuity of vision and implementation in the organization.

## Britannia

Britannia's organizational design was as follows:[396] from the traditional sales management and brand management activity in the brand function, the overall brand management activity now comprises packaging, brand management, key account management, channel management, innovation, and manufacturing and logistics.

In the words of the COO, Neeraj Chandra, earlier, there used to be a stable career track in sales and brand management. This changed to people rotating between the six areas outlined above. While reporting relationships converge to a head of marketing and operations (Neeraj), who oversees all six activities, day-to-day decisions are taken on a project basis by a designated person on a team that would include personnel from (as the case may be) the brand manager, the key account manager, the manufacturing manager and the innovation person. Logistics and packaging also come on board as required. Decision-making is not restricted to the brand manager in the team (unlike in HUL, where the brand manager will get to take the call most of the time). Depending on the level of the decision, it can escalate to the level of Neeraj Chandra.

There is job rotation between the different activities. Compensation varies by level. At higher levels, it is about 30–35 per cent variable, while at lower levels, it is about 10–15 per cent variable. Performance metrics are situation-dependent. In some instances, it could be sales and market share, in some it could be awareness creation, in some it could be cost-related. Over the course of a year, a composite score is created. Being in the FMCG space, small gains count a lot.

The company allowed 99,999 shares of Rs 2 each upon exercise of options under Britannia Industries Limited Employee Stock Option Scheme in 2018–19 to give effect to its new initiative, thereby linking employee performance and company performance.[397] The platform element of the MOE structure can be said to have been implemented—though the hierarchy is very much present.

## Nestlé

The Nestlé portfolio of more than 2000 brands is organized by geographical status and role.[398] These two elements together create a 'hierarchy of brands', in which every product is related to least two brands at various levels in the hierarchy. The geographical criterion allows three groups of brands to be distinguished—international, regional and local brands.

These brands fulfil different functions and roles, depending on the customers, and represent the principal families of brand architecture. There are 'family brands' (or source brands), range brands, product brands and endorsing brands.

- 80 per cent of Nestlé Group's activity is brought together under six strategic corporate brands :
  - Nestlé
  - Nescafé
  - Nestea
  - Maggi
  - Buitoni
  - Purina
- Seventy strategic international brands, designating either ranges or products, come under or even outside the umbrella of these six corporate brands. They include Nesquik (an extensive range of chocolate milk products), but also product brands such as Kit Kat, Lion, Friskies and the mineral waters Perrier, San Pellegrino, Vittel and Nestlé Pure Life.

- A third category groups together eighty-three brands known as 'strategic regional brands', which are regional rather than international, such as mineral waters like Aquarel and Contrex, the Nuts bar and Herta cold meats.
- Finally, there is a fourth category of local brands sold only in their country of origin.

Thus, the Nestlé brand refers to several levels and roles:

- It is a corporate brand and as such, acts as an endorsement for all the products and brands in the group. This endorsement function means that the corporate brand usually appears on the side of the packaging or on the labelling on the back.
- The Nestlé brand is also one of the six strategic corporate brands, with the status of a family brand or source brand. It covers categories as diverse as baby products, products for children, chocolates, ice cream, chocolate bars and fresh dairy products.
- The Nestlé brand is sometimes simply a product or a range brand, as in Nestlé chocolate or Nestlé condensed milk. These are the basic products, the symbolic products that lie at the heart of the Nestlé galaxy.

It is worth pointing out that 20 per cent of Nestlé's turnover is not produced under the six 'strategic corporate brands'. This is the case with mineral waters. For example, Perrier, which is classified as a recreational drink for adults, is indeed managed with the Nestlé Water Division. But this division does not have a brand—its identification is a matter of internal organization. For clients the world over, Perrier is simply Perrier.

Brand managers are often likened to small business owners because they assume full responsibility for a brand or brand family. It is their job to distil the brand's essence, map out the competitors in the brand's category, identify marketing opportunities and be able to effectively communicate the unique benefits of that product or service with the help of a cross-functional team. [ii]

The following career path is quite common within marketing at Nestlé (as well as at many of the established large global fast moving consumer goods firms):

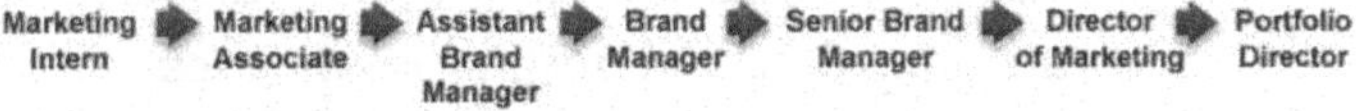


The following career path of a current brand director in marketing, Carla, gives an idea of the tenure in each of the above roles:

- Marketing Intern (summer)—Purina ONE®
- Marketing Associate (one year)—Purina ONE®
- Assistant Brand Manager (two years)—Purina ONE®
- Brand Manager (one year)—Purina ONE®
- Brand Manager (one year)—Pet Promise®
- Brand Manager (two years)—Friskies®
- Senior Brand Manager (two years)—Fancy Feast®
- Brand Director (current)—Dog Chow®

Nestlé's structure is a legacy of its history—and unlike Unilever which rationalized from 1800 to 400 brands worldwide, Nestlé continues to keep its roster of brands and very different levels of scale (both of volume and geography). This leads to a complex structure and less clearer lines in the organization. As a product that is for individuals with little service component, this has worked for Nestlé. And is quite unlike the MOE structure.

## Burberry

Founded in 1856, Burberry is a luxury fashion brand based out of London, UK. It has a matrix organizational structured by a democratic leadership that aims to create 'democratic luxury' for its consumers. The previous CEO, Angela Ahrendts, maintained that, 'If you're going to be democratic, then you have to get that out to everyone and by doing that, it unites the culture.'[399] Her vision allowed the company to improve upon its matrix organizational structure to accommodate more and more employee engagement. Reportedly, 87 per cent of the employees are proud to be working at the company.[400] In 2017, the company found itself undergoing another phase of changes and 'inspired employees' form a part of its two-phase plan to rejuvenate the brand and achieve a firm hold in luxury fashion. The company and its leadership strongly believes that its employees are major enablers of change and innovation and treats them accordingly.

Until the recent past, the company was associated with old men. Burberry leveraged the power of digital media to reach millennials and they continue to utilize digitalization to cater to their clientele better.[401] To align the company's brand value or the 'Burberry behaviours' of 'Putting Customers First, Being Bold And Open to New Ideas, Being One Team, and

Being Accountable And Responsive', Burberry launched their Leadership Development Programme to accelerate the delivery of the revamping strategy.[402]

Decision-making, however, remains the job of the leadership and is then mediated down, as in a corporate hierarchy. Employees enjoy the benefits of setting their own goals, which are reviewed once a year and evaluated for a bonus. The company also prefers 'internal promotions' to encourage employees and keep the talent in-house. Despite the hierarchical way of decision-making, the company encourages creativity and innovation, and is a 'young old company.'[403] It has encouraged small groups to come up with ideas.

All in all, Burberry's marketing strategies have targeted millennials and the democratic matrix organizational structure has helped keep its core values the same and in sync with the values of millennials, and also to evolve into a brand that is a leader in luxury fashion, particularly in its trench coat segment, when only a couple decades ago, it resonated with old men.

## Maruti Suzuki

Maruti has a divisional structure where there are five departments (or directorates, as Maruti calls them): HR, marketing and sales (including service and support), supply chain, production, engineering and R&D (design). As it appears, there is a good amount of interplay between these directorates to facilitate the overall image of the organization. Marketing is responsible for identifying trends in industry and identifying gaps (the classic customer orientation). They then go to engineering and discuss the initial requirements. This leads to debates and discussions within the organization over price, features, etc. A product committee comprising marketing, supply chain and engineering gets into an iterative process of deleting or adding features and then arrives at some consensus on the product specifications. The design team then assesses the practicality, feasibility, etc. The entire process can take from four to eighteen months.

Branding often resides in the hands of the different product groups, called PGs. These groups are headed by brand managers, who typically have MBAs reporting in to them. Brand managers are responsible for all activities related to the brand (positioning, advertising) and trends, and detailed research is done exclusively by the brand manager. The PG head would actually take the decisions (he is thirty-five to thirty-eight years old) with inputs from the brand managers. It is apparent that crucial activities such as branding are driven by people who have educational backgrounds in marketing, etc., and thus are typically MBAs.

The outsourced MR personnel and brand managers interact with the product planning group. The open plan office interacts with the media teams and the MR teams on a regular basis. Senior management gets involved (at times till the level of the chief executive) for brand-related decisions.

As an engineering-driven organization, Maruti still manages to have a very close ear to the ground on matters related to customer thinking. The organizational structure is closer to the traditional functional organization with a very strong Japanese cultural influence rather than an MOE.

## Infosys

Infosys follows a matrix organization structure. The organization structure for the company is business model-driven. There is a high volume of customer interfacing touchpoints in the organization due to the nature of the business. So while there is no explicit attempt to make a 'brand-oriented' organizational structure, it clearly has been a factor in deciding the organization structure.

Infosys has people from diverse backgrounds with multiple skills who have worked to build the brand. The company is a globally built one so it has leveraged the multiple strengths of different people to get where it is today. However, there are two traits that have been found to be most effective in individuals who have helped to build the brand:

1. **Good storytelling ability:** Infosys acknowledges that people who have been the most successful in helping to build the brand or to strengthen the brand further are those who are very good storytellers. The reason for this has been attributed to the ability of good storytellers to tell stories about anything that they want to market or sell.
2. **Ability to demystify complexity without reducing the significance:** The company believes that the people who perform client-facing roles and also those who have regular interaction with the customer need to have the ability to reduce the complexity while maintaining the significance for the work that is being done or for any suggestion being made. This ensures that these people talk the language that customer understands. Consequently, they enhance the overall brand value of Infosys in the eyes of the customer.

Infosys has a matrix structure and is a flat organization as far as inter-departmental exchange of ideas is concerned. The company has mechanisms to listen to the voice of customer from every corner of the organization (typically the project delivery teams). For branding there is a corporate branding team that takes inputs from the delivery side as well and hashes out the relevant data. Also, the company has a fairly open culture that ensures that there is easy exchange of information and ideas.

Overall there is a corporate branding group that defines overall corporate branding and image of the organization to the extent of colour, the font and the style of the logo, etc. This is under the direct supervision of the top management and all top leaders from the sales and marketing function are involved in decision-making around branding. This group of leaders meets periodically to review the brand attributes and make decisions. Once any branding-related decisions are taken, relevant communications are made to the teams affected and they take it forward in forms that are relevant to them.

Apart from the traits discussed above, the front-end staff (typically the client engagement groups) is encouraged to gather client testimonials, etc., and make the customer an evangelist of the brand. The company also makes conscious efforts to ensure that the change in strategy, such as 'Building Tomorrow's Enterprise', percolate to the lowest level and become part of day-to-day conversations. There are significant awareness campaigns that are run to ensure this. A fair amount of leeway is given in encouraging more acceptable risk-taking to help build a stronger brand and with the overall branding strategy in place, tactical efforts are made by different groups independently.

The marketing department itself is scattered but has a strong governance structure. The group is committed to business and brand. The brand values are measured through the voice of the customer and other channels. The marketing department makes efforts towards understanding the shifts in customer demands and to see 'what is surfacing'.

There is a direct linkage between the incentives of brand managers and marketing managers and brand enhancement. This is tied to their goal sheet in their annual performance reviews. Marketing managers can have up to 40–50 per cent linkage of their incentives with branding. For non-brand and non-marketing managers, the linkage is much lower (in the range of 1.5–2 per cent). Client relationship managers have objectives that assess consistency and staying with corporate branding and also how they are able to change customer behaviour in favour of the Infosys brand.

## The Tata Group

The Tata Group in India is a conglomerate that is managed by a private company—Tata Sons Ltd (TSL). TSL has a group that is called the Brand Custodian group, which is responsible as a steward for the Tata brand across all the group firms. Group firms pay TSL a royalty for the Tata brand. And the Brand Custodian group is tasked with the responsibility of maintaining consistency across the different group firms with the core of the Tata brand—that revolves around the ethos of trust, caring and ethical behaviour from a brand that has demonstrated high levels of customer engagement and empathy many times over the decades (consider for example, the exemplary behaviour by Taj Hotel employees when under the gun of terrorists in 2008 and the famous Tata Steel campaign—'We also make steel', to emphasize the commitment of the Tata Steel firm to its people).

Each group company manages its own product brand independently within the larger Tata brand. So, Tata Motors has a bunch of cars that are badged both as Tata and as Jaguar. Tata Global Beverages sells Tata Tetley tea. TCS is the group's flagship $25-billion-revenue firm that is India's largest software firm. Tata Cliq provides upmarket products to a select clientele with a group of service providers that go the extra mile to be empathetic to their customers. Tanishq provides quality, reliable and the latest gold and diamond jewellery to Indians who are obsessed with gold and jewellery. The Brand Custodian of the group may sit on some boards to harmonize the practice of the ethos of the brand that is based on the culture, values and practices of the individual firms in the group. Arguably, the values, ethos and culture are a reflection of J.R.D. Tata and Ratan Tata who between them have been custodians of the group for eighty-four years.

In summary, different companies have created different structures that have come from a combination of legacy, history, market requirements, the primacy of marketing in the organization and the nature of the product or service that the firm is selling. The common themes across these different firms and their organizational forms for brand management can be summarized as follows: First, companies have built sound feedback mechanisms so that they get to hear the voice of the customer from the remotest corner of the firm. For example, Maruti has a system that provides a daily score to top management about the company's service satisfaction levels. Similarly, Infosys has defined mechanisms to gather data from the delivery side to ensure that they get inputs from all the levels of the organization. Second, the brand manager has both the responsibility as a steward of the brand and the authority to make decisions on behalf of the brand. Third, either explicit contractual incentives or cultural norms drive the brand management process. Fourth, there is relative consistency in brand management practices over time from the brand organization. The organizational structure itself may or may not be MOE, but the systems, processes and the values and ethos that are inculcated matter.

Companies may even influence the outsourcing and suppliers to align with their own processes (to the extent of organizational structure in the supplier firm) to enhance their brand.

The incentive structure of managers has a direct linkage with their motivation to contribute to branding. This applies to both the sales and marketing workforce, which is primarily responsible for branding activities, and also to the non-marketing managers, who contribute indirectly to branding. The ones who have greater impact on branding due to the nature of their jobs have a stronger relation of their incentive structures with the branding contribution.

In product-based companies such as HUL, Britannia and Maruti, the brand managers, sales managers and product group managers have up to 30 per cent of linkage in their incentive to branding contribution.[404]

Service companies such as Infosys, Wipro and DRL also demonstrated direct linkages of incentives with branding contribution for the sales and marketing workforce. However, these companies also have incentives for the non-marketing managers for their contribution to branding. It could be attributed to the nature of the businesses that these companies have. These companies have far more direct touchpoints with the customer as compared to the product companies and these touchpoints also require skills for involving and influencing the customer. However, DRL had a different mechanism of incentivizing the efforts of non-marketing and non-sales managers. The company has installed a reward and recognition mechanism that encourages branding-related behaviour in non-marketing managers.

Brand champions are external and internal storytellers who spread not only the brand values and brand vision, but also nurture the brand in an organization. Every organization needs committed and passionate brand champions. The more employees the organization can turn into brand champions, the better equipped it will be to build and maintain strong brand equity. Singapore Airlines, L'Oreal, Harley-Davidson, Nike, Google and LEGO are well-known examples of companies that benefit tremendously from their employees being strong and dedicated brand champions.

However, silos or divisions within the culture of an organization can frustrate the achievement of brand orientation. An organization implementing a major brand-revitalization strategy, despite having a strong brand vision and high level of management commitment, saw how functional silos associated with different mindsets contributed to the failure of the new brand strategy.

Silos generate inefficiencies and conflicts and act as barriers to implementing a coherent brand strategy; there are also other significant and less obvious factors and divisions at work within the organization, which deserve further investigation. The barriers between silos cannot be removed easily; brand leaders must acknowledge and work with silos, creating KPIs and vision statements and developing values across the whole organization that are relevant to each silo in an attempt to create a commonality between them. Silos are not going to disappear overnight. Some suggest that we should create a chief customer officer (CCO)[405] and a chief marketing officer

(CMO)[406], in order to overcome silo thinking. The question is whether this is a realistic option and whether it would be effective. As researchers have pointed out, most CCOs have been created on top of a traditional structure, which does little more than create a new veneer. Some argue that the most efficient and realistic means to execute successful brand management strategies is to acknowledge and work within the silos, and that the following factors are critical:

1. Creating a shared vision for the brand that is manifested within the different mindsets and cultural divisions across the organization.
2. Organizational, management and financial commitment to implementing commonly agreed and understood long-term strategic brand strategy and KPIs across silos. Short-termism based on sales and cost reduction targets is probably doomed to failure.
3. Communication and information-sharing across divisions that allow silos to monitor the activities and goals of each other in terms of the brand strategy. The development of common knowledge structures to facilitate the sharing of knowledge.
4. The development of formal and informal organizational structures to allow this and to promote more common, silo-spanning communication and behaviour across the organization, something that requires trust between the different departments.[407] Activation in the caudate region of the brain has been observed to be related to the amount of reciprocity observed and is seen to encode the 'intention

> to trust'.[408] Trust between different parts of the organization is a key driver of brand-appropriate behaviours with customers.

Clearly, the right organizational form will lead to better trust between departments and better brand outcomes. A 2015 study illustrates how a flexible organizational form like an MOE, for example, essentially makes every employee a leader. The 2015 study argues that a manager's roles of 'sensing', 'seizing' and 'reconfiguring' are important cognitive capabilities.[409] Exploring and exploiting are two important phenomena our mind utilizes to traverse through decision-making, governed by rewards attained through the two ways. In fact, the two processes are important ways in which our brain learns to make decisions. Reinforcement studies have shown that a rat learns to navigate a maze by exploring new options in the beginning and then settling upon specific explored options to exploit them regularly for maximum reward. In the face of a new decision, humans also try to explore all the options and our prior biases may direct us to exploit the one most closely resembling previously explored options. Over a period of time, we learn from the rewards and punishments encountered while exploring different options and we exploit our experiences to choose those options that maximize our rewards.[410, 411] Brands with which the customer connects are those that 'reward' customers (dopamine, serotonin, BOP#3, BOP#4, for example). Similarly, organizational forms need to 'reward' people so that their positive actions support the brand. Scientists have observed that we associate negative emotions with inequity and non-reciprocity.[412]

Leaders and managers are required to build a 'paradoxical cognition', one that embraces the exploring–exploiting dilemma, and understand the trade-offs that accompany their every decision.[413] One could conclude that leaders should be able to explore current technologies for the company to remain relevant and exploit their core technologies and mission to remain consistent. However, the jury is still out on this. The authors of another study[414] have argued that such engagement may be detrimental due to prior biases, and that leaders may be better off understanding strategic market opportunities.[415] My own view leans in the direction of the former based on the right recruits into the relevant departments and the provision of the 'right' incentives to the employees to enable the required behaviours that support the brand positioning.

## Cognition and Neuroscience Bases Emphasized by Neuroscience

Let's now examine how these various steps translate neurally and cognitively. How sensing, seizing, reconfiguring, free will, curiosity, creativity, social and personal identity, values and collaboration of the relevant employees are cognitively demanding and/or neurally rewarding. And how these can contribute to the process of building and sustaining the firm's brands.

1. **Sensing:** Two important phenomena, perception and attention, facilitate an employee's ability to sense opportunities before they materialize, and therefore predict the future needs of consumers. Sensing future opportunities would involve taking in the environment

as a whole, making sense of it and developing a plausible narrative which demands innovation today.[416] This process could be summarized as the ability to perceive. A typical brain combines past experiences and memories with current environment, recognizes patterns, envisions a future and reacts to it accordingly. The more familiar a person is with the past and the present, the more successfully one can sense and comprehend the future. Attention orients us to sensory inputs, detects signals for conscious processing and helps maintain alertness.[417] It aids perception through pattern and contrast recognition. The employee needs to be incentivized to process this information and act on it. Southwest Airlines' employees exemplify this behaviour through their actions with customers—actions that flow from very consciously fostering a culture.

2. **Seizing:** Seizing current market opportunities is enabled by, among other things, problem-solving and reasoning. These two are among the executive functions a brain engages in. To be able to form strategic moves and exploit market needs, an interplay of 'fluid intelligence', 'rational thinking' and 'heuristics processing' is activated.[418] They help individuals locate the problem and move towards a plausible solution through exploit–explore and biased–unbiased approaches. How much does your firm encourage this form of thinking? HUL in India has been able to seize opportunities time and again and has now a portfolio of really strong brands.

3. **Reconfiguring:** Reorientation and restructuring of a company requires individuals who embrace change and have a growth mindset.[419] Having a rigid mindset can lead to the death of companies due to a resistance to change. Microsoft under Satya Nadella is an excellent example of a company that encourages a growth mindset. He encouraged the company to move away from PCs and acknowledge the fact that the world has moved on from there. Instead, he pushed innovations in mobile and cloud technologies. A 2018 study[420] hints at an interplay between a growth mindset and intrinsic motivations. A neuroscience study suggested that growth mindset people are more responsive towards corrective feedback reception, exhibit a high Pe (error positivity) and therefore have heightened awareness and pay greater attention to mistakes.[421] Are you recruiting the right set of people who will have intrinsic motivation and will help build the brand?
4 **Free will:** Research by Sheena Iyengar suggests that just having options and having the freedom to choose among them makes us feel empowered because of the perception of control over ourselves and our decisions. It leads to improved moods and motivated efforts.[422] Free will may even lead to enhanced creativity. An interesting, decades-old study[423] noted that when children were given choices among material with which to make collages, they created collages that were evaluated as more creative than control subjects. In fact, Iyengar goes on to advise managers to provide employees with free will and choice to make

them feel empowered.[424] How empowered are the brand-responsible employees in your organization? Simultaneously, how well are they aligned with the brand vision?

5. **Curiosity:** In Chapter 7, we inspected how the innate curiosity of humans can be utilized to make interesting ad campaigns. Curiosity engages our brain because our brain feeds on novelty and activates striatal reward circuits[425] which is consistent with Brain Operating Principle (BOP) #4. Researchers argue that curiosity is often internally motivated.[426] This research implies that encouraging curiosity to drive innovation is indeed a rewarding experience.
6. **Creativity:** Our brain has the ability to think, and with that come important implications. We can think about things, people, situations, and even those subjects we have never encountered before. Creativity results from combination thought (deliberate and spontaneous) about two types of information (emotional and cognitive). Novel ideas originating from these neural computations are processed by the prefrontal cortex, leading to creative behaviour.[427] Employee creativity is important for enhancing brands in the marketplace, for creating the novelty in the brands that keep them interesting for customers (BOP#4).
7. **Social and personal identity:** In Chapter 5, we saw that people can be aligned with the brand if it provides them a sense of belonging by giving them a social identity—a classic example of the use of mirror neurons in branding. Free will and encouragement to

create furthers the personal identity of an individual. To belong and to be are essential feelings for the survival of a social animal like a human being.[428] Neurally, the dorsal medial prefrontal cortex (DMPFC) facilitates the expression of both 'social identities' and 'personal identities'.[429] Are your employees aligned with the brand? Arguably, Maruti Suzuki has personnel that are very aligned with the brand through a combination of culture and organizational structure.

8. **Values:** In Chapter 5, we also saw that decision-making that goes against our values and morals creates friction during the process and therefore, when brand and company purpose resonate with that of an employee, the latter is able to find purpose and fulfil their values through the company purpose.[430] This would motivate employees in an organization structure to be better brand champions. It is important for the brand to be consistent with its values and beliefs. Camper shoes provide a great example of this consistency—a brand that does not want you to buy it unless you really need it. It fits the pattern of customers who want a slower, more stable life (BOP#3) and is consistent with the values of the firm.
9. **Collaboration:** Given that we are a uniquely social species, it is not unlikely that we collaborate in unusual situations for personal or social gains. It involves understanding others' point of views, building a trusted relationship with others and working together to achieve one goal. While our goal-directed instincts may facilitate the latter, the first two involve completely

> different factors. Understanding others means that we have to acknowledge that others have their own thoughts. Essentially, we delve into the theory of the mind. rTPJ (right temporo-parietal junction) enables this process of making sense of and acknowledging others' minds, and that they are different from ours.[431]

Flexible organizational structures allow a unique expression of the brand. First, through the free will and creativity its leadership encourages, it makes the employees brand evangelists. It makes the employees working at these companies truly believe in the brand mission by providing them with non-restrictive environments. Employees are increasingly growing accustomed to this notion and it won't be long before it becomes the new normal. Second, the undertone of every innovation and solution is that the brand mission should be expressed through it. The brand mission forms the key core values, with allowances for growth in its relevance. Three, treating the customers to a glimpse of the future today is enabled by market-oriented organization forms and it helps the customer believe in the brand values that enable this company behaviour. It makes the customers believe that the company is there for their needs, future or current, and is able to meet them, thereby increasing the company's utility quotient. Overall, the agility enabled through flexible organizational forms is the key.

In this chapter, we have tried to see how different companies motivate, incentivize and encourage their employees, how they try to cater to the demand scenario, how the leading companies of the world have organized themselves to take on the challenge of the evolving world head-on by relying on agility, responsiveness and direction with a view to nurturing, growing and sustaining brands. An evolving organizational structure enables an evolving brand, one that remains relevant to the times that a company operates in. Not only that, a brand should be able to anticipate the needs of the customers even before they have realized it. Such ideas, after all, come from within and from outside the brand, and they do so only when the people involved are encouraged to pursue the path of innovation. A proper organizational structure resonates with its brand and is able to make both its employees and customers believe in the brand.

The appropriate organizational form needs to use the right neuro tools to advance its brand agenda. In the next chapter, we turn to which neuro tools to use, when and why.

# Chapter 10

# Neuromarketing Tools and Measurement in Managing Brands

In this chapter, we first develop an understanding of how and why neuro tools can add a powerful new dimension to the brand-building process. Then, we examine the various neuro tools that are currently available, how they are used, what they can do and not do. Finally, we explore how one may use neuro tools to build and manage brands.

## Introduction

The use of neuromarketing tools has met with interest but also scepticism from marketing managers. Some see in it great potential to gain insights that are hard to access with traditional approaches. Others have raised concerns about efficacy and ethical issues. Leading firms in various sectors—Facebook,

PepsiCo, eBay, Intel, Time Warner, ESPN, Ferrero, New Balance, Uber, Heineken and Formula One—are now using neuromarketing tools. However, it's important to emphasize that they are no silver bullets, simply a complementary way to probe for answers to market researchers' questions and a useful tool to develop brands.

Interest in neuromarketing was sparked in the mid-2000s with the publication of several academic studies on how the human brain responds to marketing actions such as branding and pricing. In a seminal paper (2004) referenced earlier in the book, a team led by Read Montague and Sam McClure[432] used fMRI to investigate how the display of the brands Pepsi and Coca-Cola influenced people's liking of soda. They found that knowing the brand was Coca-Cola (not Pepsi) enhanced participants' preference for this brand of soda, an inversion of the renowned Pepsi Challenge. And also that when participants consumed an identical drink labelled Coca-Cola (vs an unlabelled drink), there was increased brain activity in the memory circuit (but not when it was labelled Pepsi). These findings suggested that participants had unique brand knowledge about Coca-Cola but not Pepsi.

Another oft-cited fMRI study investigated why high price tags increase the enjoyment of wines. The study found that a higher price tag on an identical wine led to increased activity in the brain's liking centre.

Since neurometrics access the way consumers process information directly, they can deliver insights to questions that you might not have thought about asking. For example, a study led by Uma Karmarkar[433] asked if it mattered whether consumers saw the price before the product, or product before the price and why. Using fMRI, Karmarkar and colleagues found that it did. When the price was presented beforehand, it activated judgements of whether the product was a good deal, as compared to actually liking the product, which was the primary concern when the price was shown last.

Brands need to be nurtured and rejuvenated, and increasingly, brands form a large proportion of the value to the customer. Simultaneously, as customers become more familiar with brands, they tend to develop ennui with brands faster than before; the dopamine spikes that came early in the engagement with brands tend to decrease faster. Many brands never graduate to the level of being an unconscious habit. Since brands are, at their core, a set of patterns that exist in the neural networks of the customers who like them, any insights that a brand owner can generate that allows the brand owner to understand directly what is happening inside the brains of their customers should be helpful.

The neuro tools that are now available help us to directly understand the decision-making process of the customer better. Is it coming from the conscious or the unconscious? Is the decision being driven primarily by reason or by emotion? Such an understanding would help develop marketing interventions that are more likely to be able to continue to provide the cocktail of neurotransmitters that will more likely lead to continued customer engagement and loyalty. There is some evidence that suggests that neuro tools can improve marketing results by up to 20 per cent.[434] One sign that neuro tools have transcended their era of hype and hucksterism: Nielsen now has sixteen neuro labs globally, including five in the US; there is now one in Cincinnati, Ohio, the heart of client country and home to P&G, which is among the marketers that now have neuroscientists in-house. In 2017, Mars released a study of 110 TV ads showing that neuro research by MediaScience predicted sales impact from ads accurately 78 per cent of the time, versus survey research predicting results only 58 per cent of the time (which isn't much better than guessing).

Using neuro tools, marketing managers can design interventions of different kinds that would ultimately benefit the brand. The interventions can take place at the level of:

1. Understanding the customers' engagement level with the brand.
2. Understanding the effectiveness of a marketing intervention in the brain of the target. Customer for the brand; did the advertising message, for example, increase the liking for the brand? By how much? How can one build the brand further?
3. Designing interventions that are more likely to have the desired impact in the brain of the target customer with respect to the brand. The interventions themselves can be on product features, packaging features, pricing, advertising, retail display, etc. The impact of the interventions can lead to increasing liking, increasing purchase

probability, reinforcing and rejuvenating the brand in the brain of the consumer and so on.

4. Making predictions about the future intentions of the customer.
5. Understanding the key drivers of the brand attitude in the mind of the customer.

While these are also possible using traditional marketing tools like survey research, FGDs, thematic apperception tests, A/B tests, lab research and so on, neuro tools offer the additional dimensions of helping to understand the how and why, with higher granularity and certainty. Where do these tools fit into the overall set of marketing activities for a firm?

Marketing activities, including the sale of and interaction with brands, leads to the impact of 'on' activity in various parts of the brain. Neuro tools capture this activity in various forms. Using neuroscience, marketers can map brain activity to motivations and future intended behaviour. Customer behaviour captured in the form of big data can be used to infer the motivations of the customer, which can then be checked using neuro tools. Self-reports and surveys capture attitudes and intentions, which can sometimes be at variance with behaviour; this is not possible when a respondent is providing data to neuro tools, because these tools capture the activity of the sensory organs (eye), activity of the facial expressions, many of which happen automatically and are not in our control (face tracking) and activity of the brain (which can be at variance, sometimes, with what a respondent is saying or giving in a self-report).

Figure 1 below shows the different activities relative to one another.

## Figure 1

## Neuro Methods in the Overall Marketing and Branding Toolkit

| **Marketing Instruments**<br>Brands<br>Sales<br>Targeting<br>Distribution<br>Advertising | **Big Neurometric Data**<br>Electroencephalogram (EEG)<br>Functional Magnetic Resonance Imaging (fMRI)<br>Skin Conductance Response (SCR)<br>Functional Near-Infrared Spectroscopy (fNIRS)<br>Eye Tracker<br><br>*These brain mapping tools gauge an individual's intentions, attitudes, interests and awareness.* | |
|---|---|---|
| **Marketing Actions**<br>Packaging<br>Segmentation<br>Concepts<br>Promotion | **Self Report Survey Data**<br>Surveys and questionnaires also gauge intentions, attitudes, interests and awareness. | **Big Digital Behavioural Data**<br>Product Reviews<br>Purchase History<br>Credit Card History<br>Digital Invoices<br>Shopping Carts<br>Search History<br>Social Media Posts and Likes<br>Web Browsing Duration |

Essentially, neuro provides a direct access to the brain activities. Arguably, it can also predict better and earlier. Big data, which is now increasingly available because of the explosion of digital and social media platforms and usage, can reveal patterns of thinking and behaviour that can drive questions that can be tested using neuro tools.

Neuro, therefore, is one more weapon in the brand marketer's arsenal.

So what are the different neuro tools that are available to the marketer to help in the cause of brand development? In the following pages, we will have a closer look at what the different neuro tools are, along with potential tools of the future. In addition, we will see how brands can use such tools to further their strategies and how such processes can seamlessly occur as a part of the organizational structure. Lastly, we will have a quick look at emerging neuromarketing and consumer behaviour companies and the tools and schemes they have developed.

## 1. Existing Neuromarketing Tools

We briefly examine the following tools to better understand their utility from a marketing and brand building viewpoint.

1. **fMRI (functional magnetic resonance imaging):** This is, as of 2022, the gold standard of tools in terms of the level of insight that it can obtain about the brain areas' activities relating to a stimulus, including brand stimuli. Perhaps the most referred to method used in the studies we have discussed in this book, fMRI measures the BOLD (blood oxygen level-dependent) contrast to detect activity in regions of the brain. The response is a proxy for neural activity as changes in blood flow are known to reflect changes in neural activity. A standard approach is to capture a resting contrast and then to observe signal changes in particular regions. An increased blood level implies positive association with the stimulus and that region, whereas a decreased level would imply negative association. When McClure and others conducted their famous Pepsi vs Coca-Cola experiment, they observed an increase in activity in the VMPFC during the blind taste test. This implied that the VMPFC, which had already been strongly associated with evaluation of all options before, was engaging

in the calculation when the subjects tasted their drinks;[435] the VMPFC was also known to be a centre for affect. Researchers have developed Matlab and such codes that convert the resultant fMRI images into computational models to be able to understand the image data better. Some of these include GIFT[436], BCT[437] and CAT SPM.[438]

The major strengths of this approach are that (a) it is able to measure brain activity in response to a stimulus in all parts of the brain, including in the deep brain area (it, therefore, captures what is happening in the conscious and unconscious and can provide insights into the mix of reason and emotion driving a decision), (b) it has a high spatial resolution (a 3 Tesla machine can give a resolution of 1 $mm^3$ ), and (c) once a subject is comfortable in the laboratory environment, the responses are a true reflection of actual brain activity that is driving behaviour. Two weaknesses of this method are that (a) it is quite expensive and (b) its temporal resolution is limited; one can take multiple snapshots over time (to overcome the temporal disadvantage) but not in continuous time, as is possible in EEG.

One can use this method to make predictions. Berns et al.[439] demonstrated that neural responses of a small group of adolescents at one point in time to songs from unknown artists predicted the purchase behaviour of a much larger number of people many years later. The activity in the caudate nucleus of the adolescents correlated with the liking for the songs. They also found that the tendency among those they studied to change their evaluations of a song in line with its popularity (i.e., as a function of the ratings of the peer group) was positively correlated with activation in the anterior insula and anterior cingulate cortex (ACC). In a follow-on study, Berns and Moore (2012)[440] went on to show that the individual neural responses (in the orbitofrontal cortex [OFC] and nucleus accumbens [NAcc]) to the songs in their initial study could be used to predict purchase decisions by the general population assessed via the total number of units sold several years later.

One can also use this method to understand the drivers of a decision in the brain of a customer. Was the decision accompanied by an anticipation of gain? Or a feeling of regret? Did it lead to a heightened level of risk perception? We can infer these from the activation of particular areas of the brain. These are critical questions that a brand needs to track and answer. The answers to these questions can lead to design of, for example, relevant marketing communication interventions that are more likely to work to build or rejuvenate a brand.

2. **Eye tracking:** Perhaps one of the most affordable and convenient methods that allows mobility is eye tracking. When subjected to visual stimuli, different aspects of the stimuli catch different amounts of attention, and this is reflected in the way our eyes take in the entire stimulus. If our vision lingers for a relatively longer amount of time on a particular aspect, it is seen as an attention-grabber. Most of it is unconscious attention and we often don't realize

that some aspects are being attended to more, and therefore are more attractive than others. Because a fair proportion of our decision-making is unconscious, eye tracking can be a useful tool to evaluate visual stimuli. Screen-based, mobile glasses and VR are three ways in which subjects' attention is encoded as they explore the visual stimulus on a screen while roaming around a store and the world of virtual reality, respectively. This device can be used along with an EEG cap to encode the brain activity along with the attention to understand why something attracts us. Three metrics, namely, gaze replay, heat-map and area of interest are used to understand attention. Gaze replay encodes the path our visual focus takes when observing a scene. A heat map encodes the amount of attention different aspects of a scene grab, population-wise. The area of interest method figures out defined areas that grab attention and contrasts them with other areas. This method can aid in understanding brand equity, new product development, pricing decisions, placement (of products in a store) decisions and promotion decisions.[441] A 2014 review study discusses how eye movements while viewing advertisements can show a professional how a particular ad composition attracts attention and how originality and repetition are perceived, among other things.[442]

Eye tracking can be a very useful tool to evaluate and test different elements of brand messaging implementations as well as the effectiveness of elements of packaging given that it captures unconscious attention as well. Using an eye tracker in combination with an EEG enhances the utility of the output considerably in evaluating brand elements with the target customer. Which brand elements are adding to the strength of the brand? Which are not? Today, it is possible to take a combination of a mobile eye tracker and a mobile EEG into the field to collect customer data.

3. **Electroencephalography (EEG):** EEG is basically electrodes placed on one's scalp that transmit the brain waves that encode the cognitive processes during a stimulus. Unlike the fMRI, which uses the blood oxygen as proxy for neural activity in a particular part of the brain, the EEG uses the electrical waves that are generated in the brain by its electrical activity. These waves are the alpha and beta waves and the N200 waves. For our purposes, by using a 64-channel or a 128-channel EEG, one can localize the waves to within a square centimetre in the external areas of the brain—within a centimetre of the scalp (but not the deep brain areas). These can then be mapped to the behaviour of the respondent. When connected to existing knowledge of what different brain areas do, this can provide powerful insights for marketing action.

There are several advantages to using EEG as a neuromarketing tool. One, it provides us with excellent time resolution, albeit at the expense of relatively (compared to an fMRI) poor spatial resolution. Two, it allows mobility and the use of the tool in the field, lending greater face validity. Three, it is a cost-effective method. Four, when paired with other tools like eye tracking devices, it could provide an immense amount of relevant data pertaining to attention, motivation, alertness, excitation, etc. A 2012 study illustrated how EEG can be used to predict purchase decisions when price and brand are varied.[443] Another study concluded that two ad campaigns that only slightly differ in one of their scenes are responded to differently and that slight difference is captured through neurophysiological measures. This study used EEG in combination with Galvanic Skin Response to monitor viewers' responses.

The EEG essentially provides correlations between brain activity and behaviour. This correlation can be used for prediction as well. fMRI in contrast can be used to detect causation by itself.

From a brand perspective, EEG is an effective tool to measure consumer reactions to the brand and brand experiences. From neuroscience, we can connect the activations in particular areas of the brain to particular emotions, an integral part of all branding as brands try to build up affect and the relationship dimensions.

4. **Facial coding:** The method does exactly what its name suggests. When exposed to visual or other

sensory stimuli, our reaction is also expressed through our faces, which in turn reflects our emotions. We have seen that emotions play a huge role in decision-making, therefore, through a webcam-based experiment that uses facial coding software to discern different emotions, one can understand responses to the stimulus in perhaps the most convenient and cheapest way available. When it was used along with an EEG, a popular study concluded that facial coding methods could be depended upon to understand emotional responses to stimuli.[444]

5. **Galvanic Skin Response:** GSR meters measure the change in skin conductance on the palms of our hands when we are emotionally aroused. Unconscious emotions (both the valance and the magnitude), especially fear, anger, etc., are reflected in the sweat on the palm, which changes the skin conductance and which can be measured by the GSR meter. This method is used to measure the level of emotional response to a stimulus. GSR can measure the magnitude of the emotion but not the valence; however, it is possible sometimes to infer the valence from the stimuli. GSR is inexpensive to procure and use and does not require a high level of skills.

Table 1 below provides a brief comparison of the methods discussed.

**Table 1: Comparison of different neuro methods**

| | fMRI | EEG | Eye tracking | Facial coding | GSR |
|---|---|---|---|---|---|
| Level of detail/depth | Very high | High | Moderate | Moderate-Low | Low |
| Cost/time investment | Very High | High | Low | Moderate | Low |
| Expertise required | Very High | High | Low | Moderate | Low |
| Participants' compliance | Very Low | Low | Very High | High | Very High |
| Allowance for context | Very Low | Low | Very High | Moderate | High |
| Cost (setup + per-participant - ballpark) | 500$/hr + 100$/subject | 1000–3000$ | 500–1000$ | 2000–3000$ | 100$ |

For studying healthy humans, the three most widely used methods are magnetoencephalography (MEG) and EEG, the aforementioned fMRI and positron emission tomography (PET). A common feature of these methods is that they measure brain activity indirectly. MEG and EEG capture electromagnetic effects of neuronal activity across large areas of the brain that propagate through the scalp and have excellent temporal resolution in the milliseconds, but poor spatial resolution. In contrast, fMRI captures oxygenation effects of neuronal activation on blood flow and has superior spatial resolution (in the order of mm) but poorer temporal resolution, in the order of seconds. PET, which uses radioisotopes to label molecules in the brain, has poor temporal and spatial resolution but can detect specific neurotransmitters of interest. Transcranial Magnetic Stimulation is a tool that can be used to deactivate a particular part of the brain for periods between thirty minutes to three hours to conduct brain response tests for comparison when the particular part of the brain is inactive.

In commercial applications, EEG is currently the most popular method, largely due to its being relatively less expensive. In contrast, fMRI, which is widely used and more popular in scientific and clinical use, is less often used in marketing and other business-related applications. PET, TMS and MEG are used more in clinical settings because they are invasive and not yet accepted for use in commercial settings for business research applications.

## 2. Using Neuro Tools to Improve Brand Management

What are neuromarketing tools primarily used for? The main uses, actual and potential, as of today, are as follows:

1. Evaluation of different marketing interventions (advertising executions, pricing, packaging, sales pitches, etc.) in the brain of the customer; which alternative works better?
2. Neural correlates of brand attributes
3. Evaluation of the different drivers of a brand decision
4. Brand diagnosis
5. Predictions

Of these, the first two are being used commercially, the first more than the second. The third and the fourth are largely in the research phase in academic institutions with limited commercial use at the time of writing of this book. The fifth is just taking its first steps in academic research settings with still some distance to get robust results in the field.

### Consider Some Examples

The idea of a 'brand personality'—attributing human-like characteristics to the brand (e.g., sincere, competent, rugged)—is influential in shaping branding strategies (on which billions are spent). Traditionally, brand personality has been measured by a self-report scale (see critiques of the conceptual validity of brand personality), yet whether consumers really relate brands to personality traits is unclear. Ming Hsu and his team's fMRI study found evidence that brands that share similar personality traits activate similar neural patterns in the brain. This somewhat 'validates' the concept of brand personality—it does indeed make sense for brand managers to focus their communications on relating their brand to distinct human traits.

Using N200 wave outputs, groups working with Dino Levy and with Ryan Webb found neural activity in a passive product-viewing task that predicted which products were later chosen by the participants. The portability of EEG as a neurometric tool also allows for the study of consumers 'in the wild', e.g., using a technique called inter-brain correlations to measure the extent to which consumers' brains are 'in sync' while watching movie trailers in a cinema. A study by Samuel Barnett and Moran Cerf predicted the recall of those trailers after six months and average weekly ticket sales.

Building a brand is about the customer's experience with the brand. In the in-store context, neuro tools can contribute strongly to how to design the point of sale and in-store experience—online or offline—with portable devices. For online stores and, more generally, website optimization, eye tracking plus AI-enhanced attention models have been the method of choice to capture attention and engagement. Similarly, for brick-and-mortar store design, understanding the customer's attention patterns using mobile eye trackers seemed to be the most appropriate application. Ikea's store design, for example, is a classic application of key brain operating principles (BOP#1, BOP#2 and BOP#3), as are their promotional messages to their customers.

Interestingly, however, for the design of grocery stores, Ferrero's Shopper Neuroscience Unit also applied fNIRS and EEG to capture emotional responses to, for example, different types of store lighting. Along those lines, outside the area of typical business activities, they also surveyed interior designers and architects using EEG to improve the aesthetics of rooms and spaces. The key in the case of online and offline store optimization is to complement neuromarketing research with field experiments and A/B testing.

AI (Artificial Intelligence), AR (Augmented Reality) and VR (Virtual Reality) are unboxing newer methods that can be used to gain insight into the consumer brain. One can combine these tools with different neuro tools to enhance insights. Eye tracking is already using VR to accomplish this goal. The emergence of 5G is only going to increase the utilization of AR and VR when every ordinary person owns a mobile phone. Lenskart, an e-commerce site for eyewear, for example, uses the simple technique of screening your face and then augmenting it with the eyewear of your choice, which allows a consumer to better visualize their look! This 3D try-on is only the beginning of the exploration of AR. AR can, therefore, soon also be utilized to study consumer experience in a completely different way.

Other potential innovations could be an improvement in the imaging segment that could allow better real time data[445] to be captured and analysed or a decrease in the size of a typical fMRI or MEG machine manifold—perhaps, innovations that can allow analysis of active consumer participation while an imaging machine is at work.

The evaluation of different drivers of a brand decision involves the study of decision-making with respect to a brand using tools such as fMRI. For example, research suggests that when consumers buy a weak brand (in direct comparison to a strong brand with equivalent attributes), then there is activation of the anterior cingulate cortex, which is known to be involved in regret and conflict resolution.[446] The same study also indicates that relative to when choosing the strong brand, the DLPFC (a centre for reasoning and logic) has a higher level of activation in the brain, than when the customer chooses the weaker brand. Further studies like this would need to be conducted to make robust predictive models that allow a path to be shown between an external stimulus (advertisement, packaging, WOM, user experience) on one hand, brain activation on the other and the final customer action as the final outcome. As we saw earlier, Berns and Moore (2012)[447] showed that the individual neural responses (in the orbitofrontal cortex [OFC] and nucleus accumbens [NAcc]) to the songs in their initial study could be used to predict purchase decisions by the general population assessed via the total number of units sold several years later. To make this result more robust, we should consider triangulating different studies that could lead to interesting and even more predictive models.

## 3. Fitting Neuroscience and Neuromarketing into the Organizational Process

With abundant evidence of its usage, it is only valid to ask how a company can fit neuro tools in their organizational structure to improve branding strategies. It would appear suitable to explore the buy, build and borrow options here because at this point in time, there is no template that can be applied across firms and sectors. Interestingly enough, Facebook has explored all these options.

a. **Buy:** GSK, P&G, Unilever, Deloitte, BMW and Mondelez International use this approach towards neuroscience and buy their equipment from iMotions, a global consumer neuroscience firm that also sells exceptional items like eye tracking glasses, GSR wristbands and EEG headbands. This action would require hiring people skilled in understanding the process of conducting a neuroscience study, which would involve the ability to analyse related data and to understand it. Some methodologies, like using a facial coding module and implicit response testing, may only require re-skilling of the existing market and brand research team. Another 'buy' option could be to acquire independent labs or small consumer neuroscience firms. Facebook, for example, acquired an AI start-up which uses methods based on facial analysis programming to understand human emotions.

b. **Build:** Multi-millionaire companies can even opt to develop a research centre devoted to understanding consumer behaviour. Facebook, in 2017, made waves by announcing an intention to open such a centre to understand user interaction with advertisements.[448]

c. **Borrow:** Collaboration is, perhaps, one of the most realized options of all. Many consumer neuroscience and behaviour companies have sprung up in the past decade that are up for hire. Many times, university and independent research labs accept corporate propositions to understand the company's brand. Facebook commissioned a study at NeuroFocus, a Berkeley-based firm, to understand and compare consumer reactions to Facebook, the *New York Times* and Yahoo's interface.[449] Smaller companies like Ghadi detergent bar in India have begun using the findings from neuroscience to develop neuroscience-based interventions in marketing communications and packaging. Academic institutions like Duke University, Stanford University, Indian Institute of Management Ahmedabad and Imperial College London have collaborated with firms on projects of mutual interest.

In existing marketing organizations, it is possible to set up a small unit to explore the uses of neuro tools for brand management.

Smaller firms can start with collaborations with neuro firms. Many large firms (especially consumer goods MNCs, automotive firms and global pharma) are already using neuro tools extensively.

## 4. Examples of Neuromarketing Firms and their Approaches

The abundance and range of the available neuromarketing tools imply that there's something in it for every kind of company, whether big or small, whether one with a billion-dollar evaluation or one with a more modest estimation. Companies like Coca-Cola, Pepsi, Hyundai, Daimler, Google, the Weather Channel and eBay have, in the past, utilized these tools.[450,451] Hyundai, for example, studied the EEG results of subjects experiencing a prototype of a car and did analysis to make changes to the car. eBay's Paypal realized that speed mattered more to people than security and safety and as a result, their ad campaigns shifted their focus towards speed. Pepsi's neuroscientific study concluded that matte beige bags of Frito-Lay chips didn't trigger the anterior cingulate cortex—the centre engaged in making us feel guilty[452]—whereas the shiny bags do. This led them to shift to shiny bags for packaging in the US!

Others have opted to hire neuromarketing and consumer behaviour firms to aid them. For example, Vodafone, Spotify, NBC, Booking.com, Pinterest, Google, Tesco, etc. are some of the clients of a Danish neuro firm called Neurons Inc., founded by Dr Thomas Z. Ramsøy, a leading consumer neuroscientist.[453] Indian Railways have used the services of finalmile.in, a boutique consulting firm that uses inputs from neuroscience to generate interventions in the field.

Table 2 below provides a list of companies and the tools that they have used and for what purpose. As we can see, quite a few firms offer services that are related to branding.

**Table 2: Companies Offering Neuro-Tools Based Services**

| COMPANIES (COUNTRY OF HQ) | SERVICES | METHODS |
|---|---|---|
| Alpha One (Netherlands) | TV commercials, static posts/ads, packaging, branding and user experiences customer journey and product usability | EEG, fMRI, eye tracking, AI-based eye tracking |
| Bitbrain (Spain) | Branding, packaging, digital surroundings, website design, gaming and entertainment | EEG, Virtual Reality, eye tracking |
| BlackBox (Slovenia) | Branding, packaging, pricing, advertising, website design | EEG, eye tracking |
| Brain Impact (Belgium) | Product development, fragrance testing, shopper experience, advertising and branding | fMRI, EEG, Virtual Reality, eye tracking |
| Brainsights (Canada) | Analyse and advise on advertising, branding, campaign effectiveness and concept creation | EEG, eye tracking, SCR |
| Brain Intelligence (China) | Advertising, product usability and games | EEG, eye tracking, SCR |
| Brain Research Innovation (Korea) | Advertising, shopper journey, new product development, branding and pricing strategy | EEG, eye tracking, SCR, Implicit Association Test |
| Buyer Brain (UK) | Customer loyalty, customer satisfaction, virtual shopper journey, branding and packaging and employee engagement | Eye tracking, EEG, Virtual Reality, Implicit Association Test |
| Buyology (USA) | Advertising, packaging design, concept creation and branding strategy | EEG, fMRI, eye tracking, Implicit Association Test |
| Emoreader (Turkey) | Analyse and advise on branding and advertising | EEG |
| Entropik Tech (India) | Packaging, advertising, product development and user experience | EEG, eye tracking, FAR, AI-assisted eye tracking |
| Forebrain (Brazil) | Product development, packaging design, branding, advertising, user experience | EEG, eye tracking, fMEG, ECG, EEG, Saliva Analysis |

| COMPANIES (COUNTRY OF HQ) | SERVICES | METHODS |
|---|---|---|
| Gamma Research (Georgia) | Packaging design, pricing, value proposition, and shelf display | FAR, EEG, eye tracking |
| ICN Agency (Portugal) | Branding, shopper experience and sensory marketing | EEG, SCR, eye tracking, FAR |
| Incore (Germany) | Branding and concept creation | fMRI, EEG, Implicit Association Test |
| Ipsos (Global) | Branding strategy, new product development, advertising, customer experiences, corporate reputation, social research, market predictive analysis | EEG, FAR, eye tracking, Biometrics (e.g. SCR, HR), Virtual Reality |
| Kantar Emor (Estonia) | Branding and advertising | EEG, eye tracking, SCR |
| Neural Sense (South Africa) | Shopper journey, website usability, shelf display, branding and product development | Eye tracking, Virtual Reality, FAR, fEMG, EEG, NIRS, SCR |
| Neurotrend (Singapore) | TV commercials, static posts/ads, packaging, branding and user experiences | Eye-tracking, EEG, Biometrics (e.g. SCR) |
| Neurons Inc (Denmark) | Branding strategy, new product development, advertising, customer experiences, in-store design | fMRI, EEG, eye tracking, FAR, SCR |
| Nielsen Consumer Neuroscience (Global) | Advertising, positioning, packaging and shelf layout, media, product development | Eye tracking, EEG, FAR |
| Netvalue S.M. (Greece) | Advertising | |
| Promosapiens (Croatia) | Advertising, concept creation, user experience | EEG, eye tracking, FAR |
| The Sixth W (Italy) | Packaging, advertising, product usability and branding | EEG, eye tracking, SCR |
| Neurons Inc. (India) | Packaging, advertising, branding | EEG, eye tracking, SCR |
| Finalmile.in (India, US) | Packaging, branding, advertising | Micro interventions based on neuro research done by others. |

With these large number of providers of neuromarketing-related services, clearly, a large number of client firms are using neuro tools.

Figure 2 below provides a sense of the firms in various sectors that are using neuro insights and neuro tools in their marketing and branding.

**Figure 2**
**Sectoral Use of Neuro Insight Tools**

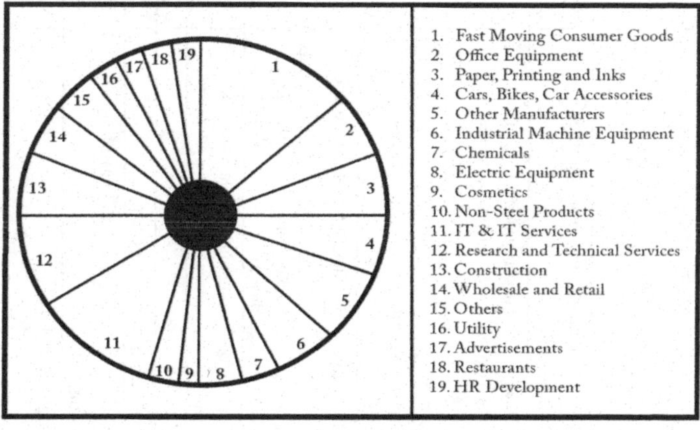


***Source:** NTT Data Institute of Management Consulting. Inc., Japan.*

## 5. Putting it all Together

As a manager, one is always concerned about the ROI of the marketing effort. Are neuro tools worth it given the expenses that one can incur, depending on the tool used?

Consider the following:

- Although the single unit cost of collecting neuro data is higher than traditional methods (like surveys), much neuromarketing research collects multiple data points per consumer, increasing their statistical power, thus requiring a smaller sample size. Neuro insights can also be more granular. Compared to a typical market research survey that requires 1000 respondents, a neuro-based effort may need only fifty respondents.
- Less costly alternatives such as eye tracking, SCR, portable EEG and facial affect encoding can be applied in more ecologically valid real-world settings (e.g., wearable eyeglasses in a retail store).
- Portable EEG and SCR devices, and user-friendly analysis packages, have been developed to facilitate the use of neuro data by firms, which often lack the technical expertise and resources.
- It would probably not make sense for smaller companies at this point to buy and maintain fMRI scanners (and more esoteric machines like PET and TMS, which are invasive in nature), but collaborations between firms and research institutes could lead to a win-win, as Ferrero has demonstrated.
- Neuro tools can be used not only to gain more granular customer insights but can also be used to make predictions about customer behaviour—at least in the six to twelve-month time frames, at a higher level of accuracy.
- Most large firms across the world in the consumer goods and automotive industries are already using

different neuro tools. COVID-19 has accelerated the use of associated tools and the need to understand how consumer brains work.

- As the cost of using neuro tools decreases, more firms will naturally start choosing to deploy neuro tools—to begin with, perhaps as a supplement.

In summary, neuro tools are a new toolbox that is available to brand marketers and can enhance accuracy of insights and predictive power by up to 20 per cent over the current methods that are available to marketers. Like all methods, however, it is important to apply it correctly. A lot of marketing research, and a lot of marketing effort gets a bad name because of poor conceptualization and execution. The same applies to neuroscience, neuro tools and their application to improve brand management practices. Neuro tools that are now available to brand marketers, hopefully, will not fall into the same category. Like any other tool, the success of neuro tools for brand management will be a function of its skilful and appropriate usage.

# Acknowledgements

This book is the result of contributions of so many people that it is not possible to list all of them. But I would like to especially mention and place on record my thanks to B.S. Meghana and Paridhi Kothari who helped with the sourcing and drafting of some of the material, Varuna M. Joshi for helping with the diagrams and figures, Tara Tiwari for making sure that the citations were done accurately, and my editors Manish Kumar and Ralph Rebello, who kept pushing me to move the project forward.

# Notes

1. https://www.livemint.com/Companies/1JKHsutTXLWtTcVwdIDg0H/The-Maggi-ban-How-Indias-favourite-twominute-noodles-lost.html
2 https://timesofindia.indiatimes.com/india/Nestle-seeks-Supreme-Court-nod-to-destroy-550-tonnes-of-Maggi-Noodles/articleshow/54448434.cms
3 https://www.abplive.in/india-news/delhi-banned-maggi-being-sold-in-black-price-hiked-by-1000-per-cent-21208
4 https://economictimes.indiatimes.com/how-maggis-aww-inspiring-comeback-campaign-came-about/articleshow/49058907.cms?from=mdr
5 https://www.firstpost.com/india/wemissyoutoo-maggi-returns-the-love-with-a-new-advertisement-2407054.html
6 https://www.business-standard.com/article/companies/nestle-comes-up-with-miss-you-maggi-ads-115082600052_1.html
7 http://www.livemint.com/Companies/rC595TZsFFMfovci6E6kEN/Nestl-sells-45-mn-Maggi-packs-within-two-weeks-of-relaunch.html
8 http://www.moneycontrol.com/news/business/companies/maggi-noodles-has-cornered-60-market-share-nestle-india-cmd-947536.html
9 https://www.businessinsider.in/business/corporates/news/marico-takes-on-nestle-with-saffola-instant-noodles-to-rival-the-iconic-maggi-brand-in-india/articleshow/81109314.cms
10 McClure et al., 'Neural Correlates Of Behavioral Preference For Culturally Familiar Drinks', *Neuron*, 44(2), (2004): 379–87.

11 https://www.ifrs.org/-/media/feature/meetings/2018/june/iasb/ap18d-gi.pdf
12 https://www.microsoft.com/investor/reports/ar17/index.html
13 www.articlesfactory.com/articles/.../the-value-of-brand-building-to-a-business.html
14 www.caribbeanheadhunters.com/building-your-brand
15 Philiastides, M.G., and Ratcliff, R., 'Influence of Branding on Preference-Based Decision Making', *Psychol Sci.* 24(7), (2013): 1208–15.
16 https://www.thehindubusinessline.com/info-tech/oneplus-captures-36-market-share-in-premium-smartphone-segment-in-q4/article26129739.ece
17 Knutson et al. 2007.
18 https://www.wired.com/2016/06/oneplus-grows-goes-invite-free-next-phone/
19 https://tech.economictimes.indiatimes.com/news/mobile/oneplus-renews-its-exclusive-partnership-with-amazon-india/55042668
20 https://www.livemint.com/technology/gadgets/oneplus-7-pro-becomes-the-fastest-selling-ultra-premium-smartphone-on-amazon-1558615161656.html
21 Keller, K.L.. 'Conceptualizing, Measuring, and Managing Customer-Based Brand Equity', *Journal of Marketing*, Vol. 57, No. 1 (Jan. 1993): 1–22.
22 Grubb et al., 'Neuroanatomy Accounts for Age-Related Changes in Risk Preferences', *Nat Commun* 7, (2016): 13822.
23 Keller, K.L.. 'Conceptualizing, Measuring, and Managing Customer-Based Brand Equity', *Journal of Marketing*, Vol. 57, No. 1 (Jan. 1993): 1–22.
24 Ibid.
25 Philiastides, M.G., and Ratcliff, R., 'Influence of Branding on Preference-Based Decision Making', *Psychol Sci.* 24(7), (2013): 1208–15.
26 McClure et al., 'Neural Correlates Of Behavioral Preference For Culturally Familiar Drinks', *Neuron*, 44(2), (2004): 379–87.
27 http://citeseerx.ist.psu.edu/viewdoc/download?doi=10.1.1.330.9744&rep=rep1&type=pdf///https://onlinelibrary.wiley.com/doi/epdf/10.1002/cb.253///https://www.annualreviews.org/doi/full/10.1146/annurev.psych.60.110707.163604

28 Esch et al., 'Brands on the Brain: Do Consumers Use Declarative Information or Experienced Emotions to Evaluate Brands? Journal of Consumer Psychology, 22, (2012): 75–85; https://www.sciencedirect.com/science/article/pii/S1057740810001002 /// Santos et al., Journal of Consumer Behavior on neural correlates of brands, (2012).

29 http://www.strategynewmedia.com/why-is-branding-important/

30 Wang et al., 'Emotional Graphic Cigarette Warning Labels Reduce the Electrophysiological Brain Response to Smoking Cues', *Addict Biol.*, 20, (2013): 368–76.

31 Knutson et al. (2007).

32 Agarwal, S., and Dutta, T., 'Neuromarketing and Consumer Neuroscience: Current Understanding and the Way Forward', *Decision*, 42 (4), (2015): 457–62.

33 Lukatela, K. and Swadlow, H. A. Neocortex. In The Corsini Encyclopedia of Psychology. (2010)

34 Catani, M., Dell'acqua, F., and de Schotten, T.M., 'A Revised Limbic System Model for Memory, Emotion and Behaviour', *Neuroscience and Biobehavioral Reviews*, Vol. 37(8), (2013): 1724-37.

35 Sinek, S. Transcript of 'How Great Leaders Inspire Action', *Ted.* (Retrieved from https://www.ted.com/talks/simon_sinek_how_great_leaders_inspire_action/transcript?language=en#t-314180).

36 Brain, S., 'Human Brain Statistics', *Statistic Brain*. (Retrieved from http://www.statisticbrain.com/human-brain-statistics/).

37 Pepperell, R., 'Consciousness as a Physical Process Caused by the Organization of Energy in the Brain', *Frontiers in Psychology*, 9 (2018). (Retrieved from https://www.frontiersin.org/articles/10.3389/fpsyg.2018.02091/full).

38 Haider et al., 'Synaptic and Network Mechanisms of Sparse and Reliable Visual Cortical Activity during Nonclassical Receptive Field Stimulation', *Neuron*, 65, (2010): 107–21.

39 Bos, M.W., Dijksterhuis, A., and van Baaren, R., 'Food for Thought? Trust Your Unconscious When Energy Is Low', *Journal of Neuroscience, Psychology, and Economics*, 5(2), (2012): 124–30.

40 Rasmussen et al., 'Neural Basis of the Rescorla–Wagner Model', *Proceedings of the National Academy of Sciences*, 112 (45), (2015): 14060–65.

41 Kotler et al., *Marketing*, 9th ed., (2013): 171, Australia: Pearson.

42 Agarwal, S., and Dutta, T., 'Neuromarketing and Consumer Neuroscience: Current Understanding and the Way Forward', *Decision*, 42 (4), (2015): 457–62.

43 Ibid. (Retrieved from https://link.springer.com/article/10.1007/s40622-015-0113-1).

44 Zurawicki, L., 'Neuromarketing, Exploring the Brain of the Consumer', *Springer*, Berlin, (2010).

45 Kotler et al., *Marketing*, 9th ed., (2013): 171, Australia: Pearson.

46 Wood 2015.

47 Gilovich, T., Tversky, A., and Vallone, R. 'The Hot Hand in Basketball: On the Misperception of Random Sequences'. *Cognitive Psychology*. 17 (3), (1985): 295–314. doi:10.1016/0010-0285(85)90010-6.

48 Davis, M., 'The Role of the Amygdala in Fear and Anxiety', *Annual Review of Neuroscience*, 15:1, (1992): 353-75.

49 Preuschoff, K., Quartz, S.R., and Bossaerts, P., 'Human Insula Activation Reflects Risk Prediction Errors As Well As Risk', *Journal of Neuroscience*, 28 (11), (2008): 2745–52.

50 This is where Kahneman's concept of System 1 and System 2 comes in. Our thought processes can be categorized into two based on the way our brain processes them. System 2 meticulously processes inputs for a well-thought-of execution, therefore, requires a lot of cognitive attention. System 1, on the other hand, is the automatic part of our processing in the brain—quick, reflexive and not very accurate. It is System 1 that learns by association.

51 Kaya, N. and Epps, H.H., 'Relationship between Color and Emotion: A Study of College Students', *College Student Journal*, Vol. 38, Issue 3, (2004): 396–405. 10p. 3 Charts.

52 Gnambs, T., Appel, M., Oeberst, A., 'Red Color and Risk-Taking Behavior in Online Environments', *PLoS ONE* 10(7), (2015): e0134033.

53 Wexner, L.B., 'The Degree to Which Colors (Hues) Are Associated with Mood-Tones', *The Journal of Applied Psychology*, Vol. 38, No. 6, 432–35.

54 Kaya, N. and Epps, H.H., 'Relationship between Color and Emotion: A Study of College Students', *College Student Journal*, Vol. 38, Issue 3, (2004): 396–405. 10p. 3 Charts.

55 Ibid.

56 Gaines, K., and Curry, Z., 'The Inclusive Classroom: The Effects of Color on Learning and Behavior', *Journal of Family & Consumer Sciences Education*, 29(1), Spring/Summer (2011).

57 McClure et al., 'Neural Correlates Of Behavioral Preference For Culturally Familiar Drinks', *Neuron*, Vol. 44(2), (2004): 379–87; Schaeffer and Rotte, 'Favourite Brands as Cultural Objects Modulate Reward Circuit', *Neuroreport*, Vol. 18(2), (2007).

58 Buckner, R.L., 'The Role of the Hippocampus in Prediction and Imagination', *Annual Review of Psychology*, 61:1, (2010): 27–48.

59 Schultz, W., 'Dopamine Reward Prediction Error Coding', *Dialogues Clin. Neurosci.*, 18, (2016): 23–32.

60 Venkatraman et al., 'New Scanner Data for Brand Marketers: How Neuroscience Can Help Better Understand Differences in Brand Preferences', *Journal of Consumer Psychology*, 22 (1) (2012): 143–53.

61 Rizzolatti, G. and Craighero, L., 'The Mirror-Neuron System', *Annual Review of Neuroscience*, Vol. 27, (2004): 169-192. (Retrieved from https://www.annualreviews.org/doi/full/10.1146/annurev.neuro.27.070203.144230#_i5).

62 Preston, S.D., and de Waal, F.B.M. 'Empathy: Its Ultimate and Proximate Bases', (2001). (Retrieved from https://greatergood.berkeley.edu/images/uploads/Preston_dewaal2002.pdf).

63 Oberman, L.M., and Ramachandran, V.S., 'Reflections on the Mirror Neuron System: Their Evolutionary Functions Beyond Motor Representation', J.A. Pineda (ed.), 'Mirror Neuron Systems: The Role of Mirroring Processes in Social Cognition', (2009): 39-59. (Retrieved from https://link.springer.com/chapter/10.1007/978-1-59745-479-7_2).

64 Rizzolatti, G., and Craighero, L., 'The Mirror-Neuron System', *Annual Review of Neuroscience*, Vol. 27, (2004): 169–192. (Retrieved from https://www.annualreviews.org/doi/full/10.1146/annurev.neuro.27.070203.144230#_i5).

65 Stillman, T.F. and Baumeister, R.F., 'Uncertainty, Belongingness, and Four Needs for Meaning', *Psychological Inquiry*, 20:4, (2009): 249–251.

66 Lacoste-Badie, S., and Droulers, O., 'Advertising Memory: The Power of Neurons', *Journal of Neuroscience Psychology and Economics*, Vol.

7(4), (2014): 195–202. (Retrieved from: https://www.researchgate.net/publication/269154992_Advertising_Memory_The_Power_of_Mirror_Neurons).

67 McClure et al., 'Neural Correlates of Behavioral Preference for Culturally Familiar Drinks', *Neuron*, Vol. 44(2), (2004): 379–87.

68 Yoon et al., 'A Functional Magnetic Resonance Imaging Study of Neural Dissociations between Brand and Person Judgments', *Journal of Consumer Research*, Vol. 33, Issue 1, (2006): 31–40.

69 Plassmann et al., 'What Can Advertisers Learn from Neuroscience?', *International Journal of Advertising*, 26(2), 151–175

70 Plassmann, H., Kenning, P., and Ahlert, D., 'Why Companies Should Make Their Customers Happy: the Neural Correlates of Customer Loyalty', *NA—Advances in Consumer Research*, Vol. 34, Association for Consumer Research, (2007): 735-39.

71 Shiv, B., Yoon, C., 'Integrating Neurophysiological and Psychological Approaches: Towards an Advancement of Brand Insights', *Journal of Consumer Psychology*. 22 (1), (2012): 3–6.

72 Agarwal, S., and Dutta, T., 'Neuromarketing and Consumer Neuroscience: Current Understanding and the Way Forward', *Decision*, 42 (4), (2015): 457–62.

73 Venkatraman et al., 'New Scanner Data for Brand Marketers: How Neuroscience Can Help Better Understand Differences in Brand Preferences', *Journal of Consumer Psychology*, 22 (1) (2012): 143–53.

74 Erk et al., 'Cultural Objects Modulate Reward Circuitry', *Neuroreport*, Vol. 13(18), (2002):2499–503.

75 Kahneman, D., *Thinking Fast and Slow*, Penguin Books, (2012).

76 https://www.vesper.ai/blog/use-neuromarketing-increase-sales/

77 Soudry et al., 'Olfactory System and Emotion: Common Substrates', *European Annals of Otorhinolaryngology, Head and Neck Diseases*, Vol. 128, Issue 1, (2011): 18–23.

78 Herz, R.S., and Engen, T., ,Odor Memory: Review and Analysis', *Psychon. Bull. Rev.*, 3(3), (1993): 300-13.

79 Kleinfield, N.R., 'The Smell of Money', *The New York Times*, (1993). (Retrieved from https://www.nytimes.com/1992/10/25/style/the-smell-of-money.html).

80 Zaltman, G., 'How Customers Think: Essential Insights into the Mind of the Market', *Harvard Business School Press* (2003).

81 Crosby, L.A., and Zak, P.J., 'The Neuroscience of Brand Trust.' (Retrieved from https://www.ama.org/publications/MarketingNews/Pages/the-neuroscience-of-brand-trust.aspx).

82 https://www.coleyporterbell.com/how-neuroscience-can-help-to-build-your-brand-as-seen-in-campaign/

83 Lawrence et al., 'Changing Abilities in Recognition of Unfamiliar Face Photographs through Childhood and Adolescence: Performance on a Test of Non-Verbal Immediate Memory (Warrington Rmf) from 6 to 16 Years', *Journal of Neuropsychology*, 2, (2008): 27-45.

84 Kragel et al., 'Developmental Trajectories of Cortical–Subcortical Interactions Underlying the Evaluation of Trust in Adolescence', *Social Cognitive and Affective Neuroscience*, (2014). doi: 10.1093/scan/nsu050. (Retrieved from https://today.duke.edu/2014/03/teengut).

85 Soon et al., 'Unconscious Determinants of Free Decisions in the Human Brain', *Nature Neuroscience*, 11(5), (2008): 543–45.

86 Dolcos, I., and Dolcos, S., (2011), Shiv (2007), Knutson et al. (2007), Bechara and Damasio (1999), Soon et al. (2008); Author analysis.

87 Schultze-Kraft et al., 'The Point of No Return in Vetoing Self-Initiated Movements', *Proceedings of the National Academy of Sciences*, 113 (4), (2016): 1080–85. doi: 10.1073/pnas.1513569112. ISSN 0027-8424. PMC 4743787. PMID 26668390.

88 Kornhuber, H.H., and Deecke, L., 'Hirnpotentialänderungen bei Willkürbewegungen und Passiven Bewegungen des Menschen: Bereitschaftspotential und Reafferente Potentiale', *Pflügers Arch.* 284, (1965): 1–17. (Retrieved from https://link.springer.com/article/10.1007/BF00412364).

89 Damasio, A.R. *Descartes' Error: Emotion, Reason, and the Human Brain*. Penguin (2005).

90 Dolcos, I., and Dolcos, S., (2011), Shiv (2007), Knutson et al. (2007), Bechara and Damasio (1999).

91 Shah, A.K., and Oppenheimer, D.M., 'Heuristics Made Easy: An Effort-Reduction Framework', *Psychological Bulletin*, 134(2), (2008): 207.

92 Nicholls et al., *From Neuron to Brain*, (5th ed.), Sinauer Associates.

93 Pessoa, L., and Adolphs, R., 'Emotion Processing and the Amygdala: From a 'Low Road' to 'Many Roads' of Evaluating Biological Significance', *Nature Reviews Neuroscience*. Vol. 11(11), (2010): 773–83.

94 Voss et al., 'A Closer Look at the Hippocampus and Memory', *Trends Cognitive Sciences*, 21(8), (2017): 577–88.

95 Grabenhorst, F., and Rolls, E.T., 'Value, Pleasure and Choice in the Ventral Prefrontal Cortex', *Trends in Cognitive Sciences*, 15(2), (2011): 56–67.

96 FitzGerald, T.H., Seymour, B., and Dolan, R.J., 'The Role of Human Orbitofrontal Cortex in Value Comparison for Incommensurable Objects', *The Journal of Neuroscience*, 29(26), (2009): 8388–95.

97 Niv and Montague, *Neuroeconomics*, Chapter 22—Theoretical and Empirical Studies of Learning, (2009). (Retrieved from https://www.sciencedirect.com/science/article/pii/B9780123741769000221).

98 D'Ardenne et al., 'BOLD Responses Reflecting Dopaminergic Signals in the Human Ventral Tegmental Area', *Science*, 319(5867), (2008): 1264–67. (Retrieved from https://www.ncbi.nlm.nih.gov/pubmed/18309087).

99 Pessiglione et al., 'Dopamine-dependent Prediction Errors Underpin Reward-Seeking Behaviour in Humans', *Nature*. 442(7106), (2006): 1042–5.

100 Carter et al., 'Activation in the VTA and Nucleus Accumbens Increases in Anticipation of Both Gains and Losses', *Frontiers in Behavioral Neuroscience*, (3), (2009).

101 Preuschoff, K., Quartz, S.R., and Bossaerts, P., 'Human Insula Activation Reflects Risk Prediction Errors As Well As Risk', *Journal of Neuroscience*, 28 (11), (2008): 2745–52.

102 Mano, H., 'Risk-taking, Framing Effects, and Affect', *Organizational Behavior and Human Decision Processes*, 57, (1994): 38–58.

103 Vuilleumier, P. et al., 'Effects of Attention and Emotion on Face Processing in the Human Brain: An Event-Related fMRI Study', *Neuron*, 30(3), (2001): 829-41.

104 Jullisson, E.A., Karlsson, N., Garling, T., 'Weighing the past and the future in decision making', *European Journal of Cognitive Psychology*, 17(4), (2005): 561–75. doi: 10.1080/09541440440000159.

105 Camina, E. and Francisco Güell, F. The Neuroanatomical, Neurophysiological and Psychological Basis of Memory: Current Models and Their Origins', *Frontiers in Pharmacology*. 8.438, (2017).

106 Ibid.

107 Graybiel, A.M., 'Habits, Rituals, and the Evaluative Brain', *Annual Review of Neuroscience*. 31:1, (2008): 359–87.

108 Dolcos, F., LaBar, K.S., and Cabeza, R., 'Remembering One Year Later: Role of the Amygdala and the Medial Temporal Lobe Memory System in Retrieving Emotional Memories', *Proceedings of the National Academy of Sciences of the USA*, 102(7), (2005): 2626–31.

109 Stuss, D.T. and Knight, 'R.T. Principles of Frontal Lobe Function', *Chapter 6 Physiology of Executive Functions*, Oxford University Press (2013).

110 Fogassi, L. and Luppino, G., 'Motor Functions of the Parietal Lobe', *Current Opinion in Neurobiolog*, Vol. 15, Issue 6, (2005): 626-31.

111 Kiernan J.A., 'Anatomy of the Temporal Lobe', *Epilepsy Res Treat*. 2012.176157

112 Ibid.

113 Dickerson, B.C. & Eichenbaum, H. The Episodic Memory System: Neurocircuitry and Disorders', Neuropsychopharmacology volume 35, pages 86–104 (2010)

114 Rajmohan V., Mohandas E. (2007). The limbic system', Indian Journal of Psychiatry 49(2) 132–139

115 Moreno-Jiménez et al., 'Adult Hippocampal Neurogenesis is Abundant in Neurologically Healthy Subjects and Drops Sharply In Patients with Alzheimer's Disease', *Nat. Med.*, 25(4), 554–560 (2019)

116 Buchanan, T.W., Tranel, D., Adolphs, R. A., 'Specific Role for the Human Amygdala in Olfactory Memory', *Learn Mem*. 10(5), (2003): 319-25.

117 The Human Memory—Types of Memory', (2020). (Retrieved from http://www.human-memory.net/types.html).

118 Schacter, D., Addis, D., and Buckner, R., 'Remembering the Past to Imagine the Future: the Prospective Brain', *Nature Reviews Neuroscience*, Vol. 8, (2007): 657–61.

119 Ranganath, C., 'Working Memory for Visual Objects: Complementary Roles of Inferior Temporal, Medial Temporal, and Prefrontal Cortex', *Neuroscience*, 139(1), (2006): 277–89.

120 Funahashi, S., 'Working Memory in the Prefrontal Cortex', *Brain Science*, 7(5), (2017): 49.

121 Jensen, O., and Lisman, J.E., 'Hippocampal Sequence-Encoding Driven by a Cortical Multi-Item Working Memory Buffer', *Trends Neuroscience*, 28(2), (2005): 67-72.

122 Ledoux, Scholarpedia, 2(7), (2007): 1806.

123 Sara 2000.

124 Nader, K., Schafe, G.E., and Le Doux, J.E., 'Fear Memories Require Protein Synthesis in the Amygdala for Reconsolidation after Retrieval', *Nature*, 406, (2000): 722–26.

125 Carter, C. S., and Porges, S.W., 'The Biochemistry of Love: An Oxytocin Hypothesis', *EMBO*, Rep. 14, (2013): 12–16.

126 Sanburn, J., 'The Ad that Changed Super Bowl Commercials Forever', *TIME* (2016). (Retrieved from https://time.com/3685708/super-bowl-ads-vw-the-force/).

127 Fürst et al., 'The Neuropeptide Oxytocin Modulates Consumer Brand Relationships', *Sci.* Rep 5, (2015): 14960.

128 Carter, C. S., and Porges, S.W., 'The Biochemistry of Love: An Oxytocin Hypothesis', *EMBO*, Rep. 14, (2013): 12–16.

129 Shiv, B., and Fedorikhin, A., 'Heart and Mind in Conflict: The Interplay of Affect and Cognition in Consumer Decision Making', *Journal of Consumer Research*, Vol. 26, No. 3, (1999): 278–92.

130 Rottenstreich, Y., Sood, S., and Brenner, L., 'Feeling and Thinking in Memory-Based versus Stimulus-Based Choices', *Journal of Consumer Research*, Vol. 33, No. 4 (2007): 461–69.

131 Ibid.

132 Sam M., 'Cadbury Dairy Milk Shubh Arambh Kuch Meetha Ho Jaaye', (2010). (Retrieved from https://www.youtube.com/watch?v=aHSxhAVCiKY).

133 Campaign India, 'Cadbury's New Thought: "Shubh Aarambh"', (2010). (Retrieved from http://www.campaignindia.in/article/cadburys-new-thought-shubh-aarambh/412460).

134 Shiv, B., and Fedorikhin, A., 'Spontaneous Versus Controlled Influences of Stimulus-Based Affect on Choice Behavior', *Organizational Behavior and Human Decision Processes*, 87, (2002): 342–70.

135 Kahneman, D., *Thinking Fast and Slow*. Penguin Books (2012).

136 Dolcos, F., LaBar, K.S., and Cabeza, R., 'The Memory-Enhancing Effect of Emotion: Functional Neuroimaging Evidence', in B. Uttl, N. Ohta, and A.L. Siegenthaler (eds.), Memory and Emotion: Interdisciplinary Perspectives, Malden, MA: Blackwell Publishing, (2006): 107–33.

137 Dolcos, F., Iordan, A.D., and Dolcos, S., 'Neural Correlates of Emotion–Cognition Interactions: A Review of Evidence from Brain Imaging Investigations', *Journal of Cognitive Psychology*, 23(6), (2011): 669–94.

138 Graybiel, A.M., 'Habits, Rituals, and the Evaluative Brain', *Annual Review of Neuroscience*, 31:1, (2008): 359–87.

139 Wood, W., and Rünger, D., 'Psychology of Habit', *Annual Review of Psychology*, 67:1, (2016): 289–314.

140 Doll, B.B., Simon, D.A., and Daw, N.D., 'The Ubiquity of Model-Based Reinforcement Learning', *Curr. Opin. Neurobiol.*, 22(6), (2012): 1075–8.

141 Wood, W., and Rünger, D., 'Psychology of Habit', *Annual Review of Psychology*, 67:1, (2016): 289–314.

142 Ibid.

143 Ibid.

144 Abraham, C., and Sheeran, P., 'Acting on Intentions: The Role of Anticipated Regret', *British Journal of Social Psychology*, 42(4), (2003): 495–511.

145 Sagi, A., and Friedland, N., 'The Cost of Richness: The Effect of the Size and Diversity of Decision Sets on Post-Decision Regret', *Journal of Personality and Social Psychology*, 93(4), (2007): 515–24. doi: 10.1037/0022-3514.93.4.515.

146 Ibid.

147 Botti, S., and Iyengar, S.S., 'The Psychological Pleasure and Pain of Choosing: When People Prefer Choosing at the Cost of Subsequent

Outcome Satisfaction', *Journal of Personality and Social Psychology*, 87(3), (2004): 312–26. doi: 10.1037/0022-3514.87.3.312.

148 Jullisson, E.A., Karlsson, N., and Garling, T., 'Weighing the Past and the Future in Decision Making', *European Journal of Cognitive Psychology*, 17(4), (2005): 561–75. DOI: 10.1080/09541440440000159.

149 Gilbert, D.T., and Ebert, J.E.J., 'Decisions and Revisions: The Affective Forecasting of Changeable Outcomes', *Journal of Personality and Social Psychology*, 82(4), (2002): 503–14. DOI: 10.1037/0022-3514.82.4.503.

150 Wood, S.L., 'Remote Purchase Environments: The Influence of Return Policy Leniency on Two-Stage Decision Process', *Journal of Marketing Research*, 38(2), (2001): 157–69.

151 Fessler, D.M.T., Pillsworth, E.G., and Flamson, T.J., 'Angry Men and Disgusted Women: An Evolutionary Approach to the Influence of Emotions on Risk Taking', *Organizational Behavior and Human Decision Processes*, 95, (2004): 107–23.

152 Wiltermuth, S.S., and Tiedens, L.Z., 'Incidental Anger and the Desire to Evaluate', *Organizational Behavior and Human Decision Processes*, 116, (2011): 55–65.

153 Han, S., Lerner, J.S., and Keltner, D., 'Feelings and Consumer Decision Making: The Appraisal–Tendency Framework', *Journal of Consumer Psychology*, 17(3), (2007): 158–68.

154 Raghunathan, R., and Pham, M.T., 'All Negative Moods Are Not Equal: Motivational Influences of Anxiety and Sadness on Decision Making', *Organizational Behavior and Human Decision Processes*, 79, (1999): 56–77.

155 Davidson et al., 'Depression: Perspectives from Affective Neuroscience', *Annual Review of Psychology*, 53, (2002): 545–74.

156 Shiv, B., 'Emotions, Decisions, and the Brain', *Journal of Consumer Psychology*, Vol. 17, Issue 3, (2007): 174–78.

157 Ibid.

158 Miller, E.K., and Cohen, J.D., 'An Integrative Theory of Prefrontal Cortex Function', *Annual Review of Neuroscience*, 24, (2001): 167–202.

159 Fishman, I., Ng, R., and Bellugi, U., 'Do Extraverts Process Social Stimuli Differently from Introverts?', *Cognitive Neuroscience*, 1, 2(2), (2011): 67–73.

160 Gullette, D.L., Lyons, M.A. Sexual sensation seeking, compulsivity, and HIV risk behaviors in college students', Journal of Community Health Nursing, 2005 22(1):47-60.

161 Lucas, R.E., and Diener, E., 'Understanding Extraverts' Enjoyment of Social Situations: The Importance of Pleasantness', *Journal of Personality and Social Psychology*, 81(2), (2001): 343–56.

162 Argyle, M. and Lu, L., 'The Happiness of Extraverts', *Personality and Individual Differences*, Vol. 11, Issue 10, (1990): 1011–17.

163 Lischetzke, T. and Eid, M., 'Why Extraverts Are Happier Than Introverts: The Role of Mood Regulation', *Journal of Personality*, Vol. 74, Issue 4, (2006).

164 Zhang, W.J., and Howell, R.T., 'Do Time Perspectives Predict Unique Variance in Life Satisfaction beyond Personality Traits?', *Personality and Individual Differences*, Vol. 50, Issue 8, (2011): 1261–66.

165 Bennington-Castro, J., 'The Science of What Makes an Introvert and an Extrovert', (2013). (Retrieved from http://io9.gizmodo.com/the-science-behind-extroversion-and-introversion-1282059791).

166 Canli T., and Amin Z., 'Neuroimaging of Emotion and Personality: Scientific Evidence and Ethical Considerations', *Brain and Cognition*, 50(3), (2002): 414–31; Canli et al., 'An fMRI Study of Personality Influences on Brain Reactivity to Emotional Stimuli', *Behavioral Neuroscience*, 115(1), (2001): 33–42.

167 Johnson et al., 'Cerebral Blood Flow and Personality: A Positron Emission Tomography Study', *Am J Psychiatry*, 156:2, (1999): 252–57.

168 Killgore et al., 'The Trait of Introversion-Extraversion Predicts Vulnerability to Sleep Deprivation', *J. Sleep Res.*, 16(4), (2007): 354–63.

169 Depue, R.A. and Fu, Y., 'On the Nature of Extraversion: Variation in Conditioned Contextual Activation of Dopamine-Facilitated Affective, Cognitive, and Motor Processes', *Frontiers in Human Neuroscience*, (2013).

170 Sahay, A., Sharma, N., and Mehta, K., 'Role of Affect and Cognition in Consumer Brand Relationship: Exploring Gender Differences in

an Emerging Economy Market Context', *Journal of Indian Business Research*, Vol. 4(1), (2012).

171 Koch et al., 'Gender Differences in the Cognitive Control of Emotion: An fMRI Study', *Neuropsychologia*, 45(12), (2007): 27744–54. (Retrieved from

172. https://www.sciencedirect.com/science/article/abs/pii/S0028393207001558?via%3Dihub).

173 Steve Forbes' quote. (Retrieved 5 October 2017 from http://www.azquotes.com/quote/1319841).

174 Holt, *How Brands Become Icons*, Harvard Business School Press (2004).

175 Fortune 2004.

176 Kay et al., 'God and the Government: Testing a Compensatory Control Mechanism for the Support of External Systems', *Journal of Personality and Social Psychology*, 95 (1), (2008): 18–35.

177 Aggarwal, P., and McGill, A.L., 'When Brands Seem Human, Do Humans Act Like Brands? Automatic Behavioural Priming Effects of Brand Anthropomorphism', *Journal of Consumer Research*, Vol. 39, Issue 2, (2012): 307–23.

178 Fournier, S., 'Consumers and Their Brands: Developing Relationship Theory in Consumer Research', *Journal of Consumer Research*, 24(4), (1998): 343–73.; Park, C.W., and Lessig, V.P., 'Familiarity and Its Impact on Consumer Decision Biases and Heuristics', *Journal of Consumer Research*, 8(2), (1981): 223–30; and Laroche et al., 'How Intangibility Affects Perceived Risk: The Moderating Role of Knowledge and Involvement', *Journal of Services Marketing*, 17(2), (2003): 122–40.

179 Santos et al., 'Neural Correlates of the Emotional and Symbolic Content of Brands: A Neuroimaging Study', *Journal of Consumer Behavior*, 11(1): (2012): 69–94.

180 This table builds on the works of Batra, R., Ahuvia, A., and Bagozzi, R.P., 'Brand Love', *Journal of Marketing*, Vol. 76, (2012): 1-16; and Fournier, S., 'Consumers and Their Brands: Developing Relationship Theory in Consumer Research', *Journal of Consumer Research*, 24(4), (1998): 343–73.

181 Fournier, S., 'Consumers and Their Brands: Developing Relationship Theory in Consumer Research', *Journal of Consumer Research*, 24(4), (1998): 343–73.

182 Fournier, S., 'Consumers and Their Brands: Developing Relationship Theory in Consumer Research', *Journal of Consumer Research*, 24(4), (1998): 343–73.; Park, C.W., and Lessig, V.P., 'Familiarity and Its Impact on Consumer Decision Biases and Heuristics', *Journal of Consumer Research*, 8(2), (1981): 223–30.

183 Email communication (14 September 2010,) with V. Kini, vice president, marketing, Global Juice, the Coca-Cola Company.

184 PepsiCo India. Press Releases. (Retrieved 12 November 2017 from http://www.pepsicoindia.co.in/media/Press-Releases/release_02_28_08.aspx).

185 Bhasin, H., 'What is Brand Ladder and How to Use It for Brand Building?' *Marketing91,* (17 December 2019). (Retrieved 12 November 2020 from http://www.marketing91.com/brand-ladder/).

186 LANDOR, 'Brands That Make You Love Them.' (Retrieved 16 November 2017 from http://landor.com/thinking/brands-that-make-you-love-them).

187 Aaker, J.L., 'Dimensions of Brand Personality.' *Journal of Marketing Research*, Vol. 34(3), (1997): 347–56.

188 Fournier, S., 'Consumers and Their Brands: Developing Relationship Theory in Consumer Research', *Journal of Consumer Research*, 24(4), (1998): 343–73.

189 Thomson et al., 'The Buy-in Benchmark: How Staff Understanding and Commitment Impact Brand and Business Performance', *Journal of Marketing Management*, Vol. 15. No. 8, (1999): 819–35.

190 Sahay, A. and Sharma, N., 'Brand Relationships and Switching Behaviour for Highly Used Products in Young Consumers', *Vikalpa,* (January–March 2010), Indian Institute of Management, Ahmedabad.

191 Ibid.

192 Fournier, S.. 'Consumers and Their Brands: Developing Relationship Theory In Consumer Research', *Journal of Consumer Research*, 24(4), (1998): 343–73.

193 Sahay, A. and Mathen, N., 'Hero Honda: Multisegment Positioning and Selling,' *IIMA Case (MAR418)*, (2010).

194 Sahay, A., Sharma, N., and Mehta, K., 'Gender Differences in Role of Affect and Cognition in Brand Relationships', *Journal of Indian Business Research*, 4(1), (2012): 36–60.

195 Kring, A.M., and Gordon, A.H., 'Sex Differences in Emotion: Expression, Experience and Physiology', *Journal of Personality and Social Psychology*, Vol. 74, No. 3, (1998): 686–703.

196 https://en.wikipedia.org/wiki/Diderot_effect

197 Schouten, J., and McAlexander, J. H., 'Subcultures of Consumption: An Ethnography of the New Bikers', *Journal of Consumer Research*, Vol. 22(1), (1995).

198 Schembri, S., 'Reframing Brand Experience: The Experiential Meaning of Harley-Davidson', *Journal of Business Research*, 62(12), (2009): 1299–310.

199 Algesheimer, R., Dholakia, M., and Herrman, A., 'The Social Influence of Brand Community: Evidence from European Car Clubs', *Journal of Marketing*, Vol. 69(4), (2005).

200 Fournier, S., 'Consumers and Their Brands: Developing Relationship Theory in Consumer Research', *Journal of Consumer Research*, 24, No. 4, (1998): 343–53.

201 Zurawicki, L., 'Neuromarketing; Exploring the Brain of the Consumer', *Springer*, (2010): 155.

202 Pribyl, C., et al., 'The Neural Basis of Brand Addiction: An fMRI.' *Gallup Management Journal* (2007).

203 Fetscherin et al., 'The Effect of Product Category of Consumer Brand Relationships,' *Journal of Product and Brand Management*, 23(2), (2014): 78–89.

204 Park, C.W., Jaworski, B.J., and MacInnis, D.J., 'Strategic Brand Concept—Image Management', Vol. 50(4), (1986): 135.

205 McClure, S.M., York, M.K., and Montague, P.R. (2004), 'The Neural Substrates Of Reward Processing In Humans: The Modern Role of fMRI.' The Neuroscientist, 10(3), pp. 260–268

206 Batra, R., Ahuvia, A., and Bagozzi, R.P., 'Brand Love', *Journal of Marketing*, 76(2), (2012): 1–16

207 Fournier, S., 'Consumers and Their Brands: Developing Relationship Theory in Consumer Research', *Journal of Consumer Research*, 24(4), (1998): 343-73; Batra, R., Ahuvia, A., and Bagozzi, R.P., 'Brand Love', *Journal of Marketing*, 76(2), (2012): 1–16.

208 Kahneman, D., *Thinking Fast and Slow*, Allen Lane (Penguin Books), (2011).

209 http://www.howdesign.com/resources-education/online-design-courses-education/4-key-reasons-branding-is-important/. (Accessed 10 May 2017).

210 Interbrand – Best Indian Brands 2016. (Retrieved from https://interbrand.com/best-brands/)

211 Shen, L., 'United Airlines Stock Drops $1.4 Billion After Passenger-Removal Controversy'. (Retrieved 10 May 2017 from http://fortune.com/2017/04/11/united-airlines-stock-drop/

212 United, Our United Customer Commitment'. (Retrieved 10 May 2017 from https://www.united.com/web/en-US/content/customerfirst.aspx).

213 How Design Live. (Retrieved 21 September 2020 from http://www.howdesign.com/resources-education/online-design-courses-education/4-key-reasons-branding-is- important/).

214 'Steve Jobs', *Wikipedia*. (Retrieved 30 July 2021 from https://en.wikipedia.org/wiki/Steve_Jobs

215 Guruprasad's Portal. (Retrieved 10 February 2018 from http://guruprasad.net/posts/part-14-thums-up-story-coca-cola-tries-kill-parle-brands/)

216 'Thums Up', *Wikipedia*. (Retrieved 10 February 2018 from https://en.wikipedia.org/wiki/Thums_Up).

217 McClure et al., 'Neural Correlates of Behavioural Preference for Culturally Familiar Drinks', *Neuron*, Vol. 44(2), (2004): 379–87.

218 Thompson, J.B., *Ideology and Modern Culture*, Polity Press, Cambridge, (1990)

219 Abhishek and Sahay, A., 'Culture and Celebrity Endorsements', *IIMA Working Paper*, (2012).

220 BikesMania, New Bajaj Pulsar 200cc TV Commercial Ad.' (Retrieved 10 August 2015 from https://www.youtube.com/watch?v=AxwUwPJh2zk).

221 Zaltman, G., 'How Customers Think: Essential Insights Into the Mind of the Market', *Harvard Business School Press*, (2003).

222 Sahay, A., and Sharma, N., 'Managing Your Brand Relationships', Working paper (2012).

223 Simon, C.J., and Sullivan, M.W., 'The Measurement and Determinants of Brand Equity: A Financial Approach', *Marketing Science*, Vol.12. No.1, (1993).

224 Keller, K.L., 'Conceptualizing, Measuring, and Managing Customer-based Brand Equity, *The Journal of Marketing*, (1993): 1–22.

225 Shanon, S., and Alexander, G.S., 'Reckitt to Buy India Paras Pharma for $724 Million.' (13 December 2010) (Retrieved 25 May 2015 from http://www.bloomberg.com/news/articles/2010-12-13/reckitt-benckiser-agrees-to-acquire-india-s-paras-for-about-762-million);

226 *The Economic Times*. (Retrieved 25 July 2012 from http://articles.economictimes.indiatimes.com/2010-12-14/news/27622293_1_paras-brands-paras-pharma-paras-products).

227 (Retrieved 21 September 2020 from http://www.howdesign.com/resources-education/online-design-courses-education/4-key-reasons-branding-is- important/).

228 Ibid.

229 Blog. 'Why Marketing Strategy is Important for Start-ups.' (Retrieved 21 September 2020 from blogs.adianta.org/why-brand-strategy-is-important-for-start-ups/).

230 Tom et al., 'The Neural Basis of Loss Aversion in Decision-Making under Risk', Science, 315(5811), (2007):515–18.

231 This is an illustrative list for a particular product brand.

232 For answers to some of these questions using neuro tools and when to use them, please refer to Chapter 10.

233 Moneycontrol, 'Edelweiss Financial Services Limited.' (Retrieved 15 October 2021 from http://www.moneycontrol.com/financials/edelweissfinancialservices/financial-graphs/return-on-capital-employed/EC01).

234 Sharma, N., and A. Sahay (2010), 'Edelweiss (B): Branding in the Retail Space', IIMA Case (MAR416B).

235 Aaker, D.A., 'Measuring Brand Equity across Products and Markets', *California Management Review*, 38(3), (1996): 102–20.

236 Bhasin, H., 'What Is Brand Ladder and How to Use It for Brand Building?' *Marketing91* (17 December 2019). (Retrieved 20 November 2017 from http://www.marketing91.com/brand-ladder/).

237 Venkatraman et al., 'New Scanner Data for Brand Marketers: How Neuroscience Can Help Better Understand Differences in Brand Preferences', *Journal of Consumer Psychology*, Vol. 22. Issue 1, (2011): 143–53.

238 Joseph, A.T., 'We Are Focusing on Branded Products to Maximise Amul's Profits: RS Sodhi', *DNA* (19 March 2018). (Retrieved 2 July 2021 from http://www.dnaindia.com/money/interview-we-are-focusing-on-branded-products-to-maximise-amul-s-profits-rs-sodhi-2057932).

239 Grubb et al., 'Neuroanatomy Accounts for Age-Related Changes in Risk Preferences', *Nat Commun* 7, (2016): 13822.

240 Tymula et al., 'Adolescents' Risk-Taking Behavior Is Driven by Tolerance to Ambiguity', *Proceedings of the National Academy of Sciences*, 109 (42), pp. 17135–140.

241 Volz, K.G., Kessler, T., and von Cramon, D.Y. 'In-Group As Part of the Self: In-Group Favoritism is Mediated by Medial Prefrontal Cortex Activation', *Soc. Neurosci*, 4(3), (2008): 244–60.

242 Decety, J., and Cowell, J. (2016, March 9), 'Our Brains are Wired for Morality: Evolution, Development, and Neuroscience', *Frontiers for Young Minds*, 4:3

243 Riedl, R., Hubert, M. and Kenning, P., 'Are There Neural Gender Differences in Online Trust? An fMRI Study on the Perceived Trustworthiness of eBay Offers', *MIS Quarterly*, Vol. 34, No. 2, (2010): 397–428.

244 DeYoung et al., 'Testing Predictions from Personality Neuroscience: Brain Structure and the Big Five', *Psychological Science*, Vol. 21(6), (2010): 820–28.

245 Ozer, D.J., and Benet-Martinez, V., 'Personality and the Prediction of Consequential Outcomes', *Annual Rev. Psychology*, 57, (2006): 401–21.

246 Clark, L.A., and Watson, D., 'Temperament: An Organizing Paradigm for Trait Psychology', O.P. John, R.W. Robins and L.A. Pervin (Eds.), *Handbook of Personality: Theory and Research.* New York, NY, US: The Guilford Press. (2008): 265–86.

247 Ibid.

248 Bremner et al., 'Hippocampal Volume Reduction in Major Depression', *American Journal of Psychiatry*, 157(1), (2000): 115–8.

249 Carter et al., 'Anterior Cingulate Cortex, Error Detection, and the Online Monitoring of Performance', *Science*, 280 (5364), (1998): 747–49.

250 Eisenberger, N.I., and Lieberman, M.D., 'Why Rejection Hurts: A Common Neural Alarm System for Physical and Social Pain.' *Trends Cognitive Science*, 8(7), (2004): 294–300.

251 Pelphrey, K.A., and Morris, J.P., 'Brain Mechanisms for Interpreting the Actions of Others from Biological-Motion Cues.' *Current Directions in Psychological Science*, 15(3), (2006): 136–40.

252 Saxe, R., and Powell, L.J., 'It's the Thought That Counts: Specific Brain Regions for One Component of Theory of Mind.' *Psychological Science*, 17(8), (2006): 692–99.

253 DeYoung, C.G., Peterson, J.B., and Higgins, D.M., 'Sources of Openness/Intellect: Cognitive and Neuropsychological Correlates of the Fifth Factor of Personality.' *Journal of Personality*, 73(4), (2005): 825–58.

254 Thomson et al., 'The Buy-in Benchmark: How Staff Understanding and Commitment Impact Brand and Business', *Journal of Marketing Management*, Vol. 15, Issue 8 (1999).

255 Välikangas, L., and Okumura, A., 'Why Do People Follow Leaders? A Study of a U.S. and a Japanese Change Program.' *The Leadership Quarterly*, 8 (3), (1997): 313-37.

256 Hommer et al., 'Amygdala Recruitment during Anticipation of Monetary Rewards: An Event-Related fmri Study', *Ann NY Acad. Sci.*, 985, (2003): 476-8.

257 Soutschek et al., 'Brain Stimulation over the Frontopolar Cortex Enhances Motivation to Exert Effort for Reward.' *Biol Psychiatry*, 84(1), (2018): 38–45.

258 Laureiro-Martínez et al., 'Frontopolar Cortex and Decision-Making Efficiency: Comparing Brain Activity of Experts with Different Professional Backgrounds during an Exploration-Exploitation Task.' *Front. Hum. Neurosci.*, 7, (2013): 927.

259 Reiss, R., '12 CEOs Describe Their Leadership Style', *Forbes* (8 October 2018). (Retrieved from https://www.forbes.com/sites/robertreiss/2018/10/08/12-quotes-from-amazing-leaders/#6f02ca3715b8).

260 Dasgupta, B., 'It's Important to Acquire People Management and Coaching Skills: Upasana Taku, co-founder, MobiKwik', *The Economic Times* (4 November 2016). (Retrieved from //economictimes.indiatimes.com/articleshow/55233679.cms?from=mdr&utm_source=contentofinterest&utm_medium=text&utm_campaign=cppst).

261 Zurawicki, L., 'Book Review: Neuromarketing: Exploring the Brain of the Consumer', *International Journal of Marketing Research*, 53(2), (2011): 287–88.

262 McClure et al., 'Separate Neural Systems Value Immediate and Delayed Monetary Rewards', *Science*, 306 (5695), (2004): 503–07.

263 Gee, R., 'Uber Launches First Major Campaign As It Looks to Widen Appeal beyond Nights Out', *Marketing Week* (3 June 2016). (Retrieved 15 August 2016 from https://www.marketingweek.com/2016/06/03/uber-turns-to-traditional-advertising-for-its-first-major-outdoor-ad-campaign/).

264 Weinstein, M., 'A Trillion-Dollar Demographic: 10 Brands That Got Millennial Marketing Right' (23 July 2015). (Retrieved 15 August 2016 from https://www.searchenginejournal.com/trillion-dollar-demographic-10-brands-got-millennial-marketing-right/135969/).

265 Kahneman, D. and Tversky, A., 'Prospect Theory: An Analysis of Decision under Risk', *Econometrica* 47, (1979): 263–291; Rabin, M., and Thaler, R.H., 'Anomalies: Risk Aversion', *The Journal of Economic Perspectives* 15, (2001): 219–32.

266 Martin, J.M., Reimann, M., and Norton, M.I., 'Experience Theory, or How Desserts Are Like Losses', *Journal of Experimental Psychology: General*, 145(11), (2016): 1460–72.

267 Sahay, A., Sharma, N. and Mehta, K., 'Role of Affect and Cognition in Consumer Brand Relationship: Exploring Gender Differences', *Journal of Indian Business Research* 4(1), (2012): 36–60.

268 Graybiel, A.M., 'Habits, Rituals, and the Evaluative Brain', *Annual Review of Neuroscience*, 31:1, (2008): 359–87.

269 Wood, W., and Rünger, D., 'Psychology of Habit', *Annual Review of Psychology*, 67, (2016): 289–314.

270 Kaas, P.K., 'Consumer Habit Forming, Information Acquisition, and Buying Behavior', *Journal of Business Research*, Vol. 10 (1), (1982): 3–15.

271 Graybiel, A.M., 'Habits, Rituals, and the Evaluative Brain', *Annual Review of Neuroscience*, 31:1, (2008): 359–87.

272 Ibid.

273 Montague, P.R., Dayan, P., and Sejnowski, T.J., 'A Framework for Mesencephalic Dopamine Systems Based on Predictive Hebbian Learning', *Journal of Neuroscience*, 16(5), (1996):1936–47.

274 Romo, R., and Schultz, W., 'Dopamine Neurons of the Monkey Midbrain: Contingencies of Responses to Active Touch during Self-Initiated Arm Movements', *Journal of Neurophysiology*, 63(3), (1990): 592–606.

275 Lew, T., 'Marvel vs. DC: Which Is the Better Comic Book Universe?' *Showbiz CheatSheet*, (6 November 2016). (Retrieved from http://www.cheatsheet.com/entertainment/marvel-vs-dc-what-makes-them-different-and-which-is-better.html/?a=viewall).

276 Retrieved from http://www.cracked.com/funny-6460-marvel-vs-dc/

277 Stillman, T.F., and Baumeister. R.F., 'Uncertainty, Belongingness, and Four Needs for Meaning', *Psychological Inquiry*, 20:4, (2009): 249–51.

278 Klucharev et al., 'Reinforcement Learning Signal Predicts Social Conformity', *Neuron*, 61(1), (2009): 140–51.

279 Song, F., 'Intergroup Trust and Reciprocity in Strategic Interactions: Effects of Group Decision-Making Mechanism', *Organizational Behavior and Human Decision Processes*, Vol. 108, Issue 1, (2009): 164–73.

280 Rilling et al., 'A Neural Basis for Social Cooperation', *Neuron*, 35(2), (2002): 395–405.

281 Cox, D., 'Predicting Consumption, Wine Involvement and Perceived Quality of Australian Red Wine', *Journal of Wine Research*, 20:3, (2009): 209–29.

282 Priilaid, D.A., 'Wine's Placebo Effect: How the Extrinsic Cues of Visual Assessments Mask the Intrinsic Quality of South African Red Wine', *International Journal of Wine Marketing*, Vol. 18, No. 1, (2006): 17–32.

283 Plassmann et al., 'Marketing Actions Can Modulate Neural Representations of Experienced Pleasantness', PNAS, 105 (3), (2008): 1050–54.

284 Stewart et al., 'Information Gerrymandering and Undemocratic Decisions', *Nature* 573, (2019): 117–21.

285 Volz, K.G., Kessler, T., and von Cramon, D.Y., 'In-group As Part of the Self: In-group Favoritism Is Mediated by Medial Prefrontal Cortex Activation', *Social Neuroscience*, 4(3), (2008): 244–60.

286 Tajfel et al., 'Social Categorization and Intergroup Behaviour', *European Journal of Social Psychology*, 1(2), (1971): 149–78.

287 Volz, K.G., Kessler, T., and von Cramon, D.Y., 'In-group As Part of the Self: In-group Favoritism Is Mediated by Medial Prefrontal Cortex Activation', *Social Neuroscience*, 4(3), (2008): 244–60.

288 Molenberghs et al., 'Seeing Is Believing: Neural Mechanisms of Action Perception Are Biased by Team Membership', *Human Brain Mapping*, 34(9), (2012): 2055–68.

289 Simson, E., 'The Psychology of Why Sports Fans See Their Teams As Extensions of Themselves', *The Washington Post*, (30 January 2015). (Retrieved from https://www.washingtonpost.com/opinions/the-psychology-of-why-sports-fans-see-their-teams-as-extensions-of-themselves/2015/01/30/521e0464-a816-11e4-a06b-9df2002b86a0_story.html).

290 Edwards, H., and Day, D., 'Creating Passion Brands: How to Build Emotional Brand Connection with Customers', Kogan Page, (2007).

291 Knoch et al., 'Diminishing Reciprocal Fairness by Disrupting the Right Prefrontal Cortex', *Science*, 314 (5800), (2006): 829–32.

292 Agarwal, S., and Dutta, T., 'Neuromarketing and Consumer Neuroscience: Current Understanding and the Way Forward', *Decision*, 42 (4), (2015): 457–62.

293 Ness, R.M., and Klaas R., 'Risk Perception by Patients with Anxiety Disorders', *Journal of Nervous and Mental Disease*, 182, (1994): 466–70.

294 Loewenstein et al., 'Risk As Feelings', *Psychological Bulletin*, 127(2), (2001): 267.

295 Zurawicki, L., 'Neuromarketing: Exploring the Brain of the Consumer', *Springer Science & Business Media*, (2010).

296 Martin, J., Reimann, M. and Norton, M., 'Experience Theory, or How Desserts are Like Losses', *Journal of Experimental Psychology: General*, 145(11), (2016): 1460–72.

297 Zurawicki, L., 'Neuromarketing: Exploring the Brain of the Consumer', *Springer Science & Business Media*, (2011).

298 Sutcliffe, A., and Hart, J., 'Analyzing the Role of Interactivity in User Experience', *International Journal of Human-Computer Interaction*, 33(3), (2017): 229–40.

299 Chan, C., and Mogilnier, C., 'Experiential Gifts Foster Stronger Social Relationships than Material Gifts', *Journal of Consumer Research*, 43(6), (2017): 913–31.

300 MarkLives, MarkLives #Campaigns: Gillette South Africa's Nozizwe, (8 August 2019). (Retrieved from https://www.youtube.com/watch?v=aoz7k8Ob8Mo).

301 Sahay, A., and Sharma, N., 'Brand Relationships and Switching Behavior for Highly Used Products Amongst Young Consumers,' *Vikalpa*, , Indian Institute of Management Ahmedabad, January–March 2010.

302 Sahay, A., and Mathen, N., 'Hero Honda: Multisegment Positioning and Selling', *IIMA Case (MAR418)*, (2010).

303 Dolcos, F., Iordan, A.D., and Dolcos, S., 'Neural Correlates of Emotion-Cognition Interactions: A Review of Evidence from Brain Imaging Investigations', *Journal of Cognitive Psychology*, Vol. 23(6), (2011): 669–94.

304 'Top 50 Brands for Millennials.' (Retrieved from http://www.businessinsider.in/The-top-50-brands-for-millennials/articleshow/47505078.cms).

305 '4 Reasons Nike's Business Will Dominate', *Business Insider*. (Retrieved from http://www.businessinsider.in/4-reasons-Nikes-business-will-dominate/articleshow/46800455.cms).

306 *The Times of India*. (Retrieved from http://timesofindia.indiatimes.com/world/rest-of-world/Chile-miners-soon-to-see-loved-ones-over-video-link/articleshow/6482890.cms)

307 'Diderot Effect', *Wikipedia*. (Retrieved 24 May 2016 from https://en.wikipedia.org/wiki/Diderot_effect).

308 The term 'brand community' was first presented by Albert Muniz Jr. and Thomas C. O'Guinn in a 1995 paper for the Association for Consumer Research Annual Conference in Minneapolis, MN. In a 2001 article titled 'Brand Community', published in the *Journal of Consumer Research* (SSCI), they defined the concept as 'a specialized, non-geographically bound community, based on a structured set of social relations among admirers of a brand'. More generically, as per Wikipedia, 'a brand community can be defined as an enduring self-selected group of actors sharing a system of values, standards and representations (a culture) and recognizing bonds of membership with each other and with the whole. Brand communities are characterized in shared consciousness, rituals and traditions, and a sense of moral responsibility'.

309 Schouten, J.W., and McAlexander, J.H., 'Subcultures of Consumption: An Ethnography of the New Bikers', *Journal of Consumer Research*, 22(1), (1995): 43–61.

310 Schembri, S., 'Reframing Brand Experience: The Experiential Meaning of Harley-Davidson', *Journal of Business Research*, 62(12), (2009): 1299–1310.

311 Au et al., 'Mood in Foreign Exchange Trading: Cognitive Processes and Performance', *Organizational Behavior and Human Decision Processes*, 91, (2003): 322–38.

312 Ibid.

313 Chun et al., 'Strategic Benefits of Low Brand Fit Extensions: Why and Why', *Journal of Consumer Psychology*, 25(4), (2015): 577–95.

314 Johnson et al., 'Good Guys Can Finish First: How Brand Reputation Affects Extension Evaluation', *Journal of Consumer Psychology*, 29(4), (2019): 565–83.

315 Kay et al., 'God and the Government: Testing a Compensatory Control Mechanism for the Support of External Systems', *Journal of Personality and Social Psychology*, 95 (1), (2008): 18–35.

316 Cutright, K.M., 'The Beauty of Boundaries: When and Why We Seek Structure in Consumption', *Journal of Consumer Research*, 38 (5), (2012): 775–90.

317 Boush, D.M., and Loken, B., 'A Process-Tracing Study of Brand Extension Evaluation', *Journal of Marketing Research*, 28, (1991): 16–28.

318 Cutright, K.M., Bettman, J.R., and Fitzsimons, G.J., Putting Brands in Their Place: How a Lack of Control Keeps Brands Contained', *Journal of Marketing Research*, 50(3), (2013): 365-77.

319 'Competing for Customers and Capital', Southwest Airlines: Put a Little LUV in Your Logo! (2 September 2007). (Retrieved from customersandcapital.com).

320 Park, C.W., Jun, Y., and Shcoker, A.D., 'Composite Branding Alliances: An Investigation of Extension and Feedback Effects', *Journal of Marketing Research*, Vol. XXXIII. (1996): 453–66; Janiszewski and DaCunha (2004), Reference Dependence, JCR.

321 Management Study Guide. (Retrieved on 24 November 2015 from http://www.managementstudyguide.com/brand-management.htm).

322 Lunfen, I., and Buhr, S., 'Lyft, Didi, Ola and GrabTaxi Partner in Global Tech, Service Alliance to Rival Uber', *Tech Crunch* (4 December 2015). (Retrieved 24 November 2015 from https://techcrunch.com/2015/12/03/lyft-didi-ola-and-grabtaxi-partner-in-global-tech-service-alliance-to-rival-uber/).

323 Davidson, L., 'Is Your Daily Social Media Usage Higher than Average?', *The Telegraph*, (2015). (Retrieved from http://www.telegraph.co.uk/finance/newsbysector/mediatechnologyandtelecoms/11610959/Is-your-daily-social-media-usage-higher-than-average.html).

324 Park, M., 'Facebook Reports Second Quarter 2019 Results', (2019). (Retrieved from https://s21.q4cdn.com/399680738/files/doc_financials/2019/Q2/FB-Q2-2019-Earnings-Release.pdf).

325 Adler, E., 'Social Media Engagement: The Surprising Facts about How Much Time People Spend on the Major Social Networks', *Advertising and Media Insider*, (2013). (Retrieved from http://www.businessinsider.in/Social-Media-Engagement-The-Surprising-Facts-About-How-Much-Time-People-Spend-On-The-Major-Social-Networks/articleshow/27488606.cms).

326 Swant, M., 'Facebook is Building Its Neuroscience Center to Study Marketing', *ADWEEK*, (2017). (Retrieved from https://www.adweek.com/digital/facebook-is-building-its-own-neuroscience-center-to-study-marketing/).

327 Helliwell, J.F., and Putnam, R.D., 'The Social Context of Wellbeing', *Philos. Trans. R. Soc. Lond. B: Biol. Sci.*, 359, (2004): 1435–46.

328 Abel, J.P., Buff, C.L., and Burr, S.A., 'Social Media and the Fear of Missing Out: Scale Development and Assessment', *Journal of Business & Economics Research (JBER)*, 14(1), (2016): 33–44.

329 Pontes, H.M., Taylor, M., and Stavropoulos, V., 'Beyond "Facebook Addiction": The Role of Cognitive-Related Factors and Psychiatric Distress in Social Networking Site Addiction', *Cyberpsychology, Behavior, and Social Networking*, 21(4), (2018).

330 Bazarova, N.N., 'Online disclosure', Berger, C.R. and Roloff, M.E., (eds), The International Encyclopedia of interpersonal Communication. Hoboken, Wiley-Blackwell, (2015).

331 Haferkamp, N. and Krämer, N.C., 'Social Comparison 2.0: Examining the Effects of Online Profiles on Social-Networking Sites', *Cyberpsychol. Behav. Soc. Netw.*, 14, (2011): 309–14.

332 Meshi D, Tamir T.I., and Heekeren H.R., 'The Emerging Neuroscience of Social Media', *Trends in Cognitive Sciences*, 19(12), (2015): 771–82.

333 Wasserman, T., 'Facebook's Secret to High Emotional Engagement? Faces [Study]', *Mashable*, (2011). (Retrieved from http://mashable.com/2011/12/07/facebook-faces-emotion/#ETecsF6JJqqJ).

334 Hof, R., 'Why Ads Grab You More on Facebook than on TV or the Web', *Forbes*, (2011). (Retrieved from http://www.forbes.com/sites/roberthof/2011/12/07/why-ads-grab-you-more-on-facebook-than-on-tv-or-the-web/#616fa6b12403).

335 Hern, A., 'Cambridge Analytica: How Did It Turn Clicks into Votes?', *The Guardian*, (2018). (Retrieved from https://www.theguardian.com/news/2018/may/06/cambridge-analytica-how-turn-clicks-into-votes-christopher-wylie).

336 Meshi D, Tamir T.I., and Heekeren H.R., 'The Emerging Neuroscience of Social Media', *Trends in Cognitive Sciences*, 19(12), (2015): 771–82.

337 Falk et al., 'Getting the Word Out: Neural Correlates of Enthusiastic Message Propagation', *Front. Hum. Neurosci.*, 6, (2012): 313.

338 Falk et al., 'Creating Buzz: The Neural Correlates of Effective Message Propagation', *Psychol. Sci.*, 24, (2013): 1234–42).

339 Cascio, C.N. et al., (2015) Neural correlates of susceptibility to group opinions in online word-of-mouth recommendations', *Journal of Marking Research*, 52, 559–575

340 Meshi D, Tamir T.I., and Heekeren H.R., 'The Emerging Neuroscience of Social Media', *Trends in Cognitive Sciences*, 19(12), (2015): 771–82.

341 Naaman, M. et al., 'Is It Really About Me? Message Content in Social Awareness Streams', *Proceedings of the 2010 ACM Conference on Computer Supported Cooperative Work*, (2010): 189–92 ACM.

342 Northoff, G. et al., 'Self-referential Processing in Our Brain: A Meta-Analysis of Imaging Studies on the Self', *Neuroimage*, 31, (2006): 440–57.

343 Tamir, D.I., and Mitchell, J.P., 'Disclosing Information about the Self Is Intrinsically Rewarding', *Proc. National Academy of Sciences, U.S.A.*, 109(21), (2012): 8038–43.

344 Meshi D, Tamir T.I., and Heekeren H.R., 'The Emerging Neuroscience of Social Media', *Trends in Cognitive Sciences*, 19(12), (2015): 771–82.

345 Alibaba group, 'Alibaba's Olympic Ad: To the Greatness of Small', (2018). (Retrieved from https://www.youtube.com/watch?v=pPIBrSk9J9A).

346 Samsung India, 'Samsung India Service (SVC)—Most Watched Video in 2017—We'll Take Care of You, Wherever You Are', (2016). (Retrieved from https://www.youtube.com/watch?v=779KwjAYTeQ).

347 Swaminathan, V., Stilley, K.M, and Ahluwalia, R., 'When Brand Personality Matters: The Moderating Role of Attachment Styles', *Journal of Consumer Research*, Oxford University Press, Vol. 35(6), (2009): 985–1002.

348 ALS (Amyotrophic lateral sclerosis), otherwise known as Motor Neurone Disease, is a rare, till date incurable, disease that affects the motor neurons of the brain. Those affected by this disease experience a decreased ability to walk, use their hands, speak, swallow and breathe. The exact cause of the disease is unknown, however, both genetic and environmental factors are considered to be equally important causes.

349 Amazon India, 'We Indians Love Jaldi! Fast & On-Time Delivery on Amazon.in', (2016). (Retrieved from https://www.youtube.com/watch?v=dpxw0-D9YE8).

350 Kasteler, J., '8 Brain Triggers Guaranteed to Boost Your Social Media Marketing', *MarTech*, (2014). (Retrieved from http://marketingland.com/8-brain-triggers-guaranteed-boost-social-media-marketing-80269).

351 Kia India, 'Kia Motors India|Magical Inspiration|Stunning Design', (2019). (Retrieved from https://www.youtube.com/watch?v=8aHVz5RKi1w).

352 CNBC, 'ASMR: Why Brands Are Using "Brain Orgasms" to Advertise', (2019). (Retrieved from https://www.youtube.com/watch?v=N9N6q9sEmOY).

353 Meri Maggi, '#NothingLikeMaggi|Hostel', (2016). (Retrieved from https://www.youtube.com/watch?v=vfJATqiT0xY; https://www.youtube.com/watch?v=-dDyEP_k65Y).

354 (Retrieved from https://www.youtube.com/watch?v=BFFrUOGB138).

355 Mandal, S., Terrano and Mahato, 'Dual Brand Personality and eWOM', *European Journal of Marketing*, (2021).

356 Weingarten, G., 'Pearls Before Breakfast: Can One of the Nation's Great Musicians Cut through the Fog of a D.C. Rush Hour? Let's Find Out', *Washington Post*, (2007). (Retrieved from https://www.washingtonpost.com/lifestyle/magazine/pearls-before-breakfast-

can-one-of-the-nations-great-musicians-cut-through-the-fog-of-a-dc-rush-hour-lets-find-out/2014/09/23/8a6d46da-4331-11e4-b47c-f5889e061e5f_story.html).

357 Old Spice, 'Old Spice| The Man Your Man Could Smell Like', (2010). (Retrieved from https://www.youtube.com/watch?v=owGykVbfgUE).

358 Adage, 'Top 15 Ad Campaigns of the 21st Century', (2015). (Retrieved from https://adage.com/article/agency-news/top-15-ad-campaigns-21st-century/2162916#stratos).

359 Rust et al., 'Measuring Marketing Productivity: Current Knowledge and Future Directions', *Journal of Marketing*, 68(4), (2004): 76–89. DOI: 10.1509/jmkg.68.4.76.42721.

360 'Rowntree's', *Wikipedia*. (Retrieved from https://en.wikipedia.org/wiki/Rowntree%27s).

361 Archives, *Los Angeles Times*. (Retrieved from http://articles.latimes.com/1988-12-19/news/mn-457_1_grand-met).

362 Keller, K.L., (1993). Conceptualizing, Measuring, and Managing Customer-Based Brand Equity', Journal of Marketing. (Retrieved from https://doi.org/10.1177/002224299305700101).

363 Simon, C.J. and Sullivan, M.W., 'The Measurement and Determinants of Brand Equity: A Financial Approach,' *Marketing Science*, 12(1), (1993): 28–52.

364 Sahay, A., Proprietary Consulting Reports on Brand Valuation, IIM Ahmedabad, (2005).

365 Dyson, P., Farr, A., and Hollis, N., 'Understanding, Measuring and Using Brand Equity,' *Journal of Advertising Research*, (1996): 9–21.

366 Keller, Kevin Lane, *Strategic Brand Management: Building, Measuring and Managing Brand Equity*. Prentice Hall International, (2003): 502.

367 Motameni, R., and Shahrokhi M., 'Brand Equity Valuation: A Global Perspective,' *Journal of Product and Brand Management*, 7(4), (1998): 275–90.

368 Tollington, A., 'Brand Accounting and the Marketing Interface,' *Management Accounting*, 73(7), (1995): 58–59.

369 Ailawadi, K., Lehmann, D., and Neslin, S., 'Revenue Premium as an Outcome Measure of Brand Equity,' *Journal of Marketing*, 67, (2003): 1–17.

370 D'Souza, G., and Rao, R.C., 'Can Repeating an Advertisement More Frequently than the Competition Affect Brand Preference in a Mature Market?', *Journal of Marketing*, 59, (1995): 32-42.

371 Rao et al., (1996).

372 Laforet, S. and Saunders, J., 'Managing Brand Portfolios: How Strategies have Changed', *Journal of Advertising Research*, 45(03), (1999).

373 Zak, P.J., Kurzban, R., and Matzner, W.T., 'The Neurobiology of Trust', *Annals of the New York Academy of Sciences*, 1032, (2004): 224–7.

374 Knoch, D., et al., 'Diminishing Reciprocal Fairness by Disrupting the Right Prefrontal Cortex', *Science*, 314 (5800), (2006): 829–32.

375 Bunge, W., *Fitzgerald: Geography of a Revolution*, University of Georgia Press, (2011).

376 Olson, E.M., Slater, S., and Hult, T., 'The Performance Implications of Fit Among Business Strategy, Marketing Organizational Structure and Strategic Behavior,' *Journal of Marketing*, 69, (2005): 49–65.

377 Pugh, D.S. (ed.), *Organization Theory: Selected Readings*, Harmondsworth: Penguin (1990).

378 Jacobides., M.G., 'The Inherent Limits of Organizational Structure and the Unfulfilled Role of Hierarchy: Lessons from a Near-War', *Organization Science*, 18, 3, (2007): 455–77.

379 Lim, M., Griffiths, G., and Sambrook, S., 'Organizational Structure for the Twenty-First Century', presented at the annual meeting of The Institute for Operations Research and The Management Sciences, Austin, (2010).

380 de Chernatony, L., and Cottam, S., 'Interactions between Organizational Cultures and Corporate Brands', *Journal of Product & Brand Management*, 17, (2008): 13–24. doi: 10.1108/10610420810856477.

381 Rust et al., 'Measuring Marketing Productivity: Current Knowledge and Future Directions', *Journal of Marketing*, 68(4), (2004): 76–89. doi: 10.1509/jmkg.68.4.76.42721.

382 A very disaggregated form where small cells are empowered to take decisions is brought out in Yeung, A., Ulrich, D. (2019) *Reinventing the Organisation*, Harvard Business Review Press.

383 Ibid.

384 Rausch, E., Eberlin, R., and Tatum, B., 'Organizational Justice and Decision Making: When Good Intentions Are Not Enough', *Management Decision*, Vol. 43, No. 7/8, (2005): 1040–48.

385 Sanfey et al., 'The Neural Basis of Economic Decision-Making in the Ultimatum Game', *Science*, 300 (5626), (2003): 1755–8.

386 Interview with Shashwat Sharma, Brand Manager, Dove, HUL.

387 Hindustan Unilever Limited, homepage. (Retrieved from https://www.hul.co.in/Images/hul-annual-report-2018-19_tcm1255-538867_1_en.pdf).

388 Shah, B., 'A Study on Drivers of Organizational Structure and Design as Tool to Enhance Organizational Effectiveness: A Case Study of AMUL', *International Journal for Innovative Research in Multidisciplinary Fields*, Vol. 3, Issue 4, (2017).

389 'Organization: Amul—The Taste of India'. (Retrieved from https://amul.com/m/organisation).

390 Jha, D.K., 'Amul Raises Farmers' Income Four-Fold in Seven Years', *Business Standard India*, (2017). (Retrieved from https://www.business-standard.com/article/companies/amul-raises-farmers-income-four-fold-in-seven-years-117061500587_1.html).

391 Prasad, R., and Satsangi, R., 'A Case Study of Amul Co-operative in India in Relation to Organisational Design and Operational Efficiency', *International Journal of Scientific & Engineering Research*, Vol. 4, Issue 1, (2013).

392 Ibid.

393 Yadav, M., 'Amul', (2017). (Retrieved from https://www.slideshare.net/MohitYadav291/amul-85007390).

394 Chowdhury, A., 'Amul Girl Turns 50: Meet the Three Men Who Keep Her Going', *The Economic Times*, (2016). (Retrieved from https://economictimes.indiatimes.com/industry/services/advertising/amul-girl-turns-50-meet-the-three-men-who-keep-her-going/

articleshow/54872391.cms?from=mdr). Accessed 12 December 2019 15:16 hrs IST.

395 Gupte, M., 'Utterly, Butterly, Even at 50,' *Business Standard*, (2012). (Retrieved from https://www.business-standard.com/article/companies/utterly-butterly-even-at-50-112060600019_1.html).

396 Telephonic interview, 13 February 2017, Neeraj Chandra.

397 Britannia Annual Report 2019. (Retrieved from http://britannia.co.in/pdfs/annual_report/Annual-Report-2018-19.pdf).

398 Brands, Nestle Global. (Retrieved from https://www.nestle.com/brands).

399 https://andrew.london/wp-content/uploads/2013/08/democratic-republic-of-burberry.pdf.

400 Gilchrist, S., 'The Democratic Republic of Burberry', (2013). (Retrieved from https://www.burberryplc.com/content/dam/burberry/corporate/oar/documents/Burberry_201819-Annual-Report.pdf).

401 Solomatina, I., '5 Times Christopher Bailey's Burberry Was Ahead of the Curve', (2017). (Retrieved from https://www.sleek-mag.com/article/christopher-bailey-burberry/).

402 Gilchrist, S., 'The Democratic Republic of Burberry', (2013). (Retrieved from https://www.burberryplc.com/content/dam/burberry/corporate/oar/documents/Burberry_201819-Annual-Report.pdf).

403 Wemby, A., 'Crafting a Dual Market Strategy—Market Strategy—A Case Study of Burberry', *Bachelor thesis*, Kristianstad University, (2010). (Retrieved from http://www.diva-portal.org/smash/get/diva2:331174/FULLTEXT01.pdf).

404 Personal Interview, Brand Manager, HUL.

405 Rust, R.T., Moorman, C., and Bhalla, G., 'Rethinking Marketing', *Harvard Business Review*, (2010): 94–101.

406 Aaker, D.A., *Spanning Silos: The New CMO Imperative*, Boston, MA: Harvard Business School Press, (2008).

407 Gyrd-Jones, R.I., Helm, C., and Munk, J., 'Exploring the Impact of Silos in Achieving Brand Orientation', *Journal of Marketing Management*, 29(9-10), (2013): 1056–78.

408 King-Casas et al., 'Getting to Know You: Reputation and Trust in a Two-Person Economic Exchange', *Science*, 308(5718), (2005): 78–83.

409 Teece, D.J., 'Explicating Dynamic Capabilities: The Nature and Microfoundations of (Sustainable) Enterprise Performance', *Strategic Management Journal*, 28(13), (2007): 1319–50.

410 Laureiro-Martínez et al., 'Understanding the Exploration–Exploitation Dilemma: An fmri Study of Attention Control and Decision-Making Performance', *Strategic Management Journal*, 36, (2015): 319–38.

411 Wilson et al., 'Humans Use Directed and Random Exploration to Solve the Explore–Exploit Dilemma', *Journal of Experimental Psychology: General*, 143(6), (2014): 2074–81.

412 Pillutla, M.M., and Murnighan, J.K., 'Unfairness, Anger, and Spite: Emotional Rejections of Ultimatum Offers', *Organizational Behavior and Human Decision Processes*, 68(3), (1996): 208-224.

413 Smith W., and Tushman M., 'Managing Strategic Contradictions: A Top Management Model for Managing Innovation Streams. *Organization Science*, 16(5), (2005): 522–36.

414 Miller C.C., and Ireland R.D., 'Intuition in Strategic Decision Making: Friend or Foe in the Fast-Paced 21st Century?', *Academy of Management Perspectives*, 19(1), (2005): 19–30.

415 Gavetti G., 'Toward a Behavioral Theory of Strategy', *Organization Science*, 23(1), (2012): 267–85.

416 Gazzaniga M., Heatherton T., and Halpern D., *Psychological Science*, Norton: New York, (2010).

417 Posner, M., and Petersen, S., 'The Attention System of the Human Brain', *Annual Review of Neuroscience*, 13, (1990): 25–42.

418 Helfat, C.E. and Peteraf, M.A., 'Managerial Cognitive Capabilities and the Microfoundations of Dynamic Capabilities', *Strategic Management Journal*, 36, (2015): 831–50.

419 Ibid.

420 Ng, B., 'The Neuroscience of Growth Mindset and Intrinsic Motivation', *Brain Science*, 8(2), (2018): 20.

421 Moser et al., 'Mind Your Errors: Evidence for a Neural Mechanism Linking Growth Mind-Set to Adaptive Posterior Adjustments', *Psychological Science*, 22, (2011): 1484–89.

422 Barnes, R.D., 'Perceived Freedom and Control in the Built Environment', J.H. Harvey (ed.), Cognition, Social Behavior, and the Environment, Hillsdale, NJ: Erlbaum, (1981): 409–22.

423 Amabile, T.M., and Gitomer, J., 'Children's Artistic Creativity: Effect of Choice in Task Materials', *Personality and Social Psychology Bulletin*, 10, (1984): 209–15.

424 Chua, R.Y-J., and Iyengar, S.S., 'Empowerment through Choice? A Critical Analysis of the Effects of Choice in Organizations', *Research in Organizational Behavior*, Vol. 27, (2006): 41–79.

425. Jepma et al., 'Neural Mechanisms Underlying the Induction and Relief of Perceptual Curiosity', *Frontiers in Behavioral Neuroscience*, 6, (2012): 5.

426 Loewenstein, G., 'The Psychology of Curiosity: A Review and Reinterpretation', *Psychological Bulletin*, 116(1), (1994): 75–98.

427 Dietrich, A., 'The Cognitive Neuroscience of Creativity', *Psychonomic Bulletin & Review*, 11 (6), (2004): 1011–26.

428 Stillman, T.F. and Baumeister, R.F., 'Uncertainty, Belongingness, and Four Needs for Meaning', *Psychological Inquiry*, 20:4, (2009): 249–51.

429 Volz, K.G., Kessler, T., and von Cramon, D.Y., 'In-group as Part of the Self: In-Group Favoritism Is Mediated by Medial Prefrontal Cortex Activation', *Social Neuroscience*, 4(3), (2009): 244–60.

430 Decety, J. and Cowell, J., 'Our Brains are Wired for Morality: Evolution, Development, and Neuroscience', *Frontiers for Young Minds*, 4:3, (2016).

431 Saxe, R., and Wexler, A., 'Making Sense of Another Mind: The Role of the Right Temporo-Parietal Junction', *Neuropsychologia*, 43(10), (2016): 1391–99.

432 McClure et al., 'Neural Correlates Of Behavioral Preference For Culturally Familiar Drinks', *Neuron*, Vol. 44(2), (2004): 379–87.

433 Karmakar, S., and Knutson, 'Cost Conscious? The Neural and Behavioral Impact of Price Primacy on Decision Making', *Journal of Marketing Research*, Vol. 52. No. 4., (2015): 467–81.

434 Knutson et al., 'Neural Correlates of Purchase,' *Neuron*, 53 (1). (2007): 147–56.

435 McClure et al., 'Neural Correlates Of Behavioral Preference For Culturally Familiar Drinks', *Neuron*, Vol. 44(2), (2004): 379–87.

436 Group ICA of fmri toolbox (Gift), *TReNDS*. Retrieved from http://trendscenter.org/software/gift/.

437 Brain connectivity toolbox. (n.d.). Retrieved from https://sites.google.com/site/bctnet/.

438 The CAT toolbox. (Retrieved from http://www.neuro.uni-jena.de/cat/).

439 Berns et al., 'Neural Mechanisms of the Influence of Popularity on Adolescent Ratings of Music', *NeuroImage*, 49(3), (2010): 2687–96.

440 Berns, G.S., and Moore, S., 'A Neural Predictor of Cultural Popularity', *Journal of Consumer Psychology*, Vol. 22 (1), (2012): 154–60.

441 Santos et al., 'Eye Tracking in Neuromarketing: A Research Agenda for Marketing Studies', *International Journal of Psychological Studies*, Vol, 7, No. 1, (2015): 32.

442 Higgins et al., 'Eye Movements When Viewing Advertisements', *Frontiers in Psychology*, Vol. 5, (2014). (Retrieved from https://www.frontiersin.org/articles/10.3389/fpsyg.2014.00210/full#h3).

443 Ravaja et al., 'Predicting Purchase Decision: The Role of Hemispheric Asymmetry Over the Frontal Cortex', *Journal of Neuroscience, Psychology, and Economics*, Vol. 6, No. 1, (2013): 1–13.

444 Davidson et al., 'Approach-Withdrawal and Cerebral Asymmetry: Emotional Expression and Brain Physiology', *I. Journal of Personality and Social Psychology*, Vol. 58, No. 2, (1990): 330-341.

445 deCharms, C.R., 'Applications of Real-Time fMRI', *Nature Reviews Neuroscience*, Vol. 9, (2008): 720–29.

446 Kapoor, et al., 'Neural Correlates of Strong vs. Weak Brand Preference', *Working Paper*, IIMA, (2020).

447 Berns, G.S., and Moore, S., 'A Neural Predictor of Cultural Popularity', *Journal of Consumer Psychology*, Vol. 22, 154–60.

448 NEUR SCIENCE Academic and Business Solutions, 'Facebook Embraces Neuroscience', (2018). (Retrieved from https://www.neuroscience.org.uk/facebook-embraces-neuroscience/).

449 Wasserman, T., 'Facebook's Secret to High Emotional Engagement? Faces [STUDY]', (2011). (Retrieved from https://mashable.com/2011/12/07/facebook-faces-emotion/#ETecsF6JJqqJ).

450 EDGY, 'Why These 4 Fortunate Companies Are Using Neuromarketing', (2016). (Retrieved from https://edgy.app/four-companies-using-neuromarketing).

451 Business 2 Community, 'Neuromarketing: Using Neuroscience to Supercharge Results', (2016). (Retrieved from https://www.business2community.com/brandviews/act-on/neuromarketing-using-neuroscience-supercharge-results-01685361).

452 Burkitt, L., 'Neuromarketing: Companies Use Neuroscience for Consumer Insights', *Forbes*, (2009). (Retrieved from https://www.forbes.com/forbes/2009/1116/marketing-hyundai-neurofocus-brain-waves-battle-for-the-brain.html#6d3c00a117bb).

453 Neurons, 'Predict Consumer Responses and Behavior'. (Retrieved from https://neuronsinc.com/products/).